WITHDRAWN

(NEV) BIO

2AH
2

D0160286

For David Feul

All my best

12/23/81

CARSON CITY LIBRARY
900 North Roop Street
Carson City, NV 89701
775-887-2244

WILLIAM FISK HARRAH

Also by Leon Mandel

Speed with Style: The Autobiography of Peter Revson
Driven: The American 4-Wheeled Love Affair
Murder So Real (with Phillip Finch)

WILLIAM FISK HARRAH

*The Life and Times
of a Gambling Magnate*

Leon Mandel

DOUBLEDAY & COMPANY, INC.
GARDEN CITY, NEW YORK 1982

Library of Congress Cataloging in Publication Data
Mandel, Leon.
William Fisk Harrah: the life and times of
a gambling magnate.
1. Harrah, William.   2. Gamblers—United States—
Biography.   I. Title.
HV6715.H37M36   795'.092'4 [B]
AACR2
ISBN: 0-385-15513-1
Library of Congress Catalog Card Number 80-2364

Copyright © 1981, 1982 by Leon Mandel
ALL RIGHTS RESERVED
PRINTED IN THE UNITED STATES OF AMERICA
FIRST EDITION

To Edna and Georges Seligmann,
my mother and stepfather,
with deepest love.

Contents

Acknowledgments

This book was written while the presence of Bill Harrah was still large in Reno. Harrah's attorney, Mead Dixon, succeeded him as chairman of the board; his first president and confidant, Bob Ring, still went to his office on occasion; so did the man who succeeded him, Maurice Sheppard. Virgil Smith, who was Harrah's partner in early ventures and who loaned him money to open his first casino, was a prominent figure in the city, as was Harrah's second (and third) wife, Scherry.

With Bill Harrah so immediate, with the memory of the luncheon during which we talked about this book so vivid, the writing took a tone of informality. Bill Harrah was too much with us all to be written about as though he were covered in moss.

If this informality imparts some liveliness, a great deal of credit is due the people who remembered Harrah and who gave their time and help to this project. They are many.

Thanks to Harrah's for opening its archives, thanks in particular to a cluster of executives who continue to hold the company to Bill Harrah's standards. They include: Mead Dixon, Dick Goeglein, Rome Andreotti, Bob Ring, Maurice Sheppard, Joe Fanelli, Holmes Hendricksen, Mark Curtis, Clyde Wade, Jim Edwards, Mike Moore, and Candice Pearce. Help came also from Ann Sigstad and Heidi Marsh.

Particular thanks to Margaret Schroter, Harrah's sister, Scherry Harrah, Mary May Burger, Roxana Cupples, and Verna Harrah.

Experts of many disciplines lent their help, in particular: D'Armand Sharp, Bob Barnet, Leonard Weissman, Myra

Hodgson, Warren Lerude, Lucinda Wade, Janet Frank, Russell R. Goebel, Eric Duckstad, and Lloyd Dyer.

I am most grateful to Sammy Davis, Jr., for his time and his remarkable insights into the Harrah character.

Other writers will understand how much it meant to me to receive extraordinarily helpful criticism from Steven L. Thompson, encouragement from the editor of *Nevada* magazine, Caroline Joy Hadley, and the forgiving of many deadlines by my own editor at *Motor Trend*, John Dianna.

My agent and friend Jacques de Spoelberch, and my editor at Doubleday, Jim Menick, were strongly supportive during the three years this book was in the writing.

The Nevada Historical Society was a rich source, as was the Oral History Project of the University of Nevada, Reno.

MaraLyn O'Neal was her usual professional self in the final preparation of the manuscript. She somehow managed to squeeze eight or nine days in each of the last weeks as the deadline grew nearer.

Susan Horton began as the principal researcher on this book. With her husband, Chris, she became advisor, helper, conscience, and friend.

As always, to my wife Olivia my love and my thanks.

LEON MANDEL

Reno, Nevada
March 18, 1981

Prologue

William Fisk Harrah's name is only now becoming known outside the gambling business. It is past time. In many ways the signs that say "Harrah's" outside hotels and casinos in Atlantic City, Reno, and Tahoe have the same implication as the signs that said "Ford" over Henry, Sr.'s early plants.

As Henry Ford, Sr., changed the way America spends its leisure time—not by inventing the automobile but by industrializing its production—Bill Harrah's legacy is a change of the same kind, perhaps even of the same magnitude. Ford's assembly line was Harrah's procedure book, Day Report, and every morning profit and loss statement. Ford's $5-a-day wage (which was not automatic, by the way) was a precursor of Harrah's employee paternalism; the Ford "sociology" department was the model for Harrah's "grievance committee." If Ford put the nation in Model Ts and made the middle class mobile, Harrah, the second largest user of buses behind the military, introduced lower income blacks and Hispanics into a social arena where they had not been welcome before.

Of course, there is no predicting in 1981 whether gambling will spread much beyond thirty or so resorts by the end of this century. Our perspective is foreshortened and if we choose to take a hard look at the analogy between Harrah's gambling methods and Ford's production procedures in hopes of predicting societal effects of Harrah's contributions, we had better view the automobile industry from a moment just after the First World War; for in terms of maturity, that's about where gambling finds itself with two decades left in the century. Still, there are many who see in gambling the potential for revolutionizing the way we use leisure as well as for creating a new revenue pool to support such institutions as schools. Gamblers are predicting these things will happen, as are seekers of state and local revenue, and they are both echoed by the preachers of social doom. If they are right, gambling's spread will be the consequence of an acquired respectability and sophistication of operation; both of which are exactly, specifically the Harrah Legacy. W. R. Eadington, associate professor of economics at the University of Nevada, Reno, and the acknowledged authority on gambling within his state, wrote: "William Fisk Harrah . . . had greater impact upon the development of the casino gaming industry in northern Nevada and, indeed, in Nevada, than any other single individual."

How did this happen? Who was the man who had such profound influence? Bill Harrah was the first gambler to see the business as a part of mainstream America. He was the first member of the green-felt establishment to push hard for controls. He was the first to take his business public.

In everything he did—including the hiring of consultants before the consultants themselves realized their role in the business community—Harrah showed stunning foresight. Perhaps in consequence of that foresight, this tall, taciturn, fastidious, Victorian man came to have an amazing capacity to change. It is one thing to be able to see a decade ahead, quite another to be able to accommodate yourself and your company to the upheavals the decade will bring.

Harrah was a man who worshiped perfection. He demanded it from himself, with mixed success. He asked it of others with less reward. Harrah was also rapacious, ambitious, materialistic, uncommunicative, oblique, and socially narrow-minded. In sum, Willim Fisk Harrah was a man of great contradiction: simple pleasures, complex tastes; backwater diction, Aristotelian thought processes; a horse trader/bargainer who didn't give a damn for Return on Investment if it constrained the quality of service; a bigot who broke Nevada's color barrier; an arch conservative who was his industry's and his state's pathfinder.

Most of Harrah's contemporaries feel his legacy lies in the three great buildings in Sparks, Nevada, which house the remarkable fourteen-hundred-car assemblage, largest in the world, that says so much about Industrial America. Harrah surely felt he had put together the central American panorama in his collection. "Henry Ford built the car; Bill Harrah built its monument," said *Motor Trend* in its obituary. No question that the Collection is a stunning cultural contribution. Still, the mind wavers; will Harrah be remembered as the most dedicated priest of the American Car Culture or will his contribution be the rationalizing of an industry?

In any case, Harrah's achievements can't be properly judged outside time and place. He learned early lessons about promotion, the whimsy of law enforcement, and audiences in the extraordinary community of Venice, California. He discovered a hospitable environment in which to bring those lessons to bear in outlaw Nevada. In his four-decade march to empire, he profoundly influenced the community in which he lived.

Like it or not, Bill Harrah also changed our lives.

Like it or not, his influence will touch the social, economic, and leisure lives of our children and our grandchildren.

WILLIAM
FISK
HARRAH

1

Arrival in Gomorrah
May–October 1937

William Fisk Harrah, twenty-six-year-old charmer, pathological
car lover, and bingo entrepreneur; William Fisk Harrah, who
would spend the next four decades building a gambling monument as marbled and sturdy as the Arc de Triomphe; William
Fisk Harrah, who was not yet but soon would be assembling
the world's most important collection of automobiles; William
Fisk Harrah, the man who industrialized gambling; *that* Bill
Harrah arrived in Reno, Nevada—which was to become the
capital of his model empire—in May 1937.

He came to a town that was then, as it is now, four or five or
six communities superimposed on one another. There was
Reno, Mecca of Divorcées. There was the City of Ranchers
and Businessmen. Another City within the City waited at the
end of the trail for every sheepherder and cowboy in northern
Nevada. There was the City of the Players. And, of course,
there was Reno, the Nation's Harlot.

Not quite $23 million in assessed property clumped in four
square miles didn't leave sloganeers much choice but to call
Reno the Biggest Little City in the World; unfortunately for
the cause of accuracy Reno wasn't big (an estimated 22,000
persons lived in the Truckee Meadows) and it wasn't little and
it wasn't a city at all in the sense easterners understood the
word—a notion that would have infuriated 1937 Renoites. Didn't
Reno have an airport with four daily transcontinental mail and

passenger flights? And almost thirty car dealerships? And ten barbershops? Not to mention twenty-seven dentists, five department stores, four libraries, two mortuaries, three newspapers, ten public schools, forty-two physicians and surgeons, one hundred fifteen lawyers, seventeen "places of amusement," and two permanent meeting places for the United Ancient Order of Druids? Talk about your haven for professionals! Fortunately, the medicos made no objection when the city directory people claimed "[In] Reno . . . the sun shines every day in the year and sickness is banished." Well, yes, but banished even more thoroughly were spouses.

In 1941 the *Reader's Digest* decided the business of divorce had started in Reno just after the turn of the century: "A New York lawyer saw the advantage for divorce clients and from the first notorious case in 1905, the world has associated Reno with only one purpose." America's favorite magazine did not get it quite right. Nevada had been watching people get divorced since 1853, when a fourteen-year-old named Mary Powell married a miner named Benjamin Cole for a day. The lady had been deposited with a local family by her father who had gone off to California. When the father returned to discover that Miss Powell had become Mrs. Cole he promptly declared his daughter divorced.

It is true that divorce was Reno's most important industry before the Second World War (thereby developing local expertise Bill Harrah would capitalize upon six times), but the great prominence of the Reno separation did not arise until a year after the *Reader's Digest* said it had. In 1906, Laura (Mrs. William Ellis) Corey, wife of the young and prominent president of U. S. Steel, a faithful spouse of twenty years, discovered her husband languishing in the arms of one Mabelle Gilman, an actress. Off to Reno she went, sued successfully, and won a settlement of $2 million, an enormous sum for the day; big enough so the case broke into headlines all over the world. What the newly wealthy Mrs. Corey didn't do to make the Reno divorce notorious, Mary Pickford accomplished fourteen years later when she went to the Truckee Meadows for the divorce that would free her to marry Douglas Fairbanks.

Understanding the value of its remunerative if eccentric cottage industry, the state engaged in a quarter-century underbidding contest with the rest of the United States—indeed the world—to keep its advantage. From a six-month residency requirement in 1915, Reno changed to three months in 1927 when the chic set began to wander in droves to Mexico City or Paris to separate. ("Reno is not fashionable . . . people with money and imagination go to Paris," said *Harper's* in 1925.) If Reno could not compete in age and culture with the Old World, it could at least counter with efficiency. Upstarts Idaho and Arkansas waited three years to watch the 1927 Reno experiment and thereupon reduced the required term of residence themselves. Nevada replied to the threatened loss of an estimated $5 million annual divorce revenue by cutting the three-month term to six weeks. That did it. Not only did divorce business pick up—and these were the Depression years during which any economic shot in the arm was welcome—but so did the supply side of the divorce equation: marriage. In the first seven months of 1936, for example, the Washoe county clerk issued 3,881 marriage licenses while the courts were entertaining fewer than half that many divorce suits. Some of the marriage business was brought in by transcontinental wedding "specials" from the east, but most of it came from California in consequence of that state's "Gin Marriage" law, which required a five-day waiting period between the issuance of a license and the ceremony, compared to Nevada's no waiting at all.

What's more, Reno made it easy—if not downright fun—to divorce. Said one national magazine during those months of 1,520 divorces, quoting a straw man it chose to call "Paiute Pete," ". . . them judges that hear the divorce cases [will] lock the doors against the public and newspapermen if you ask 'em to—hold their court sessions any hour of the day . . . Reno's danged obliging to the party that wants to get divorced, get married, or get a girl."

In particular, it was danged obliging to women who came to the Washoe Meadows. Dude ranches catered comfort and cowboys. "Reno is a masculine town . . . conceived and operated

by men—for women," said Paul Gallico in 1938, continuing
that no woman needed to feel lonely while she was "taking the
cure."

In 1976, in celebration of Nevada's going bicentennial (one
of the relatively few instances of the state's acting in accord
with the rest of the nation), Nancy J. Jackson wrote a warm,
anecdotal reminiscence for the Official Bicentennial Book
about life on the dude ranches. Crediting "Judgie" Bartlett
with easing the divorcée's path by making it no longer necessary to charge specifics and adduce evidence to support them
("In this way the present morbid practice of publicizing the
intimate details of divorce action will be avoided"), Jackson
came close to rhapsodizing about life on the divorce trail. In
the year Nevada passed its six-week residency law, 1931, dude
ranches built for the "trade" began to peek their heads above
the horizon at Pyramid Lake, about thirty miles northeast of
Reno near what is now a Paiute Indian Reservation, and to the
south of town, on the road to the state capital at Carson City.
Jackson describes the Franktown Hotel, off the Carson highway, as "a kind of home away from home" with horses, obliging wranglers, and "the best cook, Edie Riley, in the country."
The Franktown even had a bridal suite, although, says Jackson,
it was used far more by affluent divorce applicants than honey-
moon couples. (*The American Magazine*, in October 1930,
was fascinated enough by the Reno divorce phenomenon to investigate demographics: "Most divorce seekers are well-to-do,
chiefly rich easterners. On the average they have been married
about ten years. Two thirds of them are women.") Jackson
tolls the list of famous dude ranch keepers as though she were
quoting a particularly rich page from the Almanach de Gotha,
and gives them credit for extraordinary professionalism in offering "congeniality," "a pleasant atmosphere," "talking to the
guests in their own language," and, above all, "privacy." While
Jackson did not choose to address herself to the origin of the
phrase "dude ranch," she was explicit about why they were not
called "guest ranches," that being the euphemism permitted in
official language for Nevada's legal brothels.

The divorce trade added money to Reno's economy not only

as a civic profit center on its own, but also as supplier to that other Reno cash machine: gambling. Happily for Bill Harrah, who would begin in Reno as the operator of a succession of bingo parlors, putative divorcées were fanatics when it came to the game he ran. "Next to the slot machines, the favorite form of gambling among women in Reno seems to be bingo which can be played for as little as $.10 a card. I watched this phenomenon and can report . . . that bingo is merely a pseudonym for lotto, a nursery game which normal children outgrow and find boring by nine," wrote Ernest Havemann in a 1940 issue of *Life* magazine. If Harrah read Havemann on bingo, it must have elicited a wolflike smile. Nine-year-olds might have been fit for the breakfast menu, but Harrah's bingo was definitely for adults.

In addition to revenue, divorce during the '30s generated colorful language. The city park across from the courthouse was called "Alimony Park." A span over the Truckee, which runs through the city, was called "The Bridge of Sighs." Natives referred to the noon train from the east as the Divorcée Special. Monday, when default cases came up, was known as "Washday." Because of its unabashed position as a divorce capital, the *American Mercury* called Reno variously: "The Wicked Sodom," "The Gambling Gomorrah," "Love's Purgatory," and "The Great Divide." But it was left to Fred Schwed, Jr., writing in *Holiday* a decade later (1949) to add the longest-lasting label of all: "Reno the Place continues to thrive on Reno the Word. It is still the world's best-known Separation Center."

Upon all of this, the establishment city of Reno looked with jaundiced eye. Said its mouthpiece, the *Reno Evening Gazette*: "The *Gazette* has not changed its opinion about the character of [the Divorce Bill]. It is designed to further commercialize the courts and law-making power of this state and ignores entirely the social side of marriage." And that was mild compared to criticism from outside the state. The husband of one woman newly returned from Reno shed of him was typically furious. In his view, Reno was "a city where perjury and more perjury is the order of the day, a city where every effort is exerted to make the marriage institution seem like a farce and

where practically the entire populace feeds like vermin on
profits from the divorce mill."

II

Northern Nevada's ranchers, in particular, would have taken
old-fashioned western offense at being called vermin. For
them, for miners and businessmen and for their families, Reno
was the social hub of the region. These were plain, sturdy people to whom the city's two hospitals were terribly important,
who looked to Reno not only for physical but spiritual cure,
and who rode into town for wholesome entertainment as well
as a chance to pick up an Emerson radio or a few bottles of
Brilliantine hair dressing. For the soul Reno offered: Baptist,
Christian Science, Congregational, Episcopal, Jewish, Mormon, Lutheran, Methodist (white) and Methodist (black),
Presbyterian, Roman Catholic, and Seventh-Day Adventist
churches. The 1935 census had placed a value of just over $2.5
million on Reno's manufacturing output and counted 383
stores selling about $16.5 million worth of goods each year.

Reno had four movie theaters and an auditorium seating
two thousand. The University of Nevada choked with an en-
rollment of just over a thousand students.

All of this was dazzling to the visitors from the cow counties: Churchill, Storey, Mineral, Lyon, Pershing, Nye, Ormsby,
Lander, and Humboldt, whom Nevada prose laureate Robert
Laxalt described as "leathery men with quizzical, judging eyes,
women who get up in the darkness to cook huge breakfasts
. . . deeply religious [people] gentle with their children, but restrictive in a way that would shock modern parents."

It was *their* legislature that had passed the six-week divorce
bill in 1931 and *their* legislature that, in the same session,
passed legalized gambling; which is not to say there was whole-
hearted approval of either measure. But it is also not to say
that these solid folk would have much liked to read in *The
Nation* that "Few outsiders have ever heard of [Nevada's]
agriculture or any constructive activities, and no one with eyes

can see her as anything but a vast, exploited, underdeveloped state with a meager and boss-ridden population."

Nevadans who came to Reno to shop, to socialize, to worship, to study could not have ignored the goings-on in the city if they wanted to, but then, as now, there was a western tolerance for what others called "sin," accompanied by a profound resentment of outsiders—particularly easterners—who passed judgment about how Nevada lived. In addition, of course, some of the sagebrush people came to Reno to play. Perhaps because they bumped only briefly against the City of the Players, they were not inclined to condemn it.

III

In part, such condemnation was not forthcoming because upstanding citizens simply did not stay up late enough to see what there was to condemn. In part, it was because the players gambled, drank, and womanized to the exclusion of normal social intercourse; exclusion that was reciprocated by the denizens of Reno's other four communities. Of the seventeen "places of amusement" listed in the city directory in 1937, two of the three of particular consequence to the players, including Bill Harrah, did not go out of their way to make gentle folk feel at home. The third, Harolds, was an exception, but it had opened only shortly before Harrah's arrival and had not yet begun what would be a famous, landmark advertising campaign.

The Palace Club on Center Street was a monument to one of Reno's legendary early gamblers, Johnny Petrecciani. It did not run "flat" or cheater games, but it did not encourage a cross-section trade, either.

Much less did the Bank Club, epicenter for the unsavory activity in the City of the Players. The place was owned by Bill Graham and Jim McKay who, had they been born a generation later, would have sent Senator Estes Kefauver into paroxysms of delicious outrage and, in fact, did—although by the time the man with the raccoon cap got around to discovering what they had been up to, both of them were long gone. Thir-

teen years after Harrah set himself down in Reno, the Special
Senate Committee to Investigate Organized Crime in Interstate Commerce took testimony condemnatory enough to Graham and McKay that its report would say of them: ". . . for
years these two men controlled Reno politically and finan-
cially." If that was true, not much worse could have been said
about the moral climate of the city. Graham and McKay were
certified villains—felons—who had their hands in an evil stew
of embezzlement, money laundering, mail fraud, and very
likely murder. The Kefauver Hearings Report called them
"backers of [a] ring of swindlers." It went on to say of the
pair: "Graham and McKay have maintained contact with a
number of important underworld characters. This goes back
many years, even during the old Dillinger investigation in 1934
or before 1934. Baby Face Nelson, who was one of the most
notorious killers of the Dillinger gang, was a friend of theirs."
This last was understatement.

Bill Graham and Jim McKay had come up from the Nevada
boom town of Tonopah in the late '20s. Before opening in the
Bank Club, they had operated a variety of small speakeasy cum
gambling joints in Reno as well as a nightclub near the California border called the Willows—an extravagant and lavish
place catering to the western equivalent of the Newport set.
According to one chronicler of Reno gambling, Raymond Sawyer, the two took "executive offices" in the Riverside Hotel
bank, "spreading the word they were interested in *any* deal in-
volving the movement of cash." The record shows McKay and
Graham arrested in 1934 for using the mails to defraud in a
$2.5 million horse race swindle. (According to the Kefauver
testimony, one victim was an eighty-three-year-old former
United States Commissioner who lost $23,600 but who clearly
had the right names to call when he discovered he'd been
had.) After four years and three trials, Graham and McKay
were convicted, fined $11,000 apiece and eventually shipped off
for nine years each in prison. That much is certain. Also on the
record is a shooting death inflicted on one Blackie McCracken
by Bill Graham, which was instantly dismissed as self-defense.
From here, things get murky.

Robert Laxalt has no trouble at all attributing criminal innovation to the pair, giving them credit for "laundering money stolen in the rash of bank robberies that was sweeping the nation.

"Hit and run robbers of the ilk of Baby Face Nelson and Alvin Karpis headed straight for Reno with their loot. There, they turned the traceable greenbacks over to . . . Bill Graham and Jim McKay and received clean money in return, less, of course, a modest handling charge." Graham and McKay's Bank Club tables were the laundromats of their day. Although a number of memoirs and even a few credentialed histories suggest that Baby Face Nelson spent a lot of time keeping out of sight during these ad hoc banking transactions, he evidently didn't keep *that* far out of sight, which brings us back to the murkiness.

A key witness against Graham and McKay in the 1934 mail fraud case was one Roy Frisch who worked at the Riverside bank. In the classic way of prosecution witnesses of the era, Frisch suddenly disappeared. Raymond Sawyer is certain he knows what happened:

"It was revealed later that before the bullet-ridden corpse of Baby Face Nelson was recovered from a ditch somewhere in Illinois, Nelson had been traced to Reno and it was established that he was in town at this particular time, as well as on the night that Roy Frisch disappeared.

"A gangster named John Chase, in jail at Alcatraz, confessed that he and Nelson had taken Frisch from the street, killed him, and burned his body just before burying it off a dirt road in a mountain range somewhere southeast of Reno . . ."

Chase would not testify and Nelson was beyond it, so Frisch is listed as a missing person to this day.

Certainly, neither Graham nor McKay was exactly a deacon of Reno's social church, but that didn't seem to make much difference to their fellow players, including Bill Harrah. The Bank Club was a regular hangout for Virgil Smith, who would later own a very tony club of his own called Colbrandt's; for the Harolds Club Smiths; for Bob Ring, Harrah's confidant and drinking partner; and for the rest of the rather select group of carousers who made up Reno's gambling establishment.

Every night Harrah would make the rounds: Harolds, the

Palace, the Wine House, the Bank Club. A young and healthy
Bill Harrah was a thirsty Bill Harrah, and he did not stint on
the Cutty Sark. But if Harrah and his cronies were drinkers
and players, they were not opium eaters, which seemed to have
been a popular weekend diversion in the Reno of the late '30s.
In two of the memoirs of the early days in the Truckee
Meadows written by players, both mention that opium smoking was relatively common and no one took particular notice—
much less the time to criticize.

Flat games, clubs run by embezzlers, bank robbers, and contract killers, free trade in heavy drugs—it does not make for a
happy picture of the City of the Players. Add to all of those
the human scenery, in particular the victims of Reno's dark
side. "Men of Reno . . ." said a contemporary *Harper's*,
". . . they were the haunting horror, the poison in the town's
blood . . . not the solid citizens [but] the drifting males who
pace the sidewalks, who clog the hotel lobbies, who pack aim-
lessly on street corners, who sit on the park benches above the
Truckee River, regarding life with wandering, hostile eyes."

IV

The possibility that Bill Harrah looked into those "wandering, hostile eyes" is remote; he would not have passed them on
his regular rounds. Whether Bill Harrah on those rounds made
it a point to be at the Bank Club at 2 A.M. when the ladies
came up from the stockade, no one is willing to confirm. It is
more than likely. He was often there late and they were *always*
there. The players did not seem to view their company as special, or surprising, or even unusual. Said Warren Nelson, an
early figure in Reno gambling and a soon-to-be manager of
Harrah's, "In Reno . . . the 'line' was wide open. The girls
would come up from the 'cribs'; the police would let them
come up after two o'clock in the morning to play. The pimps
would come up with them. It was part of our business."

Legalized prostitution may have been in debate in the
Reno of 1937, but it was also entrenched, controlled in the city
by—of course—Bill Graham and Jim McKay. There had been
innumerable quarrels in the city council about Reno's hospita-

ble attitude toward whores; bluenose Reno was and always had been outraged by the sight of painted women within the city limits, but a permissive mayor, E. E. Roberts, and a resigned council decided that prostitution was better regulated than not, so with a collective sigh (some no doubt in relief), they confined the ladies to an undistinguished quarter of town and required them to undergo regular health inspections.

That quarter housed the old Chinatown Cribs. Nowadays the very place is the site of the main Reno plant of Nevada Bell, to the delight of old-timers. Their existence, as well as that of the Riverside Stockade, scandalized the nation and provided highly spiced copy for the sensational press of the likes of *Real Detective*:

"New York Betty was dressing. Filmy silk panties, skin tight and gossamer sheer, blended indistinguishably with the warm, pink flesh of her curvaceous body . . ." which was pretty racy stuff for the day. But special investigative reporter Con Ryan was not content to be merely descriptive; what was needed here was a little socioeconomics.

"The Bull Pen, also known throughout Nevada as the District, the Stockade, the Line, or the Old Homestead, consists of seventy-five individual cribs, each occupied by a girl in various stages of undress, plying the oldest trade in the world with the sanction of local and state law and by the grace of a shadowy Chinese known only as 'Wong' [a.k.a., as we have discovered, Graham and McKay].

"The cribs are two-room affairs, facing inward on the Bull Pen, built of red brick, with a shoddy lean-to shanty tacked on at the back. A bed occupies most of the front room or parlor . . . the door and window of each crib are always open to the passerby on the sidewalk, giving an intimate glimpse into the cribs . . ."

Using *Real Detective* expense money to lure New York Betty into conversation, Ryan conducted a purported interview during which he discovered what regulation there was in Reno. "I pay $2.50 rental for this dump," New York Betty told him. "It entitles me to operate here for eight hours. When things are humming, the Bull Pen works three shifts a day. Once a week I go in to the city health officer . . . for an examination."

"What about the law?" asked Ryan.

"What law?" Betty is said to have replied. "All the local law says is that a district like this stays at least two hundred and fifty feet away from any public street or alley. That's why you have to walk down that dusty trail and across the wooden bridge to get to us. All the state law says is that we keep at least three hundred yards from a church or school building."

Still, according to Ryan, his local source did not attribute Reno's economic health to her contributions nor those of her colleagues. "Don't let it fool you. This is small-time stuff now —a sideline to Reno's main racket." The main racket?

"We started this sex business, sure. But Reno's businessmen —the law-makers, too—made marriage and divorce the big attractions of this town."

True Detective is not a source serious researchers credit. Con Ryan may or may not have been real; New York Betty almost certainly existed only in someone's imagination. Certainly, though, most of the magazine's exposé was close enough, although it indulged itself in some gratuitous editorializing: "A whole state—its legislature, laws, and citizens—have been warped to the one end, that strangers may be lured to Reno and there sheared of his or her wealth by Nevada's legalized system of quick marriage, easy divorce, wide-open prostitution, gambling and worse."

Obviously, Gomorrah.

Which is why, in large extent, Bill Harrah literally sent a cab to California to pick up his soon-to-be first wife, Thelma Batchelor, from Venice, while he planted himself firmly and forever in Reno, Nevada, in that May of 1937. As a young man buffeted by the on-and-off enforcement of laws against the sins of bingo in Southern California, he saw Reno as an oasis of freedom. As a live-and-let-live westerner, Harrah saw nothing wrong with the likes of Bill Graham and Jim McKay, who, after all, ran straight games at the Bank Club. What they did on their own time was their business. All they wanted was to be left alone.

If anyone should have been able to understand that, it was Bill Harrah.

2

We Open in Venice

Lancaster County, Pennsylvania, 1742–1937, Southern California

Twenty-one-year-old Bill Harrah posed for what is now a revealing photo. It is in vertical format, a good thing since the young Harrah had some years since attained his growth, all six feet two of it. He stands against a sepia background dressed in jodhpurs and a hacking coat, the genteel, class-defining attire of the proper Southern Californian in the salad days of the century. He is clearly unhappy to be confronted by a camera—and he would be for the rest of his life. His expression is stern. It is the photo of a self-possessed young man, and it projects the intensity of the character; in part annoyance, in part resolve, and much stoicism.

The dress, then, is Southern California affluent-casual; the expression Calvinist, the impression that of a formidable young man.

There is no hint in the photo that its subject was, at the time, a successful gambler and a hell-raiser; instead, the image oozes respectability, which may have been a Bill Harrah joke but which also, certainly, came quite naturally.

There is neither frivolity nor scandal to be found in the leg-

acy of Harrah's family, although the young man in the photo
would spend a good deal of his life rectifying *that* oversight.

In 1938, Bill Harrah's third cousin, Lucy E. Hall, then super-
intendent of the Jasper County, Iowa, schools, set to wondering about her family. If what she discovered disappointed her,
she didn't show it other than to mail to a few selected relatives
what genealogical information she'd managed to unearth second class. Three decades later, William Fisk Harrah would undertake the same task but his research resulted in a typically
brief, dry document in no way as entertaining as Lucy Hall's.

The first record of a Harrah ancestor in America turns out to
be not a Harrah at all but an O'Hara, an émigré to Lancaster
County, Pennsylvania, from northern Ireland. For whatever
reason, upon sighting the shores of the North American continent in 1748, the first thing he did was change the spelling of
his name to "Harra," to which, given the times, his wife and
two young sons acceded. One of those boys, Charles, born in
1742, was to become a Revolutionary War private in the Pennsylvania militia and Bill Harrah's great-great-great-grandfather.
He received a land warrant for his war service and along with
it a certificate of loyalty to the new nation's government,
whereupon he hied himself off to the wild west, nineteen miles
southeast of Pittsburgh.

Lucy Hall was clearly in awe of Charles and his family:
"Their hardships as pioneer settlers none can now imagine. At
one time when both [Charles and his wife, the former Margaret Gilchrist] were working in a field, a military officer rode
up and called Mr. Harra to immediate duty in defense against
the Indians. He was gone for six weeks and during the entire
time his family heard not a word from him."

Obviously a fine, churchgoing woman, Lucy Hall gives the
Charles Harra family full marks for piety: "Charles Harra and
his good wife were zealous Presbyterians and as soon as they
had a sufficient number of neighbors, they joined themselves
together with them in the organization of the Round Hill Presbyterian Church. This is still a prosperous church and is situ-
ated three miles from Elizabeth in Allegheny County." Cousin
Lucy would spend much energy and devote considerable space
to testimony of the solid Presbyterian faith of many of her

forebears; Lord knows what she might have had to say about a relative who grew up to be the most important gambler in the country.

James Gilchrist Harra, twin brother to Alexander and Bill Harrah's great-great-grandfather, was born in 1778 (although his great-great-grandson would later decide to move his birth-date up a year to 1779), married Margaret Neill and decided to move even farther west, to Ohio, in 1803. They settled in Jefferson County, seventy-five miles from their Pennsylvania home, in a spot chosen by a "friendly Indian" who might also have been in the real estate business. For them too, faith was a source of strength; on their very first Sunday in frontier Ohio, they met with the Reverend John Rea and Daniel Welch to worship under the shade of a beech tree, near a spring. "At once they resolved to form the Beech Spring Church, which in after years became one of the strongest Presbyterian churches in Ohio." Between services at the Beech Spring Church, which James served as an elder, the family managed to produce nine children and add an "H" to the end of its name.

One of the nine offspring was William Neill Harrah, who was urged to study for the ministry but went into the tannery business instead. The later William Harrah would say little about him other than that his nephew Frank founded Harrah, Oklahoma, and that he had the good sense to move to Iowa, where the modern Harrah saga really begins.

At first, William Neill took his family to a spot near Davenport, but later they went over westward to Newton, described as it was then by Lucy Hall: "Most of the land was virgin prairie and the children [eight survivors of thirteen born, including Adam Myers Harrah, Bill Harrah's grandfather, and Sarah Harrah, Lucy Hall's mother] gathered wild plums, cherries, grapes and berries of all kinds. These were dried to a great extent as were various kinds of vegetables. It was no uncommon sight to see great strings of sliced apples hanging from the strings stretched above the fireplace or stove or to find pans of fruit on the shelves or in the ovens.

"The mother of the family usually had to be the doctor and the Harrah children gathered great masses of peppermint, spearmint, pennyroyal, catnip and various kinds of herbs, which were dried or steeped to make the needed medicines for the family."

When the Harrah family settled on the Riverside stock farm in Newton, there were just two stores in town. All eight children went to a school taught by one Colonel John Meyer, whose granddaughter, Amanda Fisk, would marry William Neill's grandson, John Garrett, and join with him to produce William Fisk Harrah.

The intervening generation was handsomely occupied by Adam Myers Harrah, second youngest of the children, whose education was achieved at two energetically named schools: Wittemberg Manual Labor and Oskaloosa colleges, from which he went on to the law school at Iowa State University. Adam Myers was a respected man in Newton, county attorney for Jasper County and partner in the firm of Harrah and Myers. In 1881, he married Anna Garrett, whose father fought with Grant at Vicksburg and after whom the Garrett post of the G.A.R. in Newton was named.

Of this sturdy Iowa citizen, who died in 1919 in California where he had taken his family, his grandson remembered typically only one important fact. Adam Myers' funeral was the first event of its kind Bill had ever attended, no surprise considering he was eight years old at the time. "The high point of the funeral," he would say later with unconscious dark humor, "was my father borrowed a Marmon automobile to transport the family, which was much classier than our family car. I remember more about the Marmon than I do the funeral."

That funeral took place in Venice, California. Adam had moved as far west as he could go in 1905, landing in Pasadena, about which the *New Republic* would say a quarter century later: "The place is not merely a community; . . . It symbolizes American plutocracy at its ripest. Here is the best spot in the United States for a good, scholarly, 100% American to ponder over the symptoms which characterized the decay of the Roman Empire."

Either Adam was not scholarly enough or not American enough, for he took himself from Pasadena to Venice shortly thereafter. It was a felicitous choice, not because the town was hospitable or gracious, but because his son, John Garrett, would take *his* family there and John and John's son, Bill, would live in symbiotic reinforcement with the community throughout Bill's early years. Venice would provide them both with a congenial atmosphere and exert great influence on the later lives of father and son.

II

Venice, California, in the years between Adam Harrah's arrival and the Second World War, was a delightfully bizarre beach town, extraordinary enough to stand out in a region that was already known for its eccentricity.

The town's founder, Abbot Kinney, claimed to be a descendant of Ralph Waldo Emerson, William Henry Harrison, and Oliver Wendell Holmes. He had served on President Grant's staff, which seems to have inspired him to speculate on the stock market, where he was properly fleeced. In the meanwhile, Kinney's brothers had started a tobacco company specializing in a new and promising product, cigarettes. Among their brands was Sweet Caporal, the Winston of its day, which would make the Kinneys rich. Nonetheless, Abbot's debacle in the stock market so demoralized him that he fell sick and decided he would take his therapy in travel. Kinney landed in San Francisco on his return via the Far East in 1880, at the very moment an immense snowstorm descended on the Sierra, which effectively prevented him from going home to the east coast. With time on his hands, he decided to wander down to Southern California, where he discovered the salubrious climate he had sought during his journey and had not found.

In succeeding years, Kinney became a presence in the region, founding a construction firm that among other projects paved and landscaped what is now Wilshire Boulevard. In the natural course of his business, he put together a land syndicate that bought 247 acres north of Santa Monica and another tract south of the same town. At the time, Kinney's foresight in the second purchase seemed suspect; the land was sand and swamp. Still, the syndicate was able to persuade the Santa Fe railroad to extend a spur to the tract and there it built a Disneyland progenitor with boardwalk, pier, golf course, and horse track.

Kinney was not an easy man to get along with, and he went through a platoon of partners and associates buying, selling, or swapping land held in joint ownership at each rupture in each relationship. He came out of all the turmoil as sole owner of the land south of Santa Monica; the land with the sand and the swamp, the pier and the boardwalk.

It was entirely in keeping with early Southern California attitudes that Kinney should decide to turn this abominable landscape into an American Venice. In June of 1904, canal construction began. In March 1905 a huge storm treated Kinney's town as a single wave would a sand castle, destroying the pier and an auditorium and damaging almost everything in sight. An only moderately fazed Kinney immediately ordered the town rebuilt, this time with a breakwater to protect it.

In their lovely book, *Fantasy by the Sea*, Tom Moran and Tom Sewell described the reconstructed Venice: "Windward Avenue was the main street . . . along [it] the architectural dreams of Abbot Kinney took shape. Three-story hotels lined the street. They were designed to recapture the flavor of the Italian Venice and featured an ornate mix of Byzantine and Renaissance influence. The buildings shared common walls and were connected by an arcade running the length of the street.

"The exterior walls were trimmed with reliefs of the Lion of St. Mark's, and Egyptian crescent flags decorated the street." And that was only a beginning. Canals Abbot Kinney wanted and canals he got, seven canals totaling seven miles, and named Grand, Aldebaran, Coral, Lion, Altair, Cabrillo, and Venus, set out in a grid pattern and connected to the sea through great pipes containing tidal gates so that the ocean could renew the water they held. .

The pier was rebuilt and went out sixteen hundred feet. At its landbound foot was a pavilion housing a ballroom and an exhibition hall; the breakwater protected the pier to seaward.

A year later, sometime during the same months that Adam Myers Harrah moved to Venice from Pasadena, one Gaston

Akoun opened the Midway-Plaisance in Venice featuring "a
long row of exhibits, amusements and freak shows," including
divertissements named, variously, the Streets of Cairo, Temple
of Mirth, Ouitta's Occult Show, Darkness and Dawn, and
what were said to be headhunting Igorots from the Philip-
pines.

Mainly there was the beach, which, when threatened by a
shifting tidal pattern established by the new breakwater, was
widened and made secure by the addition of sand from a sew-
age treatment plant.

About this time, the Abbot Kinney Company decided to
move the midway to the pier and add attractions, including
Garvey's Captive Aeroplanes and the American Racing Derby.
Moran and Sewell quote a publicity handout of the era:

"Hundreds of concessions with every sort of novelty known
to the carnival world are here . . . You may play any sort of
game with any type [sic] of pretty girl.

"There are lakes of colored soda water and oceans of root
beer and ice cream soda concoctions enough to ruin all the
stomachs in California . . .

"There are side shows which savor of the circuses you went
into ecstasies of delight over when you were a child, composing
every sort of freak, tame and wild, trained and untrained,
known to the ingenuity of mankind . . .

"There are rides with long dark canals in romantic coaster
boats . . .

"There are tubs of joy and hair-raising rides . . ." One such
ride alone clocked in 48,000 paid over an early Fourth of July.

By the time three generations of Harrahs settled in Venice,
the town had added boxing "smokers," rough water swimming
races and surfboarding (in which Duke Kahanamoku was
prominent), a Pacific Coast League AA baseball franchise
(featuring future Hall of Famer Joe "Iron Man" McGinnity),
visits by the Sells-Floto and Barnes (soon to merge with
Ringling Brothers) Circuses, and the Venice Grand Prix, a
road race through the city streets, with drivers of the likes of
Dario Resta, Ralph DePalma, and Barney Oldfield and a wonderful variety of cars: Peugeot, Mercer, Stutz, Delage, Simplex,
Maxwell, and Chevrolet.

After the First World War, a tottering infant of an aircraft industry settled in Venice, building planes with names of the past: Stearman, Crawford, Catron, and Fisk. The local airport, called either Ince or Delay field, housed a flock of stunt flyers whom Abbot Kinney Company hired to keep visitors on the beaches entertained.

In 1920, Abbot Kinney died. A month later the Venice pier burned down, once again destroying the Midway's delectations. And once again, it was rebuilt, its opening (on a July Fourth) accompanied by what had come to be expected from Venice promoters; a blizzard of ballyhoo and hype including seductive cooings by celebrities Jack Dempsey, Charlie Chaplin, and Jackie Coogan.

However much Venice glittered in the Southern California sunlight, it had its dark side. The two younger generations of Harrahs were to live in that shade from the Depression forward, and its political and economic clamminess would get the better of them both.

Recall that when Abbot Kinney decided to replicate Venice, he envisioned a self-contained community, what was to become something the state of California called a "sixth-class city." To its north was Santa Monica, to its south, Ocean Park. It was a creation of the Abbot Kinney Company, and in that sense, at least, it was a company town looking to the company to negotiate, as an example, the interurban line that brought visitors to its midway. There had been talk of annexation by Los Angeles, but when it was put to the voters, they turned it down.

In 1922 a pair of circumstances changed their minds.

City treasurer James Peasgood made off with $19,000; which set some people to questioning his honesty, as well as the honesty of the balance of the city's government.

Shortly thereafter, the Ku Klux Klan held an initiation ceremony in nearby Ocean Park Heights inducting an alleged two thousand members. That sent L.A. district attorney T. L. Woolwine into a rage, and he took up the scent. It was obviously strong, and when the investigation results became public, the smell outraged the nostrils of good Venetians. They discovered that not only was the Klan involved in the Venice police department, it had infiltrated city government. The revelations were enough to persuade voters to seek cleansing through annexation. Venice elected to become a part of Los Angeles on February 20, 1923.

If the community thought annexation would solve its political and economic problems, it was soon to be disabused. Those problems were many, they were complex, and they had been with Venice almost from the beginning.

Venice's first name had actually been Ocean Park. It was a town governed by a board of trustees and owned—at least its amusement sector—by the Abbot Kinney Company, whose powerful influence in the community sat not at all well with a segment of citizenry. When the company decided to field its own candidates for the board, calling its political arm the Good Government League after national reformers of the same name, they met opposition from not only mere denizens but also Abbot Kinney's old partners in the land purchase for the city. The Kinney people won, controlling the board through the early '20s, but the fight split the town and "Charges of fraud, forged signatures and miscounting were commonly leveled at election time." Moran and Sewell faced the issue squarely. What's more, they reached beneath the surface for the real reasons that prompted divisiveness: "The needs of an amusement town devoted to providing a good time for all who visited it often ran counter to both the law and the desires of a more staid growing residential population. Gambling dens and brothels existed as did such 'lesser evils' as roll-down games, chuck-a-luck and 'razzle-dazzle.' "

John Harrah, and soon his son as well, would become intimate with the town's schizophrenia; John as a member of the board and then mayor of Venice, Bill as operator and owner of a "roll-down" game, which he bought from his father.

From those moments forward, Venice's problems were the problems of the Harrah family. By the same token, Venice's delights were to the family's profit, although it did not seem so at the time.

3

The Family Scamp
Southern California, 1911–1937

"Every time I come to your house, I get the feeling no one's been introduced." Margaret Harrah Schroter, William Fisk Harrah's sister and senior surviving descendant of A. M. Harrah's branch of the family, sits stern and upright in a winged chair in her West Hollywood house remembering early days in Venice. Her friends were welcome to visit, she is saying, but sometimes they found the atmosphere strange.

Margaret Schroter is an accomplished guide to the past. She is seventy-four now, a Susan B. Anthony commemorative medallion with a bright eye. Hers is the dry, precise locution of everybody's seventh-grade English teacher. She is a beautifully spoken woman, at once austere, at the same time antiseptically, puritanically, chastely flirtatious. It is easy to hear echoes of the 1930s in her voice. The decade hovers over her. Her past takes shape in Margaret Schroter's house, which is not far from another house in which John and Amanda Harrah stopped for a year or so on their way from affluence to Venice.

Margaret and George Schroter, a mining engineer, bought this house soon after they were married, when Bill had gone to Reno. It is Spanish-Norman, a small place on a street of small, neat places; set back from a road so close to Sunset Boulevard it seems astonishing to find such a placid evocation of early

Los Angeles cheek to jowl with the Comedy Store and bill-
boards hawking Blondie and Supertramp recordings. It is as
though the neighborhood in which she lives decided sometime
in the mid-'40s that it had discovered contentment and waved
the rest of the city by.

Margaret was born in Newton, Iowa, but by the time Bill
came along, three and a half years later, John and Amanda had
moved to California, to a house in South Pasadena. That put
them close to Margaret's grandparents, who had gone to
Pasadena, but, as Bill would say, Pasadena was too "ritzy" for
his father's pocketbook. Margaret remembers her parents, the
young Mr. and Mrs. John Harrah, as handsome people; John
tall (five feet eleven) and slender, her mother small and vivacious. It was a quiet household. The Harrahs were not given to
small talk, particularly John, who spent much time reading.

The children were tended by a housekeeper/nanny, May
Aydelott, who had come out with the Harrahs from Iowa. She
was, in Bill's words, "an old maid [who] became just a member
of the family." May Aydelott's presence was not only a good
thing, it was probably necessary. John Harrah liked tiny babies,
but when they were able to walk and talk, he wanted little to
do with his children. Amanda Harrah seems to have been
caught between cultures, perhaps between centuries. During
the early years, when her children were quite young, she was a
companion to them and opened her house to their friends. She
was a good cook and a lavish hostess. Only later would Margaret realize how deeply troubled she was.

Bill seems to have been more sensitive to his mother's anguish: "My father wasn't too social; my mother was very social.
At one time she was voted the 'most popular girl' in Newton.
She used to go back a lot after we moved to California. She
was homesick. Her father died when she was very young and
her mother died when I was just a baby. But my mother had a
brother back there, and also she had many, many, many
friends in Newton.

"So we had a kind of pattern . . . she'd go back about every
summer for a month. Looking back later, I could see how
homesick she was." One of those very, very, very good friends

was Elmer Maytag—"Maytag Washing Machine was the heart of Newton; still is, for that matter." Amanda used to joke with her son that his name might have been Maytag.

It did not seem to a very young Margaret that her mother was particularly unhappy. If the atmosphere in the household was unusually dignified, it was still fun. "She [Amanda] was good company, although I think my mother was kind of a snob. She was pretty aloof from outsiders." Emphasis comes on the last word. Certainly within the family there was warmth. On holidays, the Harrahs, who were by then living in Venice in one of three houses John's mother, Anna Garrett Harrah, inherited on the death of A.M., all would gather in old-fashioned celebration. Christmas, especially, was a joyful time tempered by Iowa good sense which had put a limit on extravagance of the presents.

It was also a traditional family, principally because John was a curious combination of Victorian father and rogue. He was firm about language. Margaret never once heard him swear and he was an absolutist when it came to grammar. (His son, who rebelled against a great many things in his life, was selective when it came to accepting his father's view of the spoken word. Bill never used bad language in public but his grammar was atrocious.)

John had a roving eye, he spent less and less time at home watching his wife age and lose her figure, and more and more at his office acquiring deeds of trust on Los Angeles real estate and scouting up companions who could offer the youth and vivacity Amanda was no longer able to give.

Of sibling clashes there were none. After all, Margaret was sufficiently older than her brother to look on him with that quasi-maternal affection elder sisters employ to circumvent competition with adored youngest children. Her memories of Bill as a child are vivid, including one on the subject of his medical record: "[Bill] was never very robust; his blood wouldn't coagulate. I'm not sure it was hemophilia, but his health was never good." Margaret may have been just a mite jealous when her brother began to stretch his social horizons. "He had loads of clothes in the latest style—whatever it was— I never had half of what he had."

By his early teens, Bill had become a handsome young man, taking very much after his father, a fact that did not escape the girls at Venice Junior High. "I'd answer the phone," says Margaret with faint disapproval to this day, "and there was some girl calling *him*, which wasn't really proper." Still, she could understand why they called. "Bill was vivacious and good-looking and talkative." Margaret, a prudent girl as she is now clearly a prudent woman, saved her money, but "Bill was always flat. He'd come roaring into my room saying, 'All right, where d'ya keep it? I've got to have twenty-five bucks.'

"He spent it as soon as he got it."

It sounds like a lively life. It may have been, but it was also life in a shadow, for by the time Bill was going out with the girls at Venice Junior High and later Hollywood High, Amanda was in a bad way. First, her health had broken. She had such acute arthritis she could hardly use one hand. She had become fat; she began to drink heavily. One day, shortly after Margaret had left UCLA and married George Schroter, the phone rang in the then-new house in West Hollywood. It was Bill telling her that Amanda had been taken to the hospital, that "she'd swallowed something." The something was poison and it "just smothered" her.

"She had a drinking problem," Bill would say. "It just got worse and worse and finally [it got] *terrible*." Bill *did* try to help. He took his mother to a man he thought was qualified to treat alcoholics. "It was so futile that she had to die. She had a quack I'd steered her to. I thought he was a good doctor [but] he hadn't helped her a bit."

He never told anyone how his mother's suicide affected him. There is only the record. His own drinking increased; when he was deep in alcohol a lively, boisterous Bill Harrah was evident, but after his mother's death, sobriety showed a new side: the quiet, even withdrawn man he would remain throughout his life.

II

Even as a grade student at the Florence Nightingale school, Bill Harrah showed evidences of what Margaret calls his "monomania" about cars. On the middle pages of a copy book he drew "The Moter-cycle [sic] of to-morrow" and "The Auto of to-morrow." The car anticipates Buckminster Fuller's Dymaxion, which Harrah later acquired for his collection. It is in the shape of a cylinder with an airstream trailer, rounded back and a pointed nose, which a very young Bill Harrah labeled "bow, for breaking wind." It is carefully drawn, rich in details which are meticulously identified: "Driver's seat/note window," "window in streamlined back." Today we would call it a van; there is a full-width seat forward of the door, and four similar seats aft of it. The wheels are spoked; there is a ship's ladder drawn between door and ground.

Such a careful representation might have surprised his teachers; it would not have surprised Margaret. "When he was very young, he had little automobiles. He'd be crawling around with one, pushing it and making car noises." His sister thinks Bill Harrah may "have been born loving cars.

"Oh! That was his one and only interest—automobiles. Before he could *read*, his favorite magazine was *Popular Mechanics*. He'd sit and look at each page just as if he *were* reading it." She remembers her mother saying in later years that she couldn't remember when Margaret wasn't able to read and when Bill couldn't drive.

Six months before his death, Bill Harrah recalled his first moments driving a car: "I learned to drive when I was um—let's see—somethin' like eight years old. Every summer we went to Big Bear—a mountain area in Southern California. We would rent a cabin up there for a month or six weeks. My father would go to Los Angeles on Monday, come back on Friday.

"I think he was driving a Chalmers at the time. But he'd found an old Hudson somewhere, about a 1911. It was right-hand drive, which in 1916 [made it] a funny-lookin' car. You had to crank it to start it. And I could drive it fine, although I couldn't see over the steering wheel and I couldn't start it 'cause I was so little.

"So I'd park it on a hill and then after breakfast I'd want to go to the store for my mother or just go for a ride. I'd go out and coast the Hudson down the hill a ways and let the clutch out and away it would go—'chug, chug, chug, chug.'"

Harrah's memory for cars was still phenomenal. Later in his reminiscences he would talk of major events in his life and the houses to which his peripatetic family moved using the same mnemonic device: "I can remember where we lived by what kind of a car we drove 'cause [at] the second home we had a 1922 Franklin; so as I was born in 1911, I was eleven when we moved there, and [a year later] I joined the Boy Scouts. I loved the Boy Scouts."

He loved cars more. It was one thing to drive an old Hudson belonging to his father, but at Hollywood High he needed and wanted a car of his own. John Harrah had established a personal transportation precedent with his son when the boy was nine and wanted a Ranger Moto Bike.

"Somethin' I want to tell you, Bill"—the son remembered—"birthdays and Christmas are mostly for your mother and sister. But you and I, anything you want that I can afford that your friends have, you can have."

Nine-year-old Bill got his Ranger; now sixteen-year-old Bill wanted a car. He knew it had to be low-priced or there was no use discussing it. He knew it could be no better (but no worse) than cars any of his friends owned. The choice was narrow: Ford, Chevrolet, and Star. "I'd studied them, of course, every inch, and I preferred the Chevrolet." After he got it, he "dolled it up."

When one of the girls who so annoyed Margaret with her forwardness would call, Bill would dress up, "leaving his room in a shambles but looking like a million dollars," with Margaret's twenty-five dollars in his pocket, and leap into his Chevy roadster. Not for long: "[The car] was stolen and stripped, of course, and that broke his heart." Evidently he never got over the heartbreak, for he told his sister later, "he was going to duplicate every car we had had in this family." Which, in fact, he did.

This was not aberrational behavior. Bill Harrah was far from the only car nut in Southern California in the '20s and '30s. In 1927 the *New Republic* claimed that Los Angeles was "now a

completely motorized civilization. Nowhere else in the world
have human beings so thoroughly adapted themselves to the
automobile. The advertisers' ideal, two cars to a family, has
very nearly been attained, not merely among the rich, but on
the average. The number of licensed drivers is just about equal
to the adult population, and all the children above the age of
10 are bootleg chauffeurs." A year later *Harper's* concurred:
"The incessant craze for driving seems to epitomize the whole
psychological situation. So frenzied are these people [Los
Angelinos] with their own enthusiasm that they must needs
leap into the car (which they often do in bathing suits) and
drive for sheer ebullience." And not only Los Angeles, for by
the time Bill Harrah got his Chevy roadster in 1926, the entire
nation had reached a level of car ownership that England, for
example, would not face until 1966. The Lynds were writing
their extraordinary book about life in America, *Middletown*
(Muncie, Indiana), in which they would particularly remark
on the sociological influence of the automobile. Had Bill Harrah been able, much less disposed, to read the Lynds' book, he
might have sent a characteristic dry chuckle in their direction,
for his family, which had owned the second automobile in
Newton, Iowa, was part and parcel of an already established
car culture. As the family's youngest and most fanatical car
devotee, he was in the Harrah vanguard on the subject of automobiles. He made sure he stayed up front.

An immensely reinforcing incident that took place at Hollywood High stuck in his memory. He was tall and he was
skinny; apart from middling competence at baseball he was a
terrible athlete, so bad he couldn't pass the physical trials
required to qualify for Eagle Scout, a bitter disappointment.
But one day, when he sat in class, the football coach sent word
he wanted to see him forthwith. No one but Bill could start
the tractor used to keep the field in shape, and suddenly in direct consequence of his warm relationship with cars, he became
a kind of athletic hero once removed.

There was economic reinforcement, too. He earned some of
the money he spent so freely in high school—how else?—parking cars, where he encountered his first Duesenberg, which,
typically, he sneaked for a drive around the block.

Twice during those years he drove to Reno, each time paying a great deal more attention to the cars than to his destination.

Like innumerable young male products of the American car culture, Harrah grew up with the automobile at the center of his life; unlike most of the others, he never grew out of his love.

What might Harrah have done if the Depression had not forced him to leave UCLA after a year in mechanical engineering? "I think he could have designed the best car America has ever seen," says Margaret.

Instead, he built the world's greatest collection.

III

The Depression was only one part in the conspiracy that forced Bill Harrah, at best an indifferent student, to leave college. He was caught cheating on a chemistry examination, which caused little furor in the Harrah household, probably more a sign of John's own problems than his susceptibility to outrage.

The family was broke.

"It all went flooey when the Depression hit," is Margaret's memory. In their book about Venice, Moran and Sewell are more explicit: "The Depression hit hard. People with no spendable income had little need for the Dragon Slide or roller coasters of Venice. The carpeting of the Ship Cafe was worn and no music was played on its bandstand. The Ocean Front Walk seemed empty.

"One amusement continued to prosper. A few small bingo-type games existed along the beachfront." One of those "bingo-type" games was all the Harrah family would have left to provide food for its table.

Like his father, John Harrah was a lawyer, like his father he was partners in a firm, his named Harrah, Lewis, and Blodgett. Bill's recollection of his father's view of the law is unconsciously accurate: "My father was a very good lawyer—it didn't bother him at all." That is to say he was a good lawyer when he was lawyering but lawyering was not enjoyable to John Harrah. The result was that he spent most of his time investing in real estate. He was spread thin even during the palmy days; when things got tough, his world collapsed. Property values plummeted. "So [my father's] $50,000 piece of property with its $25,000 mortgage became a $15,000 piece of property with a $25,000 mortgage." There were forty or fifty or eighty such pieces of property. "So anyway, overnight he owed all this money, and it was just a tragedy. He lost everything—all of the property except our home.

"All he had left was this lease on a building in Venice, on the Venice pier right at the corner of Ocean Front."

It was a large building, filled with concessions: a hot dog stand, shooting gallery, pool hall, and a milk bottle game. And something called, of all things, the Reno Game.

When, many years later, people would ask John Harrah how he happened to find himself in the gambling business, he would remind them of the desperation he—and millions of others—felt at the onset of the Depression. He would tell them about his lease on the Venice property and about the Reno Game: "The only damn thing I could think to do was put that damn game in," said the man who never swore around his children. Neither Bill nor Margaret remembers it quite that way; Bill in particular thinks the game was there and that his father took it over and changed its name to the Circle Game.

It did not take long for Bill to become an employee of his father's. "I had no direction [in college] and then I got into the Circle Game. I think I was just lookin' for a summer job and [my father] said, 'Well, you want to work?'

"I went down and looked. Then I studied, of course. And when I found I was goin' to work I got real interested."

The chemistry exam felon found out he was going to work because he wasn't given much choice. "It didn't bother me a bit to stay out [of school] and make a buck because I just wasn't doin' too good in my engineering career."

The Circle Game was bingo with a twist; players sat in a circle on one of thirty-three stools. In the middle of the table was a roll-down hopper connected to a flashboard. Players would buy cards from the dealer, then try to roll a ball into the

hopper in such a way that the flashboard would register a card
of a suit and number that would match the cards the players
had bought, filling in a four-card sequence. The effects of the
ball, once it reached the hopper, were evidently random; still,
Circle was considered a game of skill.

This last was enormously important. Bingo was illegal in Los
Angeles. But games of "skill" were not against the law.
Depending on the interpretation by whichever district attorney
was in office, the Circle Game was only sometimes legitimate.
John, the former mayor of Venice and a tenacious defender of
his legal rights, found himself in a siege with the enforcement
establishment over the interpretation of what constituted
"skill."

It wasn't only the law trying to tree John Harrah, his son
was also hounding him. By this time, Bill had been operating
the Circle Game for some time. In his careful way he had
looked at other games in other places. In his own mind he was
sure of the reasons for lack of success of his father's game compared to the others.

"It was a group game. If you have house players or shills,
then they play when play gets slow and the shills win the
game. Shills who play ruin the game . . . people see [them]
winning. You can fool the public for about two days, then they
don't play with you anymore.

"We had shills at my father's insistence."

Not only shills, but cheap stools to sit on, which infuriated
young Bill, even then a stickler for quality. Mainly, though, it
was the presence of the shills that set him off. John was insistent that "You get rid of the shills, you're gonna lose your
shirt!" His son thought he was missing the point.

"Any bingo player knows when there's a small crowd the
pots are just the same, but you have a better chance, so they'd
rush in and play." John Harrah was intransigent. On one hand,
he would not get rid of the shills, he would not upgrade the
game by adding comfortable fixtures; on the other, the shills
were costing him so much he was making only $100 a week.
"The time came when he was fed up. I bought [the game]
from him for $500 and fired all the shills immediately."

Bought it from him for $500, fired the shills immediately.

This was a twenty-year-old boy speaking; a twenty-year-old who so knew his own mind and had so carefully "studied" the Circle Game that he was willing to go mano a mano with his own father.

And not just about the Circle Game. John Harrah had gotten involved with a small group of men who needed a lawyer to polish a partnership agreement in a small theater chain. They were sufficiently impressed with John's lawyering that they offered him a piece of the business, which he promptly accepted. This delighted most of the family—free passes to the movies—but it didn't delight the heir. First off, the movies were never shown on schedule. In fact, the seats were often not even in place when the film was supposed to begin. Bill, who may or may not by that time have begun to exhibit his lifelong preoccupation with promptness, was outraged. It was the wrong way to treat people. It was the wrong way to do business. It was a variation on cheap stools and he would have none of it.

A revelation about the Right Way of Doing Things had already come to Bill Harrah. It was there and it was real and it was uncannily on the mark. "I remember the first day [of ownership of the Circle Game] was kind of scary. Then it started to go and it started makin' money.

"And then I improved it. About the first thing I did, I bought some good stools. I put in drapes."

That first year [Bill was keeping careful books] the game made between $100 and $200 a week even though the winter of 1932 was a dismal one in Southern California, doing everything it could to discourage people from playing on or near the Venice pier.

"Then in the spring, none of the games were legal."

The Circle Game had drawn competitors; there were, Bill remembered, "maybe twenty bingo games operating in Southern California and they were all closed. That's where my father came in, being a lawyer." It was merely the first in a five-year stretch of bingus interruptus. John hired Jerry Geisler, then and later the exemplar of show business lawyers, flamboyant and popular, for his successful defense.

But just as John had made friends as the mayor of Venice, so he also made enemies; the years would be filled with attacks on his son's games. Over and over they would be closed, only to be opened, only to be closed again. When he was permitted to operate, Bill Harrah was as successful a young man— measured by income—as any twenty-three-year-old in California. In 1934 he "made between $25,000 and $50,000, which was an awful lot of money." He used part of it to buy out one and then another competitor, only to find that if the authorities could close down one Circle game they could close down three. "It was political. If the district attorney said you could run, you ran; if he didn't, why you didn't. For years I kinda blamed it on Santa Anita race track. I had no proof except Santa Anita always opened on Christmas Day and ran for two or three months," during which time, by coincidence, the D.A. would close the Venice games. "Around the middle of December we'd get closed. It was never directly Santa Anita but, you know, *post hoc ergo propter hoc,* or whatever it is."

Whatever it was, it was also the beginning of the Harrah style. To remind his customers he would be back when Santa Anita closed he used a mailing list and sent them Christmas presents. That extraordinarily tender treatment of his clientele set a precedent. So did his behavior toward one of the girls who worked in the game.

Her name was Thelma Batchelor, described by Margaret forty years later, as a "girl-next-door type." Bill may have taken issue with his father as a businessman, but he also took him very much as a role model. John's feelings about women must have influenced Bill strongly when he decided to bring Thelma to Nevada three years later and to marry her. "Women were for childbearing and for decorating a scene," in Margaret's words. Thelma, who is now remarried, living in Reno, and determined to be forever silent about her first marriage, must have fit the description, although her photos show a plainish young woman, and there was no issue of the marriage.

By now, Bill Harrah was getting fed up with the on-again and off-again law enforcement habits of the locals. A high school friend, Kay Dietrich, had gone to Reno with her

mother, who was divorcing her father, and had come back sing-
ing the town's praises. Bill was not impressed; he told Kay Dietrich he had been to Reno "in a Model T."

"Well," she replied, "you haven't seen it lately. They've got
gambling and they've got bingo. They've got this and that.
And oh! it's fun." So Bill jumped into his Lincoln Zephyr and
went off to find out for himself. He remembered telling a
friend how struck he was by the change. "That's a place!" he
said on his return. "Look at that; they don't close the bars and
they don't close the games. They leave you alone."

Within a month, he received a letter from a failed Reno
gambler asking if he wanted to lease space for a bingo parlor.
"So I came up and bought it real cheap, not knowing it was a
terrible location.

"And that's a whole long story."

He did not know it then, but the "whole long story" would
become intertwined with another whole long story belonging
to his high school friend's father. Kay Dietrich's father was
Noah Dietrich and Noah Dietrich would become a strong
right bower to Howard Hughes, along with William Fisk Harrah, the sometimes largest gambling presence in Nevada.

4

An Earlier
and Wilder West
Nevada, 1820–1931

In pointing the nose of his Lincoln Zephyr toward the northern sagebrush, Bill Harrah—whether he knew it or not—was making his first great career play. He was betting (with the house) on the continuation of a stubborn western tradition: Freedom to Gamble. It was a tradition almost as long and socially tainted as that other western institution, prostitution.

Inherited from the earliest risk-taking behavior of primitive man, developed to an art in the ancient civilizations of the Mediterranean basin, swallowed with difficulty by English common law (John of Salisbury, in the twelfth century, howled publicly about "the damnable art of dice-playing"), transplanted to the Colonies where it spread like a social potato beetle, gambling made its way across (as well as up and down) the Mississippi to cast its sinister shadow upon the West. Trouble was, at least so far as the guardians of western rectitude were concerned, not many people in the early American West thought there was anything sinister about it. "Eastern people find it difficult to reconcile gambling with respectability, but when custom permits a thing—when, in fact, gambling takes the rank of an industry—the social crime disappears," wrote C. Bancroft in his history of Colorado.

Although not particularly sympathetic to this view, a passel of easterners at Cornell, commissioned by a trio of federal executive agencies, produced as felicitous a history of western gambling as there is. Said the Cornell Report ("The Development of the Law of Gambling: 1776–1976"): "Before 1850, the West was a crude region, populated almost exclusively by men. There were no laws, and no formal government to restrain anti-social behavior. In fact, the early West was more a collection of individuals than any sort of coherent society."

These individuals, the Report adds in a pixieish way, spent most of their leisure time entertained by CBS. In this case the acronym stood for combined "casino, bordello and saloon." And then the Report betrays the bias of its writers: "Gambling, whoring and drinking took place openly, and was welcomed in the early boom towns for the fat profit it yielded." Note the disagreement between plural subjects and singular verb and pronoun. At the moment of writing, it must have seemed to the Report's authors that "gambling, whoring and drinking" were one indistinguishable sin, though Prohibition had been repealed even above Cayuga's Waters and Bill Harrah had long since received the blessings of the New York Stock Exchange.

If in this early West there were antigambling laws, they had a selective purpose. Texas, for example, went out of its way to distinguish between public and private gambling. Citing Title 13, Chapter Four of the Texas Penal Code, a state court said as late as 1876: ". . . prohibited games are divided into two classes, to wit: '1st, playing cards in particular places; 2nd, gaming tables or banks everywhere.'" Playing cards in particular places was just fine with Texas, even if allegedly prohibited; gaming tables or banks everywhere were not. This made sense both to Texans and Cornellians: "Western gambling laws were meant neither to save gamblers from their own folly nor to condemn wicked and wasteful behavior . . . they were enacted in an effort to curtail the worst abuses of public and commercial gambling.

"As legends of the Wild West have it, gambling often resulted in disorderly conduct and even violence. These abuses had to be controlled before farmers would move their families into the towns. Since lawless behavior was directly associated with gambling, gambling was declared illegal as part of a concerted effort to eliminate the prevailing unruliness."

Then the Report coppers its own bet. Was there a real threat to frontier communities posed by gambling, a threat of such magnitude that it warranted blanket condemnation? Here the historians get pensive; Dodge City, they say, is everyone's example of western lawlessness. But between 1870 and 1885, there were said to be only fifteen homicides there, not many of them traceable to gambling. Bat Masterson, who was hired to tame a town run amok, never killed anyone in his years as sheriff. "While myth implies that the frontier townsfolk were besieged by armed desperadoes who flocked to the casinos, brothels, and saloons, the record suggests that this was simply not the case."

A seeming contradiction in the Report, that gambling was tolerated in the West except for that part of the West west of the Mississippi, is explained by differentiating between regions. If the Great Plains states went to great lengths to keep gamblers in their place, if many of their neighbors were more liberal but still restrictive, the Far West spent what time it took to address the problem wondering what all the fuss was about. It was a region that had little consideration for farmers since farmers had no wish to put down roots there, settling respectability upon their communities at the same time. To Far Westerners, gambling represented two important additions to their lives: revenue and pleasure. Territorial legislatures levied fees (in Montana, for example, it cost an owner of a gambling house fifty dollars a month to satisfy the levy) and, while complaining loudly about instances of fraud at the tables, found most of the inspiration for encouraging straight games in the members' own insistence on a fair chance with the cards or dice.

II

This was certainly the Nevada view. A backwater region that became a backwater territory and a wrong side of the sheets state, Nevada had grown up with gambling. Its own history almost preordained a state that would become a great hostel for gamblers on both sides of the table.

Early Nevada, a part of the Great Basin that formed the bed of a prehistoric sea called Lahontan, was a brutal, desolate place. Lucy Hall, whose sympathy for the pioneer trials of Charles Harra in Pennsylvania was so poignant, would have broken into tears had she been able to read the brave but pathetic memoirs of early settlers. The place was a huge sand and sagebrush barrier between civilization and California. In the 1830s and '40s, Jedediah Smith and John C. Frémont made exploratory probes of what would become Nevada. Mormon trappers crossed from the eastern edge as far as the shadow of the Sierra.

Then the Treaty of Guadalupe Hidalgo was signed in 1848, Mexico ceding the area formally to the United States, and this encouraged arrival of the first settlers, who were Mormons. They went to a tiny place called Genoa, southwest of the present capital at Carson City. Had they stayed, Nevada might have become as respectable as Utah, but when the federal government threatened Brigham Young with invasion because he refused to accept Washington's suzerainty, he recalled the faithful to repel boarders and the place his followers had named the State of Deseret was left to wallow in the shiftless values and fantasy hopes of prospectors and miners.

"Virginia City is where Nevada really began," says Robert Laxalt, and the discovery of the Comstock Lode in 1859 is what began it. Gold prospectors had been cursing and fuming over the sludge they had to muck through to reach their ore until one day, perhaps in desperation, one of them had the mud assayed. "The 'mud' was incredibly rich in silver. Until that day, all the wagon roads had led to California. Now, they changed directions and converged upon . . . Nevada."

Virginia City was to produce almost $300 million in silver and gold. "In the process, a fantastic town of stately mansions, luxurious hotels, gourmet restaurants, schools, churches, stores, an opera house, roaring mills and sophisticated mine operations arose out of nondescript shanties.

"It was here that the stage celebrities of yesteryear—Sarah

Bernhardt, Lillian Russell, Lotta Crabtree, and John Wilkes Booth's brother Junius—trod sloping stages . . . And it was here, as a Virginia City newspaperman, that Mark Twain got his start." Yes, but that romantic image is of a Nevada boom town in full flower. Full flower came later, clawing and scratching came first. There were distinct stages in the growth of a Virginia City, and Laxalt talks about them, too.

When a promising chip was found, assayed, and proved out, the prospector suddenly found himself the first resident of a nascent town. After him came other miners, panting to get their claims staked. In turn, merchants followed, with freight wagons carrying provisions, tools, and lumber "for the builders who threw up one-room shacks, flophouses where a man could buy a few hours' sleep in a real bed before surrendering it to the next man, bathhouses with hot water in wooden tubs in preparation for the Saturday-night wingding." The principals in the wingding were the prospectors but they got lots of help, for after the merchants came the whores and the saloonkeepers and the gamblers.

"Gold prospecting did not draw men seeking stability and long-term work. The affinity between gambling and prospecting for gold is clear. Either way, one is seeking to strike it rich. Besides, in the nineteenth-century mining towns there wasn't much else to do. Men without families could drink, whore, gamble, and fight; and they did all of these." So says Jerome Skolnick in *House of Cards*, the definitive analysis of Nevada gambling. Skolnick could have added that the men who came to Nevada in the middle of the last century were also gambling their lives. It was inhospitable terrain; it was dangerous work.

And so they risked their lives and then they winged and they dinged at poker, roulette, monte, faro, and dice. Out of this freewheeling life came an attitude that was to stamp Nevada from then on, discovered only a hundred years later by the *Reader's Digest*: "Nevada's laws are founded on the theory that each man should be capable of looking out for himself. If he wants to gamble the prerogative is his. But he must not hang around whining if he loses, nor ask the state for a free living afterward."

With the Civil War came statehood—for the most prag-

matic of reasons. Nevada was rich in silver, and Lincoln had
no intention of seeing it go to the South, much less lie
unassessed by Washington. Furthermore, he needed all the
votes he could get in Congress to move the Emancipation
Proclamation. Thus, with about one tenth of the required population, with a history as brief as a mayfly's, Nevada found itself a staunch—and contributing—part of the Union.

Statehood conferred remote respectability. The coming of
the railroad in the late 1860s offered far more: suckers. Said
one observer, "The railroad proved a further boom to Nevada's
professional gamblers by making it unnecessary for them to
await the arrival of their victims at overnight stage stops along
the way . . . they regularly rode across the state on the
through trains, affably offering other passengers an opportunity
to relieve the tedium of the journey by joining in friendly
games . . . it was widely believed that the railroad management was in partnership with the swindlers and shared in their
profits."

All of this was classic western boom town behavior, a scene
filled with rich characters, pouches of gold, bedraggled miners
being fleeced by flat games, extravagant monuments to instant
wealth; the lot.

Virginia City's decline was equally classic. Again Robert
Laxalt: "This was the town and this was the wealth that were
to transform Nevada from a neglected part of Utah Territory
to territorial status of its own, precipitate early statehood in
1864, a mere five years after the discovery of silver, and enrich
an impoverished Union treasury in the Civil War.

"And then, late in 1877, the decline began. The veins of the
Comstock Lode and the Big Bonanza ore body—one of the
richest in recorded history—started to pinch out, silver prices
skidded, the mines and the mills fell silent, and the exodus
came.

"By 1900, Virginia City, the Queen of the Comstock, was a
shabby dowager stripped of her elegance and reduced from
10,000 courtiers to a few hundred faithful who refused to give
up obeisance to the glory of what once had been."

With the exodus came the depression. The great naturalist
John Muir saw dead towns wherever he traveled in Nevada,

and gave thanks. "The fever period is fortunately passing away. The prospector is no longer the raving, wandering ghoul of ten years ago, rushing in random lawlessness among the hills, hungry and footsore." Fine for Mr. Muir; not fine for Nevada's miners, ranchers, and businessmen. For starters, the state's population plummeted from over 60,000 to a bare 42,000. There were fires in the mines, there were floods. In a state that offered not much more than an underground storehouse for precious minerals gathered over millennia, the dwindling of the inventories in those storehouses meant abandoning not only them but also the whole state. Nor were there home-grown philanthropists to help. Most of the money taken from the Comstock went straight to California, whose new millionaires were not in the least interested in holding out a hand to the tottering state that had provided them their wealth. Only miner John Mackay kept his money in Nevada and even he invested a great deal of it in a new and daring adventure somewhat out of state: the laying of the Atlantic cable.

From rich relation Nevada became distant beggar. For those who noticed, it was likely good riddance. By the turn of the century, twenty years of economic starvation had convinced everyone Nevada had given all she had to offer. Now she could be dismissed as a mere anomaly. Nevada's contribution was clearly in the past.

Except not quite.

III

Southwestern Nevada has survived, even boomed, despite itself. It gives away no edge in bleakness to the rest of the state; in addition its climate is crueler. If water is at a premium below the Donner Pass and along the Truckee in the northwest, it is like gold in the southern part of the state. The region has a perverse unwillingness to die, and this contrariness has been encouraged by a long history of inducing the keepers of federal life-support systems to keep it alive. Over the last fifty years the feds planted that grossly spectacular concrete garden called Boulder Dam at Nevada's southern border and then, having brought encouragement through water to the area, put down a nuclear test site one hundred miles or so to the north.

Not that the private sector has ignored the region. In 1945 industrial America in the form of the Mafia set down roots in what had been a quiet desert town and turned Las Vegas into an American Monte Carlo (in Tom Wolfe's words) "without any of the inevitable upperclass baggage of the Riviera casinos." Thus, the place that Bugsy Siegel built became a vital city in the middle of the desert, flanked to its south by the dam, to the north by the test site; a model example of federal reclamation working hand in hand with private capital.

Still, it was the hand of God, assisted only minimally by the hand of man, that, as the new century began, primed the pump. James Butler was a Nye County rancher who had done a stint prospecting and had been so discouraged that he was willing to look to some of the most arid, desolate land in the west for agricultural salvation. It seems barely credible, but the great Tonopah strike was discovered by a donkey. On the night of May 19, 1900, Butler's burro, one of several he had taken out into the desert on a casual prospecting trip, wandered off. Butler found it standing placidly near some rocks that looked uncommonly rich. They were. In Belmont, he gave a sample of the rocks to one Tasker Oddie, with the promise that if it proved out, Oddie would have a share. It was a happy arrangement and it put Butler in clover and Oddie in the Senate of the United States. In the way of boom towns, Tonopah, as Butler would call the place using the Indian word for "spring" (not only gold in the ground but water nearby!), sucked up an army of fortune-seeking rabble. By 1904 it was a boomer, all right, particularly since the railroad had extended a spur and Tasker Oddie proved it accessible by automobile—driving a car across the desert to the new bonanza.

Butler sold out early at a very decent price. The buyers, easterners who set up a company called Tonopah Mining, would take many millions out of the ground over the next fifteen years of what Nevada historian James Hulse calls the "stable and sedate" life of the town. But before that post-1908 stability, the region was given another shove by God and man.

Early on, Butler was approached for a grubstake by a pair of prospectors. William Marsh and Harry Stimler proposed to go as far as fifty miles south of Tonopah in the hope that gold-bearing rock was a southwest Nevada contagion. It was and it traveled wonderfully. Stimler and Marsh discovered ore that would be worth over $100 a ton and some so rich it was worth $12,000; this in comparison to Tonopah's average of $40 and compared also to an average from the Big Bonanza during Comstock days of about $65.

The twin discoveries were lifesavers for a state in decline. They would contribute not only to the economic well-being of Nevada but also marvelously to its maverick legend, Goldfield's in particular. That town began its raucous career fighting a new battle in the western arena, the labor movement. The Industrial Workers of the World (IWW) and the Western Federation of Miners—both of which were given life in Goldfield by the arrival of miners from all over the West—began grumbling when members were subjected to search at the end of their shifts. Matters came to a head when mine-owners began paying not in gold or silver but in scrip. The miners' union struck, the town fathers panicked, Governor John Sparks howled for federal troops, and pacifist President Theodore Roosevelt shipped them along. That signaled the mineowners the time had come to break the unions, and with federal troops camped in Goldfield, the owners brought in miners from surrounding states and replaced the rebels.

If miners and mine operators had become worldly and hard-headed in the years between the Comstock and the strikes at Goldfield and Tonopah, so had promoters and speculators. "[They] were forced to come up with new schemes to keep investment money flourishing," says Robert Laxalt. "The old ranks of potential stockholders who had suffered in the swin-dles of earlier times were predictably wary of Nevada mining stocks. The name of the game came to be . . . keeping a boom town's existence before the public."

In that endeavor, Goldfield was blessed by the presence of one of the great promoters of the century. He was an ex-cow-boy, ex-Klondike miner named George Lewis "Tex" Rickard, owner of the Great Northern, "the biggest and fanciest saloon and gambling hall" in town (and in which Wyatt Earp was a pit boss). In 1897, Nevada Governor Reinhold Sadler signed a bill authorizing prizefighting in Nevada—making it the only western state to encourage the sweet science. This was of particular interest to James J. "Gentleman Jim" Corbett and Robert "Fighting Bob" Fitzsimmons, respectively the heavyweight and middleweight champions of the world. A variety of promoters had tried to make their fight since 1895, only to be ushered out of state after state proposed as its location. With the passage of the Act, the fight was finally set for Carson City on St. Patrick's Day, 1897. The crowd was disappointing but Fitzsimmons was not; he unleashed his "solar plexus" punch in the fourteenth round, sending Corbett to the canvas and defeat. "The fight brought little money into Nevada, but the enormous publicity it engendered was not forgotten by the state's boosters and businessmen . . ." concluded the editors of Time/Life Books.

Rickard was both booster and businessman. Of all Nevadans the Corbett/Fitzsimmons lesson was not lost on him.

"Goldfield was afire with plans to publicize its attractions and sell stock in its mines. In July [1906] civic leaders met to discuss a number of proposals, including one to dig a huge pool in Main Street and fill it with fresh beer twice a day.

"Then Tex Rickard came up with the more practical public relations scheme of . . . a title bout between two well-known lightweights, Battling Nelson and Joe Gans," said the Time/Life editors.

Nelson, the champion, was white, Gans black; a stroke of luck for Rickard and Goldfield. The hard-nosed citizens of the Far West who would make up the audience were characteristically racist and they came out in large numbers. They also came out behind, at least those who bet on Nelson. Gans won on a foul in the forty-second round. Rickard profited both from the fight (although by less than $15,000) and in the outlines of a new career; he would go on to the promotion of the famous "million-dollar gate" in New York, drawn for the match he made between Jack Dempsey and Jess Willard in which Dempsey won the heavyweight championship.

Goldfield won much more: attention, acclaim, notice, and the misplaced confidence of investors who poured money into its mining stocks. By 1910 they and the town were flat, devastated by flood, fire, and the depletion of the mines.

Another boom, another bust—but this time a difference, for Goldfield's legacy to Nevada was a generation of politicians who would hold power in the state through the critical years during which Nevada struggled successfully for disrespectability.

IV

"From 1864 until about 1905, most outstanding Nevada political figures were identified with the Comstock Lode . . . When the Comstock declined, so did its domination of state politics. To a large extent, the towns of Tonopah and Goldfield supplied the political leaders of the next generation," says James Hulse. So if ballyhoo and hoopla were refined in southwestern Nevada for consumption by the rest of the state (with strong influence on the attitudes of many other westerners), so too were Nevada politics, which would have even more profound effect on Nevada's neighbors.

The operative word is "refined." The names were different, the point of view was not. It was sharpened; it became more ingrained. But it revolved around the same few issues, the most prominent of which was an undying allegiance to silver and a growing sense of alienation in consequence of what Nevada politicians saw as a near conspiracy to deprive the state of the value of this precious resource. Recall that Abraham Lincoln wanted Nevada wearing the union label because of her silver. Was it peculiar that the new state's representatives in Congress would be Silverites? Not to Nevadans. A succession of senators, representatives, and governors agonized as the price of the metal began to plummet in the early 1870s. It was no accident. In 1873, Congress declined to authorize the continued minting of silver dollars, an act that came to be called the "Crime of '73" by Silverites. "[Nevada's senators] argued that the low price of silver was artificial, and that it was a conspiracy of eastern businessmen and bankers—'gold bugs' who wanted to deflate the economy by having a gold standard," says Hulse. Over the next half a century and beyond, Nevadans sent to Washington would pound their desks in demand after demand for silver support; time after time they would see their efforts turned back, first by repeal of the Sherman Silver Purchase Act and then by two presidential election defeats of their standard bearer: William Jennings Bryan.

The long and bitter silver battles had their consequence. A state already distant from and suspicious of the federal government became outraged, man and boy, by what seemed arrogant and high-handed behavior. Long after the fight over silver had dropped into Congressional archives, the disaffection remained.

So Nevada found itself pitted against the seat of federal power; it had for some time known it was also at war with itself. "The thing to understand about Nevada," said the *Saturday Review* a long time later, "is that it simply never got over its frontier days. Gaming has always been part of the scene . . ." Yes and no, for it was over exactly this issue that Nevada found itself engaged in internecine warfare. In 1865 the Nevada legislature passed a bill recognizing reality. It legalized gambling. When the bill arrived on the governor's desk, it was promptly sent back to the legislature stamped "veto" by Henry Blasdel, a governor already on the record as considering gambling a "vicious vice." Four years later the sequence was repeated: the legislature passed another legalization bill, the governor vetoed again, but this time the state senate and assembly overrode. By its provisions, the new act required that gambling be kept out of sight and that gambling establishments pay a quarterly fee ranging from $250 to $500. In the meantime, of course, Nevada had already become an island of sin in the West by allowing boxing, about which Robert Laxalt says, "If one were to choose a date when Nevada consciously began playing with the idea of flouting social convention on a national scale it would have to be 1897," the year of the Carson City fight between Corbett and Fitzsimmons.

Legalized gambling, legalized boxing, flourishing prostitution; it was enough to drive a reformer berserk. The bluenoses waited until 1910 to strike. "Though gambling was first legalized in Nevada in 1869, the mood of the era at the turn of the century was for general reform. Gambling and drinking were thought to be the decadent evils of the day. In 1910 Nevada succumbed to this do-gooder movement and outlawed all forms of gambling. The San Francisco *Post* reported this incident by stating: 'With the close of the gambling houses in Nevada, one of the worst relics of the wild and wooly west has passed out.' Games of chance continued operating in this state, illegally, and authorities were paid to look the other way," Nevada's Bicentennial Book would say. Nonetheless, the state's inner turmoil over the issue tended to entrench attitudes; the players dug in. Their reaction resulted in institutionalizing another Nevada peccadillo.

That wasn't the worst of it so far as the reformers were concerned. The 1910 law authorized police to break down doors, seize and destroy gambling equipment found on the premises, and arrest proprietors of the games as criminals. Such outrageous purity was unconscionable to most Nevadans. In consequence, "The seemingly tough new antigambling law did not have the effect its sponsors had intended. The law attracted underworld gamblers skilled in the arts of cheating and of bribing officials. Not only was public revenue from licensing lost, but a chain of surreptitious joints began to develop that conducted every known game without controls and corrupted public officials . . ."

The Comstock strikes followed by a twenty-year depression followed by Tonopah/Goldfield had made a lasting impression on Nevada attitudes. Already alienated from mainstream American points of view, Nevada and Nevadans turned even more stubborn; if the nation would swallow the state's silver and offer the back of its hand in payment, if the country would consider Nevada an outlaw in consequence of its hospitality to eccentric social behavior, the state decided its recourse was to accept the verdict.

Twenty years after the puritans outlawed everything from poker to faro the Nevada legislature legalized gambling. Six years after that Bill Harrah arrived to take advantage of the New Enlightenment.

5

Pilgrim's Progress

Reno, 1937–1946

On the seventy-third anniversary of Nevada's admission to the Union, in celebration of Halloween, 1937, Bill Harrah opened his first bingo parlor in Reno. Two months later he closed. D. W. Shoemaker, proprietor of the Owl Club, had been first to make application for a license under the new legalization act; Bill Harrah's place may have been only two blocks away from the Owl, but it was also two blocks from the action—which meant he was that far distant as well from the Bank Club, the Palace, Harolds, and—worst of all—customers.

It was his initial Reno lesson, and it would not be forgotten. Bill Harrah would leap across streets—up mountainsides—in a quarter-century expansion program, he would be accused of buying towns in the wilderness and trying to open major league gambling to the Tahoe outback, but never again would he pick the wrong location.

Harrah might have chosen the wrong address; early on he exercised far better judgment in choosing an ad hoc adviser. Virgil Smith was the very model of a western wheel and table man; quiet, unflappable, determined, and ambitious. Smith made no judgment about people unless it involved the movement across his baize of the money they held in their hands. Today, one of the last survivors of the post legalization pioneers, he sits staring behind his prominent glasses at the tape recorder, not quite trusting the discretion of this strange device, and charting the outside of his lips with the tip of his tongue, around to the right, around to the left; the image of a retired small-town supermarket owner—which he very well could have been. Except that Virgil Smith's life took a strange spin one night at a Carson City social during the very month that the Nevada legislature—two weeks before, just down the street from the hall in which the dance was held—put the state's imprimatur on gambling.

Virgil was in Carson prepping for a job with Skaggs-Safeway, for whom he worked in the little town of Lovelock. He was twenty-one. He had grown up in a farming family imbued with a work ethic that would have put Cotton Mather in awe. He had been taught values, precepts, poker, and 21 by the local Catholic priest (and practiced in the back of the church using matchsticks *and* money). That moment during intermission at the Carson Social came as preordained. His friend Gene Sullivan was doing a turn at the wheel while the dealer took a break. It turned out the dealer had already taken a great deal more than that. He tossed the bankroll to a confederate, leaving Sullivan and the rest of the players—not to mention the concession owner—standing at the altar. At that moment Virgil Smith wandered over for a little conversation. What he got was a change of life.

It was an entirely appropriate beginning to a career that would see Smith retire to a fiefdom adjoining Bill Harrah's. In the meanwhile, Virgil Smith would spend the same years during which the Harrahs were tossed to and fro by Southern California legal typhoons making his bones in Reno. Virgil Smith was neither a Graham/McKay nor an unknown table soldier. Almost as though he were planning a careful course through a corporate maze, Smith carefully wended his way toward the center of the gambling establishment in northern Nevada, beginning at the Palace Club to arrive—at about the time Harrah hauled into town—at a proprietorship of his own. By 1937 he was running the games at Colbrandt's, not the biggest club in town, nor the smallest, but certainly one of the more caring of its clientele; a place with the view of the Player's Reno and to which, in the course of events, Bill Harrah came to drink.

Smith and Bill Harrah were two years apart, Smith the

elder. Harrah was half a foot taller. Smith was a country boy to whom Reno was a formidable city, while for Harrah, coming to the Truckee Meadows was almost dropping out. Both were players. The friendship beyond that is hard to explain unless it is seen as a relationship in which Smith was mentor; inconceivable given the Harrah character—unless, given the Harrah character, this was merely opportunistic behavior. If so, Bill Harrah was as thorough about opportunism as he was about everything else. Virgil Smith remembers: "We were players together, not constant but nearly every night." Every Sunday they'd get in their cars—each in his own—and drive to a small town nearby; a courtesy visit during which one or the other would reach into the case of Canadian Club both carried, pull a bottle for the tavern they were about to visit, give it to the house, and then buy it back by the drink. "As a result, when people from Lovelock or Fallon, Portola or Alturas came to town, they'd come to see us." By this time, the boisterous Bill Harrah was almost inaudible: "Bill was the quiet type. He'd buy ten rounds of drinks almost without you knowing it; he'd just give a little wave of his finger to the bartender. If he wanted everybody in the place to have a drink [and he frequently bought for the house] he'd give the bartender a kind of round motion.

"We got along very well. We never had an argument in our whole lives."

Virgil Smith and Bill Harrah went to the Fortune Club, the Palace, and to the Bank Club where they played Jim McKay and Bill Graham's games with never a thought: "The mob was in Reno but Graham and McKay weren't crooks. They went to jail, although not for a shooting or putting the finger on anybody. At one time they might have been crossroaders. There were a lot of people like that, guys who used to be cheaters then turned into very honorable people you couldn't get to cheat anyone if you tried."

Virgil Smith's friendship with Bill Harrah was important but secondary, for if Smith was a serious player, he was also a serious gambling proprietor. His clientele was select. He remembers heavy players like Jim Slingerland, "a big insurance man," and Harry Swanson, Slingerland's brother-in-law, and Abe Harper, the liquor dealer. He also remembers a tall young man who was courting the niece of a local cattleman. Together they'd wander into Colbrandt's, the man would stake his lady friend to $25 and $50 plays at the wheel while he'd stroll over to the low roller's "21" table. It is the first memory anyone has of Howard Hughes in Reno. Smith remembers the *town* as touristy. Not so his clientele: 80 percent, he thinks now, were local. The rest was split between divorcées and tourists. He could tell the difference because the tourists were at the tables, the divorcées at the bar.

When Bill Harrah's first bingo emporium went bust, he cast a newly educated eye on what was not much more than an open area between two buildings, just around the corner from the Palace, hard by the other clubs he and Smith frequented. Envision the downtown of a small city as a large rectangle, within that rectangle, sharing the larger part of its base, a smaller rectangle, and you have a picture of the two-block gambling area of central Reno. The long sides of the gambling rectangle formed the western (Virginia Street) and eastern (Center Street) boundaries of the central area. It was closed off to the south by Second Street, to the north by Commercial Row.

It was at this northern end, in a Commercial Row interstice, that Harrah decided to open. "I spent that winter tryin' to raise some money, which I did a little bit, and movin' the equipment from Center Street to Commercial Row—a place that we called the Plaza Tango."

From the Plaza Tango (not long after Harrah would change the name of his games from Tango to Bingo—exhibiting an early understanding of name recognition) he moved west and south—around the corner to Virginia Street. In the years that followed his invasion of Virginia, he leapfrogged his neighbor (Harolds) to take space in the back of a clothing store for a bar he would call Blackout (by this time the war had arrived). Then he drifted eastward again across a longitudinal (north/south) alley toward Center Street while keeping the property on Virginia; so that Harrah's, as it began to take the shape of its present incarnation, occupied space that fronted Virginia on the west, Center on the east, and was smack in the middle of the more northerly of Reno's two gambling blocks.

His progress during those years was not so much geographic as socioeconomic. He was learning the gambling business. He was discovering the quirks and cranks of his adopted city, he was discovering himself—and his competitors were finding out that in Bill Harrah, Reno had given home to a new sort of citizen.

II

This Harrah-seep into Reno's gambling fabric occupied nine years: from 1937 until he opened the progenitor of the present empire in 1946. It was an exciting and typically perilous nine years of business growth. It is a critical period in the development of the professional persona—as importantly illustrative of the maturation of a new style of gambler as his personal life during the same period (as we shall see later) was indicative of his persistent failure to pursue adulthood.

Harrah had political savvy packed in his overnight bag when he arrived. He was laconic later about the manner in which it came to his aid during those first days in Reno. He seems to have made his decision to open in the wrong place based very much on his experience dealing with pols in Southern California: "Bob Douglass, the collector of Internal Revenue, was the landlord. I needed a license and he had a lot of clout politically." When Douglass forgave him the lease on Center Street, Harrah discovered he was dealing with a different breed of man in Nevada from those who wandered the political halls of Los Angeles. From that moment, Harrah showed that he had learned not only a lesson in business geography, but also a political one, that in Nevada the political tides swept not against gambling interests but with them. Throughout his career, Harrah would work behind the scenes with city government and with the state legislature; prompting, pushing, probably occasionally bribing his way ahead. The old days of bucking the flow were over.

Before he could direct political traffic, however, Harrah had to learn the direction of its natural bent. He would discover the bumps, rocks, and swirls in the stream bed the hard way.

Harrah had made clear to the skeptics that he was in Reno to stay with a typical Harravian gesture: instead of buying the conventional space heater for his new shed on Commercial Row, he had invested $600 in a genuine, for-real oil heater. "Well," said the heater consultant, "you can get just a heater in the corner for $30. But you can get a furnace—basement, the whole bit—for $600."

"But it was a first-class job. So we bought it. We did need heat and we wanted the people to be comfortable. They're not goin' to play if they're not comfortable." The Harrah Touch again, and in that winter of '38 it warmed the hearts and feet of his bingo customers. The Harrah Touch failed him, however, in the case of the lima beans.

When Harrah opened on Commercial, he had markers made up for his bingo cards, nice ones, too, and expensive. For a reason he didn't at first realize, his players (80 percent locals, as with Virgil Smith's place) complained. It had been traditional to use lima beans, and if Harrah wouldn't supply them, his customers would bring bags of their own. To his chagrin, Harrah was forced to give up his fancy markers and replace them with odd-shaped legumes.

Bowing to pressures from the lima bean lobby was one thing; he was not at all willing to go along with less benign convention. Harrah's first dollar slot was a machine he put in the Blackout Bar. Not long after it arrived it disappeared at the same time as a good deal of whiskey. The culprit was easy to finger—when liquor is missing look to its keeper. Sure enough, Harrah was able to establish the guilt of the bartender. Trouble was, the man was under the protection of Jack Sullivan, who had taken over as manager of the Bank Club during the enforced vacation of its owners, Bill Graham and Jim McKay.

This Sullivan was a hard case. He was, by then, a large, portly, formidable figure, addressed, in contravention of the casual western manner of equals, as "Mr." Sullivan and Harrah were on a collision course.

"We lost some liquor which was replaceable (although it was very hard to get) but the dollar slot machine was irreplaceable. I called a cop right away, which you weren't suppose to do. But that's the way I was brought up.

"Then [everybody] is tellin' me, 'Gee, Bill. Why don't you let it go?' 'No way,' I said, 'I'm mad.'

"So then Jack Sullivan called me up and Jack Sullivan never called anybody up."

"Hello. Bill Harrah?"

"Yeah."

"This is Jack Sullivan."

"Ooooh! Yes, Mr. Sullivan."

"Could I see ya for a minute?"

"Oh, yes, sir. I'll come right over."

"No, that won't be necessary, I'll come and see you." Almost half a century later Harrah remembered Sullivan's size, his syntax, his cane, and the glower in his presence. "I was really impressed. It would be like President Carter or somebody comin' to see you. It was—you know—*Jack Sullivan.*" The moment might have been impressive, but it was not awesome: "He turned on all of his personality. He didn't have too much but he turned on all he had."

Sullivan wanted Bill Harrah to forget the little incident of the thefts. He wanted Harrah to know that in Reno the players overlooked pranks, that he, Bill Harrah, would have to come to an appreciation of the tolerance requisite as a kind of commercial lubricant in the world of gambling.

"I really stood up to him. I was amazed at myself. 'I respect you very much Mr. Sullivan,' I said, 'but this guy deliberately, soberly stole my slot machine and a lot of booze and I'm gonna get him!'"

"If you want to get along in Reno," Harrah remembered Sullivan answering, "I think you're makin' a mistake. Here we scratch each other's back." Bill Harrah did not scratch Jack Sullivan's back. Instead, he took himself to the witness stand and testified against Sullivan's protégé, who was sent to prison. "I guess some people thought [the bartender] might get even with me and I should have worried about it. Maybe, but I never did." Even in the early days, then, if someone was foolish enough to bite Bill Harrah he soon discovered tooth-marks on his own buttocks.

III

Harrah also bared his fangs—and didn't hesitate to use them—with less provocation, as in the case of the Great Bingo Wars. In the course of moving from Center to Commercial and Virginia and leapfrogging Harolds, Bill Harrah cam-paigned in the grand tradition of Napoleon's generals.

He was resolute in his battle with Ed Howe, resolute and sneaky.

With Mrs. Carey and the Russian, he used geopolitical bluff and conspiracy.

He took the Japanese by a flanking assault—with a little help from Admiral Yamamoto.

Ed Howe's Heart Tango on Virginia was around the corner from Harrah's new place on Commercial (still a shed, but at least now a warm shed). In the way of high finance, Harrah decided he would price his product as he had in Venice: two cards for a nickel, six for a dime. "And Howe stayed two for a nickel, which was kind of a mistake. [Because if a player had a choice—as he did at Harrah's—he'd play six for a dime every time.] Besides, we gave drawings."

Tom Smith, "a nice fellow—he became a friend of mine," was Ed Howe's manager. From Smith, Harrah discovered the number of players at the Heart Tango and no doubt its take. "I cultivated Tom," said Harrah, but he did not say much more about how he suborned him. Long afterward, during the days of empire, Smith was a Harrah employee performing pretty much the same service on Harrah's behalf in Las Vegas as he had in the early days in Reno—spying. "Tom would—well, I gotta meet Tom after work. And it was, oh, maybe kind of secretive."

Smith told Harrah that Howe was a tired man, perhaps a man willing to sell: "He'd run his place real good for ten years or so. [Smith] would tell me a little bit, maybe a little more than he should, but he still wouldn't tell me everything. [Anyway] that's where I got the feeling he [Howe] wanted to get away." Harrah concluded that Howe didn't have the stomach for competition. "He'd had the only two-for-a-nickel in town and he just had it his own way. Now he had some serious competition. It was hard work and he had to kinda change things. We ran longer hours, he had to run longer hours.

"And I learned somehow [sic] that he had been thinkin' about retiring." At which point Harrah decided to muster the legions and charge. "I went over and he had a little bitty office. When Ed and I walked into his office, why, everybody [there] was amazed to see me and word was 'bzz, bzz, bzz,' all the dealers and all the customers too. 'What's goin' on?' "

What was going on was that Harrah was pushing Ed Howe against the wall. Would he sell? Well, Howe didn't know about that, but maybe. For how much? $25,000.

"So I said, 'Well, unh, I'll have to think about that.' " The thinking was as much about the source of money as the price. "I sat at the bar and I started drinkin' and I thought, 'Gee, that's terrible. Darn guy. It's his place. He can ask what he wants for it. He can't make any money there with us runnin'. If he would sell at a low price we could just close and move into Howe's and run it. He'd be down in Arizona with his trailer; he'd be happy.' "

Having thus decided on Howe's behalf why Howe should want to sell and having planned Howe's retirement, Harrah felt ready to go back to negotiate. ("I'd really gotten kinda mad at Ed because of my thinkin'. It was almost like he was selfish.")

"Okay, Ed, I've thought about it. I'm not gonna give you $25,000 for this place, I'm gonna give you three. And it's not gonna be cash, it's gonna be $1,000 down, $1,000 in thirty days and $1,000 in sixty days." Howe took the deal and the Heart Tango was captured without a shot.

Harrah closed the place on Commercial. The Heart Tango proved to be "instant money." But Harrah could not simply collect revenues, he had to put his stamp on the new place. "We fixed it up. He had crummy little stools, we put nice stools in. We made money just from Day One there."

Bill Harrah at Big Bear, a Southern California resort dear to the family, pre-Depression. He appears to be about at the age he took up serious driving: eight. (Courtesy Margaret Schroter)

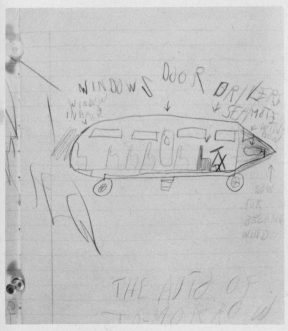

Harrah, the automotive stylist, drew this Dymaxion-like van as a grade-schooler. Notice the purpose of the streamlined bow. (Courtesy John Adam Harrah)

Inside the notorious Bank Club, Reno, in the early '30s. The games were said to be straight, but the proprietors, Bill Graham and Jim McKay, were anything but. This was the gambling atmosphere prevalent when Harrah came to town. With the Smith family of Harolds, he changed the ambiance totally. (Courtesy Nevada Historical Society)

The cadre in Harrah's second bingo parlor. Comparisons with a laundromat precursor are irresistible. (Courtesy Harrah's)

William Fisk Harrah, age eleven. (Courtesy Margaret Schroter)

Bill Harrah started his gambling career in Venice, California, in something close to bingo called the Circle Game. The drawing is by Harrah's sister. (Courtesy Margaret Schroter)

An earnest Bill Harrah and his wife-to-be, Thelma Batchelor, pose less than convincingly behind a prop at the Venice Pier. (Courtesy Margaret Schroter)

Of Virginia City's boom there are no photos. This is "C" Street after the Comstock and before the tourists. (Courtesy Nevada Historical Society)

Reno in 1907. This is a shot of downtown Virginia Street where Bill Harrah would establish his first casino and where he would fall out of a car — dead drunk — and land on his head at 80 mph. (Photo Courtesy Nevada Historical Society)

It could be a motor court somewhere in the Midwest. In fact, it's Reno's notorious Stockade just before it was torn down in 1977. Nevada sins efficiently. (Courtesy Nevada Historical Society)

Reno in 1938. The gambling zone or redline was not then an ordinance, but custom had the force of law. (See shaded area.) (Courtesy Nevada Historical Society)

A dashing Bill Harrah in Southern California uniform circa 1936, the year before he moved to Nevada. (Courtesy Margaret Schroter)

Battling Nelson (left) lost to Joe Gans in Goldfield, 1906, but the fight made Tex Rickard as a promoter and kept the town high on the bluenose hit list. (Courtesy Nevada Historical Society)

Tonopah in March 1907 with the red light district in the foreground. The Tonopah/Goldfield strikes hauled Nevada out of a post Comstock Depression. (Courtesy Nevada Historical Society)

George Lewis "Tex" Rickard, who made the great early fight in Tonopah/Goldfield between Battling Nelson and Joe Gans, and went on to become one of the most dazzling promoters in America. (Photo courtesy Nevada Historical Society)

A standard ground-breaking shot for Jack Dempsey; little did he know that the onlookers, Bill Graham (center) and Jim McKay (right), were about to be sent off to the federal penitentiary. (Courtesy Nevada Historical Society).

What has happened to the romance of divorce? The Hidden Wells Ranch about 1937. (Courtesy Nevada State Museum)

In the '50s, Harrah's was dwarfed by the Hotel Golden. Today almost the whole block is Harrah's, which also extends across the street. (Courtesy Nevada Historical Society)

Harrah's in the foreground of Virginia Street looking northeast in the '50s. The skyline has gotten considerably taller. (Courtesy Nevada Historical Society)

Harolds, owned by the Smith family, brought gambling out of the closet with a worldwide (literally) ad campaign. (Photo courtesy Nevada Historical Society)

Raymond I. (Pappy) Smith, patriarch of the Harolds Club family and inventor of mouse roulette. (Photo courtesy Nevada Historical Society)

Mayme Kandis Lucille Teague Fagg, a.k.a. Scherry soon-to-be Harrah, dealing "21" as Bill Harrah must have seen her from the bar in his Virginia Street Casino where he perched for a week before he sent someone over to ask her to meet him for a drink. (Courtesy Scherry Harrah)

Lake Tahoe, near the state line, c. 1950. George's Gateway Club, soon to be bought by Bill Harrah, is the first club on the left. (Courtesy Nevada Historical Society)

Bill Harrah was an early believer in the future of Lake Tahoe. He went way out on a limb to collect the several pieces of property to convert into this predecessor of his two-bathrooms-in-every-room hotel. (Courtesy Harrah's)

Banker days. Harrah hated to speak; he had not yet gone contemporary in his clothes. He might not have believed it at the moment of the photograph, but he would survive a good many years. (Courtesy Harrah's)

Bob Ring, early friend, constant echo.
(Courtesy Harrah's)

Bill Harrah (left), Maurice Sheppard
(right), and a vehicle attendant on his
way to park a customer's transportation.
(Courtesy Harrah's)

Frustrated in his effort to build a hotel at the Lake by cost projections that terrified everyone, including himself, Harrah came back to Reno, bought most of a city block, and put up his downtown hotel on the skeleton of the old Golden in 1969. (Courtesy Harrah's)

Harrah congratulates the late Ken Miles, a world-class racing driver he hired for one event in his Ferrari GTO. Ever a car cuckoo, Harrah entered only two cars in as many races, He did run an unlimited hydroplane for a season and sponsor an event, but Harrah always preferred driving to watching. (Courtesy Harrah's)

It would be easy to criticize Harrah for using Howe's manager Tom Smith as a fifth columnist, particularly easy to make too much of it, except Smith as infiltrator set a pattern. From then on, Harrah made it a point to have people in Harolds; for all Virgil Smith knew, in Colbrandt's, in every place against which he could measure his own success or from which he could learn. Spies became regulars in the Harrah Table of Organization.

While Harrah was storming the Heart Tango, another Southern California bingo operator had come to Reno and opened at the southeast corner of the Virginia Street block which Harrah had invaded and from which Howe had retreated. After a month of trying the competition, the newcomer fled. "But there [the place] sat. There's nothing more dangerous than a fully equipped bingo parlor sitting vacant with a sign in the window." It would not sit vacant for long. A caricature of a rich widow sponsored a caricature of a gigolo as its operator. "If you want to draw somebody's sweet old grandmother—like on TV—that's what Mrs. Carey looked like, kinda chubby and round cheeks.

"And then this fella came along, a promoter. He looked like a Russian. His clothes were like a hustling Russian. He wore his hair very long. He had a kind of flowing tie like an artist and a hat with the brim tipped up on one side and down on the other. He kissed hands and clicked heels and things like that." Clearly not Bill Harrah's kind of man, particularly when he mesmerized the rich Mrs. Carey and persuaded her to sponsor him in the abandoned bingo parlor.

"It was instant turmoil in the bingo business. He was hurtin' everyone. The place was full—we'd checked 'em very closely— but, well, they just weren't makin' it. And then they were gettin' robbed 'cause he didn't know anything about the business and the dealers can steal if you don't know how to watch 'em." Unfortunately for Harrah, either the dealers weren't stealing enough or Mrs. Carey's bank account was inexhaustible. In the first instance Harrah had to trust fate; the second he could find something about. Typically, and in his first admitted use of Intelligence outside the gambling business, Harrah managed to measure the boundaries of Mrs. Carey's wealth. "I think we

found out she had a couple of hundred thousand dollars in the
bank—just a huge amount for those times." By the time Harrah was willing to talk freely about a matter long since buried,
he had become *almost* willing to tell all. "And then we got
into her other—" At which point he stopped, clearly condi-
tioned by a life of secrecy. He simply could not bring himself
to talk about the surreptitious way he did his "checking." He
was willing only to say, forty years after the fact, that he discovered Mrs. Carey was heiress to the Molybdenum Company
of America fortune. "It was a zillion-dollar company and she
owned a big chunk of it. So we thought, well, she can go on
forever." The solution lay in an alliance. "So the three of us,
Joe Zemansky [of the Fortune Club] and Freddie Aoyama
(who was the manager of the Reno Club) and me—we
worked together. And finally it got so desperate we met daily."
The topic was always the same: the lady and the Russian. First
the three went to the city council, hoping to use them as Hes-
sians. "They said, 'No—once we get into that we'll have to tell
'em how to run their craps and all,' which was a pretty good
point," not to mention one that threatened Harrah's ox as the
next creature to be gored. Having failed to hire governmental
mercenaries, the three decided to concentrate on the Russian.
"We're workin' every angle we could. So we got somebody to
get to the Russian. We didn't bribe him. He was interested in
something like a dance school or something she [Mrs. Carey]
didn't like for some reason.

"We got all this out, you know, which you can do—snoopin'
and everything. There was something he wanted to get into
she didn't want him to get into and so we found that out."
How they found it out Harrah would not say then or later.
What they did with the information, he seemed almost proud
about. "Of course, he was fed up with her. He didn't like her.
She's hangin' on him every minute. You know—just kind of
hard way to make your money. So he was susceptible and listened."

At this point, Harrah made another strategic decision. The
conspirators would not ask that the place be closed down or
that the Russian leave town—that would be blatant. All that
was required was some common sense in the size of the pots

offered by Mrs. Carey's bingo emporium. If she would agree to
lower them to the level of the competition—meaning Zemansky, Aoyama, and Harrah—they would compete as honest
citizens. Notice that Bill Harrah was more than willing to put
his bet on the unfair advantage he was able to give himself
through his own diligence, his own research, his own meticulous business methods. Nothing more. Besides which, the
strange disappearance of so noticeable a character as the Russian would have been noticed. No indeed, no rough stuff; instead, a little cooperation coaxed forth by well-intentioned
blackmail. But how were the conspirators to be able to trust
each other? Obviously, they would draw up an agreement, and
in order to do that, they went to Joe Zemansky's lawyer. With
the agreement in place and the problem solved there remained
only a technicality; somewhere there had to be a consideration
—money. "Freddie still had plenty of money. The Russian
and Mrs. Carey had plenty of money. Joe and I are broke.

"The Russian was pretty cocky still and he said, 'Well, I
think we should each put up $2,000 in cash. The first one that
violates [the agreement] loses his $2,000.' And Freddie says,
'That's fine with us.' "

It wasn't fine with Joe Zemansky and Bill Harrah, neither of
whom was even close to having $2,000. Zemansky stalled, Har-
rah stalled, and everyone agreed to meet later in the afternoon.

The Fortune Club, Zemansky's place, was mortgaged to
First National Bank of Nevada; the choice was to knock it over
or walk in as customers seeking a loan. In defiance of everything Harrah had learned in Southern California, Eddie
Questa, the banker, was happy to oblige. "Anyway, we put up
the $2,000 and went back to the schedule. Then, of course,
their place being in a bum location, [it] only ran a week or so
and folded up." Better still, they were rid of the Russian. "I
don't think we ever had to do anything [with him]. I think
maybe he'd stolen some money when the thing was goin' on;
but he disappeared and that was the end of it."

That left the Japanese.

Bill Harrah had no compunction about stamping out the
Yellow Peril. It was simply a variation on the Black Peril or
the Female Peril or the Jewish Peril Theme. This despite the

fact that the money from the First National Bank had come on the recommendation of a Southern California banker named Phil Simon, "The only Jew we knew and of course we were a little suspicious. There are Jews and there are Jews but there are many Jews that are kinda chiselers." Simon wasn't a chiseler because he came through, but that did not lessen Harrah's suspicion. It was fortunate for him that his only Jewish acquaintance wasn't female. Harrah might have been able to stomach a Jew but a woman was another matter. He would not have a female dealer of his own hiring until well after other clubs in Reno, and he wouldn't have a woman executive until very late in the company's growth. No woman would sit on the board until late in the day. As for Asians, particularly Japanese who happened to be in competition with him, Harrah had even less use. "Freddie was arrogant. The Japs had all the money they needed, they just could call Japan or L.A. and get more." There was worse to come by way of rationalization. "This Freddie was [also] a little treacherous (so I understand how Pearl Harbor happened) . . ."

If Harrah had been able to bring himself to the requisite level of anger to assault Ed Howe, a harmless senior citizen, he had a lot less trouble turning his competitive wrath on Freddie Aoyama and his Japanese backers. "[The Reno Club] was a Japanese place so after Pearl Harbor they ran maybe a week or two and they had to close.

"So with the holdover from the bingo war, I knew [Freddie] real good and I immediately went to work to get that place. I'd take him out to dinner—he and his wife—which he liked very much. He liked to associate with white people socially.

"And we made a deal with him. We couldn't buy the place but we leased it. We kept our Heart Tango; we called the Reno Club 'Harrah's Reno Club.' We got rid of the shills—same old story—and did real good. That became the best bingo parlor in Reno."

IV

Not much of this paints Harrah as admirable except as an effective businessman. He was stealthy. He did not shy at using undercover agents, or at suborning his competitors' employees. He was devious. He was a bigot. Most of these failures he simply did not recognize, the others he explained away.

It is inadequate mitigation to say Harrah was a man of great courage—evidenced in the facedown of Jack Sullivan—and shrewd. Nor does it balance the scale to notice he was meticulous and bold. If there were to be any redemption, it would have to come from Harrah's yet-to-be-proven ability to change.

In the meanwhile, Harrah began to engineer yet another complicated transaction that would end with the single documented instance of legal edgework in his long career. From the moment he opened his casino in 1946, Bill Harrah insisted he did not have a partner or partners. What was done—Harrah was saying as clearly as he could—he did himself. Alone. In saying that he was defying truth. Not only was Virgil Smith an adviser, he became a partner in concessions all over town. "Bill and I had concessions," Virgil Smith would say in 1980. "Some of them were in writing and some of them were word of mouth."

By "concessions" Smith meant the common practice of outside ownership of games within casinos and clubs. Smith himself had owned and operated the games in Colbrandt's before he bought the place. With Harrah, he owned games at the Christmas Tree, Sky Tavern, Villa Sierra, the Open Door, and the Cedars. In addition, in order to open his grand casino, Harrah found it necessary to go back to the Smith well for money. "He not only borrowed from me, but many others," Smith, who loaned him $35,000, said. He did more.

"These articles of agreement made and entered into this 25th day of September, 1943, by and between Ralph Austin, Virgil Smith, William Harrah, Ingram (Bill) Williams, and Wayne Martin . . . WITNESSETH:" In the legalese of blue-backed documents, the agreement binds them all in ownership of John's tavern and club. It was an unhappy experience and it did not last long. But the partnership, the joint ownership of concessions with Virgil Smith, the borrowing of money to open in '46, all must have preyed on Harrah's pride and his sense of independence.

Not long after the casino opened, Harrah had his books

taken to a downtown parking lot, stuffed into a barrel and burned. Almost certainly it was not an act meant to deceive the tax collector. There is no evidence it was a cover-up of theft. That leaves one answer: Harrah, who had enormous respect for the law, defied it from a sense of embarrassment that he had had to seek the help of others. His rapacious behavior throughout the early years was not bothersome to him; revealing a need for help would have been shameful. The first he would talk about, the second he would never mention.

Hubris.

6

Rounder Reformed

Jasper, Tennessee, 1926–1952, Reno

Almost at the same time that Bill Harrah was fighting the bingo wars on the Russian front, his future wife, Mayme Kandis Lucille Teague Fagg, was encountering *her* first Russian. He was part of a dance team, which was in turn a part of a renowned band of post-vaudevillians who made up Earl Carroll's Vanities. It was a cosmopolitan group. In addition to the Russian, there was a French dress draper, an All American girl singer, assorted acrobats, and twenty-one girls, all of whom were extraordinarily beautiful, and whose job was to parade around wearing fans, beads, flesh-colored bikinis, and not much else.

The *good* ones—that is to say, those with prominent features—stood on pedestals while the French dress draper draped them in front of God, and the occasional mob of servicemen.

The *best* one was the line captain, Mayme Kandis Lucille, whom Earl Carroll called "Sheila" both because he had been in love with a blond lady whom Mayme put him in mind of, and because he had rechristened her "Scherry," a name he liked but couldn't remember.

By the time she was a line captain, "Scherry" suited her far better than those names she was born and married into; she was a stunner, she was a Hollywood starlet (although in later years the only film she could remember playing in was *That's*

My Gal, whose star slipped from her memory). Her childhood, though, was tailored to fit a little girl named Mayme Kandis.

One morning in 1925 Clarabelle Worsham, a Jasper, Tennessee, divorcée carrying a baby in her arms, boarded a river ferry. More or less immediately she felt the terror of the sea and burst into tears. In accord with the tradition of sailors, the ferry captain, Clarence Teague, took immediate pity, one hundred dollars out of his pocket, and, not long after, Clarabelle to wife. Mayme Kandis was one consequence of the encounter. Scherry would come to describe her father as "a ferryboat captain, deep sea diver and bootlegger," and it would become very clear that he—at least her image of him—had a profound influence on her. Unfortunately, Captain Teague died of "plaguery" when Mayme Kandis was just three so likely the image is larger than the reality. Something, though, imbued Mayme with romanticism and restlessness. It could have been the trees; it could have been the worms.

"When the leaves fall from the trees, I feel very lonesome; I feel like the tree is lonesome." As the words of a woman remembering herself as a girl, there is genuine poignancy there as well as enough synthetic drama to revive *The Perils of Pauline.* Facts are facts, though; Mayme Kandis' mother worked as a domestic while her daughter was going off to a one-room schoolhouse in Jasper. She recalls that she did not feel deprived, although bread and gravy was likely more of an entrée than afternoon tea.

One day when she was nine years old, her class went down to the Tennessee River. It was springtime and the banks of the river were nothing but great slabs of mud as far as the eye could see. Worse yet, it was the day the worms came out to check their shadows. All up and down the Tennessee "there were *huge* worms just everywhere." Her teacher insisted the children bathe in the river. Mayme Kandis insisted that she would be damned if she'd set foot on a worm, so a gallant schoolmate carried her over the bank and into the water.

If the future Scherry was skeptical about the advantages of Jasper pre-worms, she was downright depressed about it post-worms; and so her mother arranged that she live with an aunt, Ella Allison, in Alcoa, Tennessee, a border-state town not named after a war hero. Everyone worked at Alcoa in Alcoa, and everyone had lunch in the company cafeteria—except Elmo Fagg. Elmo stood behind the counter of the grocery store where Mayme Kandis was sent to shop. By then she had left high school and gone to beauty college to which she seemed to have reacted in much the same fashion as she did the worms. At sixteen, she and Elmo, who hummed a few bars at the local radio station in between bagging bananas, got married.

The future Mayme Kandis Lucille Teague Fagg Harrah Harrah was direct even then. "I think if you're going to stay in show business, you should change your name," she told her new husband. He disagreed and enlisted in the Army instead. For nine months Mayme traveled with her new husband until the oilcloth and plywood life wore her down, and she went to live with Mr. Fagg's sister in Toledo, Ohio.

Follow now in a series of flash-forwards; a montage of Mayme Kandis Lucille in the process of becoming Scherry. She checks time cards in a trailer hitch factory in Toledo. Her social life is not much, but she remembers going out to a roadhouse with gambling in the back room; the proprietor of the place was named Lincoln Fitzgerald. He would build a hotel up the street from Harrah's in Reno but not until a quarter of a century later.

Tight shot on arched eyebrows, cupid mouth, and a flashbulb popping, as Mayme Kandis wins the John Robert Powers Talent Hunt—Toledo, Ohio Chapter—and hies herself off to New York to become a famous fashion model.

Dolly in on a Brooklyn rooming house, a place the future Mrs. Harrah has taken a room because that's where her only friend for a thousand miles lives.

And then a confrontation at the offices of the Powers Agency where, for reasons Scherry now brushes aside, Mayme Kandis turned away from a career as a model to become a hostess at a tearoom on Madison Avenue in midtown Manhattan called Longchamps.

"New York wasn't any place for a country girl," deposes a disingenuous Scherry who went west to find "a better place in life." She found Hollywood, Earl Carroll, a divorce from Sergeant Fagg, a life on the road, and that "the stories you hear about girls getting their jobs on the couch was pretty much the way it was."

Having come off the road and refusing to make the necessary couch stops, Scherry was delighted when a photographer friend told her about a reasonably high-paying one-shot. "I went on that call and saw cushions on the floor. I asked about them and they told me.

"What it turned out to be was the famous nude shot that Marilyn Monroe finally did. I imagine I went on that call before she did but when I saw those cushions I just said, 'I think I'm on the wrong call.'" On the wrong call and in the wrong place. Someone told her Harolds Club had opened an employment office on Sunset, just a block up from Earl Carroll's. She decided that rather than go back on the road as a line captain or anything else, she'd ship herself to Reno and deal "21".

These days Scherry Harrah is a housecoated, middle-aged citizen of the posh section of Reno. In 1942, she is easy to see as a willowy, stylized pinup of a blonde; her cosmetics a Veronica Lake replica mask, her hair cascading to her shoulders and polished every morning with the Shampoo of the Stars. If there had been one hundred women as striking as Scherry in Hollywood, there were perhaps two others in all of Nevada—a fact that did not escape William Fisk Harrah.

II

Harolds hired Scherry, Harrah hired *and* married her. What's more he did it without curtailing a social life that would have exhausted Lothario, gagged Henry the Eighth, and left Casanova dehydrated and swearing lifelong celibacy.

For openers, the drinking was getting bad. Scherry would say Bill was up to half a bottle before breakfast—albeit breakfast was just after noon. Harrah was a sneaky drunk; he could consume enormous amounts and show little effect, but even he had to begin to pay attention to increasingly obvious clues. He attributed the increase in Canadian Club and Cutty Sark patronage to the stresses of opening his first full-fledged casino in 1946; but he must have been given pause before by, for example, the bridge. He hit it in his new Packard conclusively enough to break his neck in 1942.

Before and after his recovery, he would wonder why, just as he felt he was about whiskeyed out, a cab driver would appear at his elbow to take him home. He did not find out until many years later that Scherry would spend night after night calling around town to find out where he was, then dispatch her faithful cab driver to reel him in. "I can't tell you how much money that used to cost me," she said later.

Their courtship might have given her a clue. He had perched at a bar near her "21" table for a solid week after she had hired on from Harolds, knocking back the booze and staring at her. "I kept wondering when he ever went to the bathroom," Scherry remembers. He interrupted his drinking and mooning only long enough to dispatch a minion to ask Scherry to meet him next door at the Wine House, where on their first date both simply stood at the long bar saying very little if anything to one another, and drank. It does not seem much of a prelude to romance. Scherry is not at all sure how their relationship matured, but before either was exactly aware of what they were about, they had become man and wife. Not particularly friendly ones, either. Every night Bill would go drinking, every night Scherry would wait, tapping her foot, for her new husband to show up for dinner. Every night dinnertime would pass, and then after-dinnertime, and then "Lux Radio Theatre," "Fibber McGee and Mollie," and "Gangbusters" time, and still no Bill Harrah. Finally Scherry would start her calls. "It got so I felt he could *wear* his dinner," and evidently there were times he did. They fought constantly. If Bill had been in any shape to focus, Scherry is sure he would have hit her; as it was, the closest he came was pulling her hair. Finally, after almost two and a half years, she'd had it and her ultimatum was pure country. "I told him if he didn't stop drinking, I'd kill him. And he believed me."

Bill Harrah's recollection is slightly different. "I knew there was something wrong and, you know, you don't like to admit it. But I went to my doctor and I said, 'Look at me,'" and he showed Dr. Vernon Cantlon how badly his hands were shaking.

"And he said, 'Oh, I can fix that.'

"So I said, 'Give me a pill. Fix that.'

" 'No, I can fix it, but I won't give you a pill.'

" 'Well,' I said, 'that's good.'

" 'Will you do what I say?' asked Cantlon.

" 'I'll do it, I'll do it!' " Harrah must have been desperate—
at least as desperate as he could bring himself to be.

" 'Go fishin'!' "

So there, Harrah would have us believe, was a physician who
had already treated a broken Harrah neck caused by an
unyielding bridge and a snootful of booze, telling his patient to
cure a severe case of alcoholism by taking off for the Idaho
backcountry to commune with some trout. Harrah's memory is
that he was dutiful in following Cantlon's instructions. He
climbed aboard his Packard 12 convertible, collected a girl
friend and took off to discover a little town called Stanley,
which he would later convert into the northernmost province
of his empire. Outside Stanley he found a fishing hole, a guide
to the spots where trout lunched, and a route back to town,
where he went every afternoon to drink. *Mirabile dictu!*
"When I came back, I think my weight had gone from two
hundred and somethin' down to one ninety. I lost my pot and
I lost my shakes."

He had lost or almost lost a couple of other things as well.
Scherry, for openers. The Great Bridge Crash was one thing;
they hadn't been married and Bill had been engaged in a
man's errand when it happened. ("We were drinkin' and I
remember Rita had [the] Green Lantern down there. Rita was
a good friend of mine; I kinda liked her. I used to hang around
there a little bit—not too much, but I liked to go down and
have a drink and maybe fool around but not too . . ." Rita was
a madam; the Green Lantern a whorehouse.) The Virginia
Street Fall was quite another matter. First, it came after the
marriage. Second, it came with Scherry in the car. Third, it
came within an inch of killing her husband. He had drunk a
bottle of Scotch, climbed into the car with Scherry, and started
a fight. Annoyingly enough, she fought right back. Worse
still, his driving 80 mph through town didn't faze her at all—
at least until Harrah got to Virginia Street, the main drag, and

couldn't make up his mind which way to turn. At the very last moment he tried to go left, the driver's door swung open, Harrah pitched out on his head, Scherry slid over behind the wheel and got the car stopped. But that was—forever, absolutely, finally, enough-is-enough—it. Scherry threw him out of the house. Bill moved to an apartment at the Riverside Hotel and Scherry, having thought the whole affair over for an hour or so, followed. Wherever Bill moved, Scherry moved with him until, when Bill finally took the cure, they remarried.

In addition to almost losing his life on Virginia Street, and his wife after it became clear that he would survive, he had also almost lost his bankroll. Although by the time of the Great Virginia Street Tumble, the incident was long since forgotten, Harrah had almost succumbed to gambling fever.

One night at the Mapes, Virgil Smith remembers, Bill Harrah summoned him over to the tables and said he needed help. He was down about $18,000 and he wanted to stake Virgil at another table to help him get it back. Harrah had parked Scherry at the bar, where so far as she was concerned, he was idling his time removed from immediate stocks of liquor and therefore from immediate danger. Little did she know. Smith recouped the $18,000, gave it to Harrah, and with a cautionary whisper that the Mapes games were not what they should have been, wandered over to the bar to join his wife and Scherry. Within minutes, Harrah was frantically signaling him to come back. He had lost another $9,000. Again Smith recovered the money through his own gambling skill, again he gave it to Harrah, again he told him not to gamble any longer; but this time he took his own wife by the arm and left the casino.

By the time Scherry decided she'd been abandoned long enough and drifted over to join Bill, he was $54,000 down—an amount way beyond what he could afford to pay, much less lose. In due time, he did pay, but he never gambled to that extent again.

Virgil Smith's explanation of the reformation is lovely. He is certain that Harrah went to a mentalist named Arthur Ellen— a sort of early version of Kreskin—who was playing the Riverside and paid a handsome amount to be cured of gambling *and* drinking. About this time too, Harrah stopped smoking and

Virgil Smith thinks now, but does not absolutely trust his
memory, that the Amazing Arthur cured him of that as well.

Bill Harrah had discovered sobriety and it changed his life.
He discovered, when he sobered up, that in Scherry he had as
much a partner as a wife. He made his first trip to Idaho, a
place that would draw him more and more toward new values
and newer wives.

He would never again be a heller—except very discreetly.
Now he had time for his business and his cars.

III

Accurately, he had always *made* time for the cars. Nor was
he discouraged by his new fellow citizens in the attention he
paid to automobiles. Many of them treated the automobile
with equal obeisance. Bob Douglass, the tax collector whom
Harrah, upon arriving in Nevada, mistakenly thought he had
to bribe, turned out to be as car crazy as Harrah himself. First
off, Douglass took Harrah for a little spin in his new Ford
south to the state capital, Carson City. Harrah had been
warned about Douglass' driving habits. In fact, the man who
sold Douglass the Ford pleaded with Harrah to make Douglass
drive reasonably—at least until the car was broken in. Nothing doing. Douglass put the hammer down outside the city and
kept it there. This, of course, commended him highly to Harrah, who began right then and there to change his mind about
the malevolence of Nevada politicians. If the man drove fast
and hard, how bad could he be? Not bad at all, Harrah concluded soon enough when Douglass told him about a Reno-
Sacramento race he'd run in his Stutz. The highway had been
suddenly clogged by snow, so Douglass decided to do the only
rational thing: take to the Southern Pacific tracks. The inevitable happened in one of the Sierra tunnels; Douglass was able
to bail out before the train hit but the Stutz was totaled.
Douglass may have lost a car, but he gained Harrah's profound
respect right then and there. The man was a *serious* car guy.

Harrah's early car exploits in Nevada are submerged in tales
of his drinking and general carousing. Only when he sobered
up did his driving style—his highway panache—begin to take

on the quality of legend. His automotive legacy seems so obvious: those 1,400 cars at the eastern edge of town, the world's largest collection, the most formidable display of American artifacts assembled in the century. But to see the collection as the only Harrah gift to the car world is to mistake the importance of example. Bill Harrah was as much or more the western exemplar of the *publicly* audacious car-worshiper as existed even during the postwar years of ferment in car-crazy Southern California. Famous customizers might have been changing American tastes in the Valley; mechanical wizards could have been inventing instant tradition for the Indianapolis Speedway in Fresno and Burlingame, but Bill Harrah in Reno was setting the tone for at least two generations of street racers.

Not that he didn't go to Indianapolis to see for himself. Memories of that first excursion are centered around the strange workings of fate, superstition, and a silver dollar. Harrah had taken back a pocketful of cartwheels, knowing perfectly well that outside Nevada people were as enchanted by them as children by candy cones. It happened that upon his arrival he looked in the mirror and decided he needed a haircut. Sure enough, when he paid in silver dollars the barber was entranced, but not so much as the man who followed Harrah into the chair. *He* was Mauri Rose, and he went on to win the 500—with one of Bill Harrah's silver dollars, given to him by a worshipful barber, in his pocket. With sly immodesty, Harrah took a small slice of credit for Rose's success.

That's as far as he ever went. Although Harrah would field a race team of unlimited hydroplanes, sponsor a sports car race near Reno, and even hire two prominent racers to run his own Ferraris, he never put his name on a car at the Speedway. That has puzzled many. Harrah was one of the most committed car devotees in North America; Indianapolis was Mecca. Why didn't the twain meet? First off, Harrah was less interested in the race than in how the Speedway handled its crowds—how the 400,000 or so race-day fans were shuttled inside the great two-and-a-half-mile soupbowl, fed, diapered, and ushered out again. It was a matter of professional assessment, doing his homework again, studying things. (See him with his quarterfold blue notepaper, gazing from a $40 seat way up in the

stands over the first turn at the seethe and swell of the crowds
in the infield, laboriously scrawling locations of port-a-johns,
remembering his breakfast menu in the Gasoline Alley Garage,
questioning occupancy rates at the Speedway Motel during the
rest of the year.)

But there was another reason Harrah never fielded a car.
Over the years he was approached by dozens of teams seeking
sponsorship and he turned down every one. Nobody ever came
up to him suggesting he set up his own racing operation. That
would have been the Bill Harrah way. To see his name
emblazoned across the side of, say, A. J. Foyt's car might have
sent chills of erotic pleasure through someone else's groin, not
Bill Harrah's, to whom a car owned and run by someone else
but carrying his name on its flanks would have been an
anathema. Now if Harrah and Harrah's people had built the
car, set up the car, tested the car, and prepared the car for the
500, *the Harrah way*; well, nobody ever asked and Bill Harrah
never stepped forth. There is not much question but that if he
had decided to go racing in the major leagues, he would have
brought the same meticulous attention to detail that he
brought to everything else. Only twenty-five years later, when
Roger Penske fielded *his* first car at the Speedway, did the racing establishment fully appreciate NASA-like thoroughness.
Penske's style made his team an enormous success and turned
him into a racing legend. Most of that success came because he
was incredibly thorough, some of it came because he was lucky
and no small part of that luck was that Harrah decided against
getting there first.

It wasn't so much state-of-the-art equipment that had begun
to fascinate Bill Harrah. He might want the fastest production
car available and then modify it so it was faster than anything
else around. But his real love was for old cars. There is much
romanticizing in the literature about this widespread addiction;
there are almost no efforts to explain it other than to suggest it
comes from reverence of the past. Or perhaps the worship of
an abstract ideal. Or even brass fetishism. Harrah was pretty
direct about the genesis of his own feelings: "When I was a little kid, Model T Fords were the new thing you bought and

drove. They were cars. I was always interested in cars. I liked them. As I got older, the Model T Fords became antiques.

"I really didn't know there was an antique car society or that there were collectors of antique cars 'cause where I lived, that was just nonexistent.

"I remember seein' a picture in the L.A. *Times* of a friend of mine, Dick Teague, who's a car collector, and I've known him forever. There was a picture of him and a 1906 Cadillac and I thought, 'Gee, look at that old Cadillac!' I didn't know there was anything that old existed. And I thought, 'Gee, it'd be fun to have something like that.'" Something like that turned into 1,400 somethings like that. The pent-up ache to own everything on wheels that had passed its twentieth birthday came upon him carefully orchestrated by providence. "An old car to me was a big rarity; whenever I saw one, I couldn't believe it. And I hardly ever saw one. It was just almost like Fate lettin' me *not* see 'em yet 'cause . . ." 'Cause he wasn't in a position to afford every one he saw quite then, and the desire to possess was not feverish on his brow, and he had not—not quite at any rate—concluded the automobile was the key to understanding America. Fate must have been playing with Harrah's friend Dick Teague, too. His interest pushed him into the bowels of a Detroit styling studio, from which, at a crucial moment in the history of American Motors, he emerged to pen a variety of cars that somehow saved the company.

Meanwhile, Harrah had discovered the Maxwell. The car, a 1911, belonged to the brother of a friend of his, Johnny Vogel. "And Johnny was kind of a—what's the word?—scatterbrained, kind of a go-go-go guy. Johnny loved cars but he was careless. I preached to him. I was a good friend about driving and car safety and good tires and don't ride in convertibles . . .

"Anyway, Johnny was a good friend and he was down in L.A. and he was comin' to Reno. He just took off on the spur of the moment, which is the way he did things. He had a big dog and a Lincoln Continental convertible. He was driving up [route] 395 at 90 mph when a tire blew. It was a faulty tire; it was a worn-out tire and he hadn't checked it. And, of course, [in a] convertible you can get killed real easy." Which Johnny Vogel and his dog did. "The funeral was a real sad thing. And all these twenty-year-old kids, and here Johnny's dead.

"Anyway, that left the Ford and the Maxwell." Harrah wanted that Maxwell but—as he would do in all his later automobile transactions—he wanted to buy it at the right price, except this time manners intruded on horse-trading. "[There] was Mrs. Vogel, who was just one of the sweetest ladies in the whole world and a very generous lady. She'd done so many nice things for me. I wanted to buy the Maxwell and it was worth around a thousand.

"After the funeral things had settled down a little and we're talkin' and she said, 'Bill, Johnny wanted you to have the Maxwell and the Ford, if you wanted them.'

"And I said, 'Well, that's fine, Mrs. Vogel, but I don't want 'em as a gift, I would like to buy them.'

"'Well,' she said, 'that's what I really meant. You can buy them.'" At which point Mrs. Vogel took out a letter that had been in her son's effects. "Johnny was always valuing everything real high. So he had the Maxwell down at $2,000, and I was kinda proud of myself 'cause it wasn't the time to bargain. She said, 'Is that all right?' And I said, 'That's fine.'"

If there is a car beginning, the acquisition of the Maxwell and the Ford point to it; but Harrah's real initiation did not come until he managed—through ignorance—to turn a genuine 1911 Maxwell into a counterfeit 1907.

By this time, though, he was bringing himself to focus on his business, and Harrah's was on the way to becoming the jewel in the most significant new leisure industry in America.

7

Gold Bars and the Red Menace

Reno, 1946–1955

One day in 1946, before the very first casino bearing Harrah's name opened, Le Patron wandered over to a newly decorated bar ("We were using an astrology theme") and asked his new manager, Warren Nelson, what he thought of the work. Nelson was no lightweight, nor was he a neophyte; it's just that he'd never seen a gold-leafed bar before and he didn't quite know how to react. "I asked the painter if it was real gold; he said, 'Yes.' It was a considerable amount of gold being implanted on the bar. When they got it laid, they covered it with some kind of resin to keep it from peeling, and when it got all done it didn't look nearly as well as I thought it would.

"Harrah came in and looked at it, and he said, 'Warren, what do you think of that?'

"And I said, 'Well, it didn't turn out just the way I thought it would, but it's all right.'

"And he said, 'Well, you don't like it?'

"And I said, 'Well, no.'

"He turned to the guy and he said, 'Take it off.'

"I said, 'Wait a minute, don't do that. That's gold.'

"He said, 'I don't care what it is, if it don't look good, it don't look good.' So they put some paint remover on it and scraped that gold in a bucket. I asked the guy, 'Could we re-

trieve that?' He says, 'I don't think so, maybe we could, maybe
we couldn't.'

"Anyway that was the end of the gold-leaf bar. But that was
the way Bill Harrah did things." Even a Bill Harrah who was
in debt to half the gamblers in Reno for money to get his first
casino started did things that way. Autocracy came naturally,
but the experience with John's tavern reinforced Harrah's natural inclination to go things alone. It had been a bitter partnership. He was adamant the experience would not be repeated.
"John's Bar was semisuccessful; it made money. But I learned
something real fast. I'd never had any partners up till that except my father [who] got difficult at times. Then when I got
on my own, I could just make decisions and run along." John's
was a railroad flat of a bar, long and narrow. "I've always
thought in terms of expansion, and there was a store next door
that became available." Had Harrah been the sole proprietor,
he would have snaffled the space next door and doubled the
size of John's. (It was later said of Harrah, as he swallowed a
substantial amount of the property in the Idaho town of Stanley,
that he didn't want everything he saw, just what was next door
to him.) Bill Williams, a Harrah partner, wanted nothing to
do with expansion. "He was a gambler, still a dime was a dime
to him." Williams wanted a concession on the rent, and there
is a strong implication that Williams balked at improving the
place in consequence of the cost involved. Worse, Williams
was cowed by wartime regulations, unlike Harrah, who saw
them as conspiratorial efforts to thwart his success. "Of course,
the war's goin' on. I wanted to tear the wall out. You couldn't
do anything in those days—everything was frozen—on the
other hand you *could* do things.

"And the way you did 'em, you just went ahead; you hired a
contractor you knew and made your plans, got all your plumbing, your light fixtures, but the big thing was the wall. Some
kind of board could stop you.

"So the trick was just to get it done before they knew about
it. Bill—no, no, he didn't want to do it that way." Williams'
position was a sound one. First off, the plumbing and the light
fixtures had to come from the black market, which meant not
only that an illegal transaction was necessary, but also that the

cost was very high. Harrah's real impatience, though, seems to have come from Williams' unwillingness to use the *fait accompli* method of dealing with bureaucracy. That was in every way Harrah's style; it did not leave room for faint hearts. They got the place but they ended up paying rent on an empty store for want of the proper permits. "So we sat there for the duration with this vacant room next door, when we could've had it full of slot machines and '21' tables and all sorts of stuff."

That would not happen with the new casino. "There's a little good in nearly everything. If it'd been a real happy partnership, I might have cut them in on the casino when I opened it because I needed money. But because of that experience I had *no* partner."

No partner, but an alter ego whose name was Bob Ring, who looks perfect these days to play the lead in a remake of *Miracle on 34th Street*. Ring still goes to his office at Harrah's. At the moment of writing, he is listed in the table of organization as vice-chairman, but his responsibilities are light. He spends much of his time attending the needs of old customers and planning the annual golf tournament. But Ring was there from the beginning. He was a superb adjutant; he was very likely the first (certainly the most enduring) of the Harrah hierarchy to understand that the commander in chief understood the uses of implications far better than he did specificity. Ring was a man of great intuition whose genius it was to understand the oblique—occasionally murky—directions Bill Harrah gave and see they were carried out.

Ring came to the Harrah inner circle in Venice, where he quickly understood his role as Harrah's shadow. He remained in Southern California, operating the Circle Game, after Harrah moved to Reno. Harrah called for him a year later to help fight the bingo wars. On Harrah's behalf, Ring had tried to expand the infant gambling empire to Palm Springs—from which Harrah later retreated. From the beginning, then, Ring was trusted. What's more, he was trusted to operate out of Harrah's sight. It was Ring, for example, whose job it was to carry the bingo bankroll back and forth to the Wine House, where it was kept when the place on Commercial Row tucked in for the night.

Very early in the corporate day, Ring and Harrah seemed to come to an unspoken—naturally—agreement. First, Ring's job was to echo Harrah. Second, it suited the management style of both to operate everything on a need-to-know basis. Third, if there was nothing important to say, neither would utter a word to the other. (Legend has Ring and Harrah driving from Reno to Los Angeles—a nine-hour trip—during which the following conversation took place: in Sacramento, about three hours from Reno, Ring mumbled something about the overall decency of the weather. At the Los Angeles city line, Harrah brought himself to agree.)

Ring's loyalty and silence were invaluable to Harrah, particularly during the rough times after the casino opened. Recall that Harrah had moved to Virginia Street, expanded the Heart Tango to an "L" shape, with the horizontal bordering the north/ south alley that split the northern block of Reno's downtown gambling area. From there, he went into the Reno Club (thanks to Pearl Harbor) and then, with a parlor on one side of Harolds Club and a lease on the back of a clothing store to Harolds southern border, opened the Blackout Bar. Maybe it was Ring's idea—he had seen the worth of serving liquor in the business in Southern California—more likely it was Harrah's; but the Smiths, who owned Harolds, agreed to cut doors between Harrah's to the north and Harolds, and Harrah's Blackout Bar to the south and Harolds. In that way, *everybody* could drink.

The acquisition that made the casino possible was that of the Mint—formerly called the Block N—giving Harrah sufficient frontage on Virginia, south of Harolds, to make a try for the major leagues.

The lease acquisition required some of the money Harrah had to borrow; the refurbishing of the place sucked up the rest. The gold leaf removal edict that so confounded Warren Nelson was just one manifestation of the length to which Harrah —with Ring's help—was going. There were also astrological decorations, terrazzo, and carpet.

"There was a bar in Los Angeles I'd heard about. Just a six-foot room but maybe sixty feet deep. A fella put a bar you can walk up to and buy a drink and still people can get by—this didn't seem possible." Harrah had to see it; he had homework to do. "There's a little bar, and the back bar up higher; they use every inch. The bar front doesn't set out over maybe eighteen inches at the most. The bar top is just wide enough for a glass. There's room for one bartender and maybe eight stools. It's just the cutest little thing you ever saw.

"So they used every inch and the fixtures were very good too. So I said, 'I want to meet the architect.'"

There is more to this than the famous Harrah attention to detail; it is one of the first instances of Harrah's openness to the expertise of others. It was no big decision to go to an architect in 1946. But to hear of efficient use of space, to discover solutions in a place of business five hundred miles from his own, to make that trip especially to see how space was used, to ask for and get the name of the man responsible; these were the Harrah traits of thoroughness that would lead him to a remarkable continuing partnership of thought with consultants about such diverse matters as busing, personal use of time, going public, buying a corporate jet, and anticipating the direction of Reno's growth.

Bob Ring remained proud of Harrah's first casino every day of his business life. He remembers its size (a 35-foot frontage, 140 feet deep); he remembered precisely the number of machines and tables (a keno game, a faro bank game, two wheels, six "21" tables, three crap games, and forty slot machines). There was a horse race book in the back end. But Ring did forget a couple of things. The *Saturday Evening Post* dropped by one day in 1948 and came away stunned: "In the basement, the Harrahs set up their own popcorn-making machines, a refrigerating system for the bars, with elevators to lift cases of beer and other liquors upstairs, and a suite of offices with as much electrical counting and auditing equipment as any bank. They built in a reserve electric system to supply light and power should there be a failure of city light and power." (For all its powers of observation, the *Post* failed to identify the true proprietor of Harrah's.) Ring could not—even from his lofty position as vice-chairman thirty years later—keep from chortling that they loosened up the slots to cut into Harolds business. He admitted to using shills although clearly this embarrassed him. Hiring house players, he rushed to add, was the product of insecurity about going into a new enterprise—the casino business. Everyone else was using shills, he said, and Harrah felt he could not risk defying convention. Obviously, it was a concession neither Harrah nor Ring could swallow and in no time the shills were gone.

"Originally we put in rubber tile, inlaid square flooring, and all our fixtures were either real fine oak or a mahogany hardwood," said Ring. Since Harrah's was advertising the new place as "The Casino to See," the rubber tiles and the inlaid squares didn't quite cut it with Mr. Harrah, as he was coming to be known. Nothing would do but terrazzo and carpet. The whole idea of carpeting a floor on which everything from divorcée's Cuban heels to cowboy shitkickers would tromp pained Virgil Smith, who had, after all, loaned Harrah a good deal of money which, he discovered to his horror, was going to pay for that carpet.

But the results seem to have been astonishing. If nothing else, the carpet set the tone for the place and it was a tone far more refined than had ever been displayed in Reno before. *Life* magazine, in fact, had called Harolds "as garish and as nakedly ugly as an unshaded light bulb hanging from the ceiling in a flophouse dormitory." Nor did it hurt to build in a steam pipe beneath Harrah's pavement so that customers would not slip on ice or snow. In fact, it was a stroke of genius, for that first winter was bitter; almost bad enough to threaten stillbirth to the new casino.

Harrah had two worries with the new casino: avoiding cheaters—which would take him years to learn to do—and cutting expenses. "You had to watch your expenses very closely. They are extremely high in a casino 'cause everybody's paid quite high compared to surrounding jobs.

"So just a few days of very slow business with a big nut (I had no idea what it was in those days, but it had to be in the thousands), why you could get in trouble real fast."

It's worth pausing for a moment before plunging into that first winter's blizzard to notice that Harrah didn't know what it cost him to open his doors every day. In part this was because he was drinking but also because he had not yet instituted the extraordinary controls that would come with the operation of the casino. There was something more: Harrah, for all his materialism, for all his fierce competitiveness, for all his attention to detail and thoroughness when it came to service, was an absolutely astonishing gambling phenomenon: an owner who didn't count his money. In every other establishment the counting room was a place reserved for only the most trusted; gambling being a business where trust was an inoperative word, money counting was done by the only people the casino owners could begin to believe: themselves. This would lead to legitimate charges of the appearance of fraud and conflict of interest, if not documented skimming. So it is fascinating to discover that even as early as the year in which Bill Harrah opened the doors of his first casino, he was cavalier about the counting of his daily take. He could leave that—in full confidence—to Bob Ring and to his father.

Harrah's counting room attitude says something else. Certainly in 1946 he needed money. He would need more and more as his tastes became increasingly extravagant. But it never seemed to occur to him, as it did to some of his competitors, that cash was flowing into a room in his own place of business, and that he could go downstairs, run his hands through $100 bills, and perhaps, with the help of some creative bookkeeping, stuff a few dozen into his pockets.

That first winter, though, he might have preferred to warm himself by burning the few dollars that came in rather than stealing them. The snow was very heavy in the streets of downtown Reno: "There was so much snow that people just stayed away from downtown. You could park anywhere on Second Street and just about anywhere on Virginia Street." And *they* were the streets that had been plowed.

"I went in the club and there wasn't a customer. But we had all our dealers and all our bartenders working. I thought, 'Brother, [with] our $8,000 nut (or whatever it was) it isn't going to take us long to go out of business.'

"That's something I learned that's almost true today. Many executives in any line of business are very slow to act; they want to quit spendin' the money but they don't want to hurt anybody and usually you have to hurt somebody." Harrah didn't want to hurt anybody either. As he would do the rest of his life, he enlisted someone else to be the assassin. Harrah would later praise his hatchetman for "cutting 'er way down and [laying] off his friends and everything," but he would not then or later ever perform such a painful act himself. Of course it worked.

"We were still in business. We [went down] to a crap table and we had a couple of '21' tables. We just cut way down where it was a real healthy little nut we had that we could maybe not meet every day—but there was no question we were going to stay in business.

"So when we had that in control, then we had promotions . . ."

Those promotions were aimed at Harolds. In perfect accord with the Harrah style, they were—at least many of them were —stolen from Harolds itself.

Harolds was an interesting place, owned by a fascinating family. The Smith clan (no relation to Virgil) was a midwestern transplant consisting of a father, Raymond I., who was a carny, and two sons: Harold and Raymond A. Harold, the younger son, had worked for his father in San Francisco and in Chicago during the Depression; he was an energetic, dedicated, huckledebuck, Calvinist-work-ethic midway hawker. Most memorialists of the era give the Smiths credit as the first casino operators to bring spectacular marketing methods to the world of slots and tables.

"[Raymond I.] suggested putting a mouse on the roulette wheel," said *Life*, "instead of the usual white ball. The mouse would run around the wheel until it got tired and dropped on a number, which was the winner. This gave Harolds business an immediate boom and [they] put in more roulette wheels and some blackjack tables." Unfortunately, the still-spinning wheels were chopping off the mice's tails; furthermore, mice made bad employees. Soon enough, Harolds dropped the gimmick. The club had made its point.

Mice to the contrary, the most visible of Harolds efforts was its advertising campaign. All over the world, literally, Harolds had bought outdoor advertising. ("The club . . . provided free evenings to graduates of the nearby Air Force Survival School," said *Holiday* magazine, "and they . . . reciprocated by erecting Harolds Club signs in the Congo and at both Poles.") From the Arctic Circle to Jerome Avenue in the Bronx there were signs that said "Harolds Club or Bust" and they flanked American highways like military escorts, much as the famous Burma Shave signs did during the same era. The key to all Harolds advertising was twofold: the challenge to go west and the total absence of any mention of gambling.

Trouble was, Harolds failed to keep its advertising promise. The message was far larger and far more promising than the medium, so that when customers trekked to Reno they found in Harolds a club that was not nearly as well run as Harrah's— although far better known.

So even if Bill Harrah had "kinda revolutionized the casinos" by upgrading the atmosphere through the miracle of carpet, customers were going to Harolds and treading on plain wood in preference. This was a clear signal to Bill Harrah that a little constructive borrowing was in order. "We started advertising with our bingo. We just wrote the ads ourselves, they were so simple then.

"When we were opening our casino, we realized that we were a little bigger and more sophisticated. We couldn't do it ourselves, we wanted a better job done." Harrah once again fell victim to his own foresight. He hired a firm that included an advertising expert as well as a lobbyist. It would not be long before Harrah's would be the most aggressive user of lobbyists in the industry, but what was needed at the moment was aggressive advertising. The small firm Harrah hired at first would provide, in Wallie Warren, a man who would be important to the growth of the company. So the lobbyist was fine; its ad guy was not up to standard.

By now, Harrah had discovered the worth of outside professionals. He went to San Francisco for the first of two ad agencies, and in short order "Harrah's" (although frequently mispronounced Har-*ahs*) became a known name. Nor was it harmful that the two clubs had names that were easily confused. The more advertising Harolds did, the more people noticed Harrah's; it would soon flip-flop to Harolds advantage, but by then it was a mere annoyance—not a matter of survival —to Bill Harrah.

The competition between Harolds and Harrah's was keen. Raymond I., the father, had aced Harrah out of the master lease on his Heart Tango building through exactly the same methods Harrah might have used himself: backdoor dealings with the absentee landlord. "I didn't get kicked out right away. It was quite an education. It was dirty pool. I didn't want to get in a fight with Raymond I.—he was too big.

"So I maintained my friendship with him. Still, I didn't feel too good. I respected him for his business ability, and we worked together till he died on all sorts of things [including] politics."

How they worked, neither said; *where* they worked was far clearer—on the far, far right. "He [Raymond I., who was also known as 'Pappy'] was a great one for the John Birch Society. He used to come and see me on that and bring all the books and talk to me for an hour.

"And I felt much like he did."

A decade later, the Smith family—by then clearly number two, if that, in Reno—got an offer for Harolds. It fell to Ed Olsen, the chairman of the gaming control board, to investigate the potential buyers. To the mystification of his field people it soon became clear that the real money behind the offer was hidden by layer after layer of front and middle men. When, after a laborious investigation, the real buyer was finally unearthed, it proved to be the American Communist Party—to the delight of Olsen, who rejected the application and was surely tempted to tweak both Raymond I. Smith and William Fisk Harrah with the information but did not.

    II

Allegiance to the national political right was one thing. Local politics was another. However idealistic Harrah was about macropolitics, he was the ultimate pragmatist when it came to his own community.

Of course he brought his philosophical baggage along on his

visits to the local pols. Harrah's benign view of the John Birch Society is as good a summary statement about his judgment of the regulatory world as there is. He did get specific particularly about those tentacles of government that reached into his world, and occasionally around his throat. The IRS he saw as made up of good and bad people; the good ones were those who came in and didn't bother him, the bad resented his success. Still, on balance, he understood that it was a needed agency performing "a thankless task." It's what the graduated income tax stood for that bothered Bill Harrah: "If they cut out all the exemptions it would be a happy day." He wanted a balanced budget, "an intelligent budget for the country to live with." He wanted to "quit tryin' to do good for the whole world," in particular "all the people that don't want to work." "A general overall tax without the deductions" made sense to Bill Harrah, say, "a straight 6 percent of your income." Of course he knew perfectly well it could never happen. "Bureaucrats don't want it simple. They want millions of people workin' for the government and makin' the life of the other people uncomfortable."

For all its seeming thorniness, this was an amazingly tolerant view considering the IRS was Harrah's constant companion. Scherry Harrah remembers Bill complaining that when he first came to Reno, bringing a stock of tax-paid liquor with him, the government pressed him to pay a second tax, which he did, and for the recovery of which he successfully sued. She—and he—spent a great deal of time trying to persuade the tax people that Harrah's increasingly large collection of cars and old-fashioned costumes to go with them (an addition Scherry Harrah put her energies toward) was not part of Harrah's personal property, and therefore taxable from Harrah's personal holdings. Bill Harrah was scornful and angry about the government's position on that one. He simply couldn't understand how the IRS could interpret the ownership of 1,400 cars as a personal fleet of automobiles. "Did they think I was drivin' all 1,400?" he asked once. He was at least as perplexed at the thought process as he was by the substance of the government's complaint.

During his career, increasingly as his business became more

important, Harrah bumped up against another federal bureaucracy, the FBI. Here—expectedly—his views were quite different. "They're super. My association with them couldn't be
better.

"They were courteous. They called. They made appointments. They showed up when they said they were going to.
They asked pertinent questions, apologized for takin' our time,
and got out." Approval was clearly predicated on the FBI's ad-
hering to Harrah's code of business conduct; it may have been
a government agency, but in dealing with Bill Harrah, the FBI
acted like a respectful supplier. And in more ways than one, for
since Harrah ran a dead-straight operation, his contacts with
Mr. Hoover's troops came only when the casino received an ex-
tortion or bomb threat. Criticism of guardian angels was not
one of Bill Harrah's faults.

One day late in his life, as he contemplated the role of government, Harrah summed it all up: "The ideal form of government is a benevolent dictatorship 'cause they just do what's
right and do it right now, without a lot of waste effort and not
a lot of waste money." Then he became wistful. "But of course
how can you arrange to have a benevolent dictatorship?"

He couldn't, but that didn't mean he was willing to still his
own voice when it came to political impingement on the gambling business.

Jerome Skolnick is matter-of-fact about what was the beginning of a great regulatory awakening by Nevada in its attitude
toward gambling control. "Until 1945, gaming control had
been the responsibility of local and county officials. The 1931
law that legalized gambling after twenty years . . . had established county license fees based on the number of games
operated. Revenues were allocated to the state, counties, and
cities, and the counties assumed the responsibility for the licensing and collection of fees.

"Twenty-five percent of the revenue went into the state's
general fund, and the remainder stayed in the county, for city
and county use. The county sheriff, district attorney, and three
county commissioners had license-granting authority." We
have seen how Harrah's misreading of the seriousness of this
law resulted in his choosing to seek a political alliance instead

and at the expense of a favorable location for his first bingo parlor. In 1945, the year before Harrah's first casino opened, the law moved gambling control to a state tax commission. Harrah had had eight years to assess the seriousness of gambling control in Nevada, to test the will of state and local pols to constrain what was becoming the largest indigenous industry in the state. How did he react to what Skolnick called in *House of Cards* a bill that "was strictly a revenue measure"?

"Well, we resented it a little like any new regulation [that was certainly due to the imposition of a 1 percent state tax on gross earnings], but in those days I was in favor of it 'cause I'd traveled around the state so much I knew there had been and were crooked places [not only] in Reno but all over the state. And I thought this regulatory body would hopefully turn things around.

"When the taxes came along, that was fine up to a point. But anyone resents taxes. When [they're] on the gross, it's a *terrible* tax 'cause you can be losing money; and we've lost money—a lot of money—day after day and still have to pay tax on it." Since this was a pocketbook issue, Harrah's position was predictable. What is fascinating, and quite different from the views Nevadans had become used to from the gambling establishment, was Harrah's judgment about the change in regulatory structure. "We could see the need for it. We were clean [so the new system made] no big change at all, at least in our operation, or in my life.

"It gave gambling a better name. The time had come. It was about right, I'd say."

Statesman Harrah had another reason for his surprising acquiescence to state control. He was not only apprehensive of the specter of federal regulation of gambling, he was lively to the political shadings within his own state and the potential for an uprising in the legislature by representatives from the cow counties. Ten years later, when a tax table distribution scheme was implemented to dole out portions of the revenues to counties where there was little or no gambling to tax, Harrah reiterated his approval: "We supported that because it gave each county something. I honestly think that those old-timers there would have voted [to keep] gambling. But why not give 'em [their share]? It's quite a bit of money to some of those little counties. It didn't hurt anybody. It was a very smart move." This approval was not entirely arm's length. Harrah had a hand in moving the legislation. "We liked it very much. [It] gave everybody a piece of the pie," and so he instructed his lobbyists to push hard, which was tantamount to telling the legislature it had the blessing of the gambling business.

If he welcomed stricter control in principle and in practice, it was in part because of his success in keeping the political wolf from the door in his dealings with local pols. From the moment he got his first license from Bob Douglass until his last great local political battle to move a bus station so that he could enlarge his sports book, Harrah enjoyed a felicitous relationship with local elected officials. His dealings with Len Harris, mayor of Reno from 1955 to 1959, make a perfect case in point. "Len was a likable guy. He wasn't the greatest mayor but he was a fun guy to be around. And he pushed you real hard to buy his lousy meat.

"I remember gettin' after our guys, 'Buy some meat from Len Harris.' And I was real serious.

"They said, 'Well, what'll we do with it?'

"And I said, 'Well, serve it!'

"They said, 'We can't! It's too awful,' which it was. And I don't know to this day [six months before his death] whether he was puttin' the muscle on you a little bit and sellin' you bum meat at a high price or he didn't know.

"I like to go by the second [theory] because he was real involved and politically ambitious."

Harrah was far less generous on the subject of Bud Baker, who succeeded Harris. "They said nobody could be a worse mayor than Len Harris and they elected Bud Baker and proved themselves wrong.

"Bud and that whole gang were just terrible . . . they were just a bunch of crooks—all of 'em or most of 'em—just terrible. There was a lot of dirty payoff stuff there, some of which I know about."

In particular, Harrah was upset with George Carr, "who I knew very well and was a good friend of mine." The bitterness had to do with the city's purchase of land for a coliseum and convention center in 1963. The responsible agency seems to have gotten a bid for the land and the construction, passed it on to the city council, and watched in wonder as the original amount increased substantially. Harrah and others were convinced much of the money eventually authorized—perhaps half again the amount of the original sum—went to some members of the council. "George Carr, he got a big chunk of money (I don't know exactly how much) on that coliseum deal. And it was common knowledge, or among my crowd of people it was no secret at the time, but nobody wanted to do anything about it.

"I thought, 'If nobody else cares, I don't want to get in where I have to look over my shoulder when I walk home at night.' So I let it pass. I don't know if I should've or not, but I did. But he's the only one I know definitely."

There was something more than civic-mindedness going on in Harrah's condemnation of the coliseum deal. He had by then commissioned a great many studies to determine the direction of the city's growth. Everything pointed south, along the extension of Virginia Street that became, as it left downtown, the highway to Carson City. Indeed, Reno sprawled to its south in the decades to come, spewing the same franchised sleaze down the Truckee Meadows as can be seen in any other McDonald's/Arby's/Wendy's-ridden town in the country. It is on this strip that the Coliseum was placed. Harrah knew all about directions of growth, but his interest was a selfish one. He wanted the convention center downtown, near his club. He fought to get it there; he lost and he was bitter about it. Harrah never held opinions in a vacuum.

III

Harrah's conservatism was measured in his dealings with government. In his handling of unions, it raged out of control. "He didn't want to be told what to do," Scherry Harrah would say after his death. No industrialist of his era did. What made Harrah's hatred of unions particularly virulent was the nature of his inventory: cash. He felt until his dying day that union

infiltration (and that is the way he saw the movement) of the
casino business would lead to a shop steward on hand in the
counting room. It was all well and good for contracts to be negotiated with garment workers. Contracts with dealers were
something else. That would be the equivalent, he thought, to
inviting the presidents of locals to sit on his board of directors;
the influence threatened to be so direct. Then there was the
problem of the *numbers* of unions with which he would have
to deal. As Las Vegas became unionized, he looked on organized labor with increasing horror, seeing as many as thirteen locals inhabiting a single hotel/casino just five hundred miles to
the south.

Three years after the new casino opened on Virginia Street,
"All of a sudden we had a strike and a union, and I don't know
how it happened. I think just because we weren't payin' attention." Harrah, his father, and Bob Ring may not have been
paying attention before the strike but they were all eyes, ears,
and elbows afterward. His motto later would be: "No matter
what it costs you, no matter *what* it costs you, . . . keep the
unions out."

It must have cost a pretty penny to organize decertification
elections; and it must have involved some considerable covert
behavior, about which Harrah refused then or later to speak,
nonetheless it was done. "Since then, we've had no unions except our musicians [who] technically aren't really Harrah's employees; they're employees of the orchestra leader."

The strike and the decertification set him off on a Right to
Work campaign—a totally sympathetic endeavor for the state
in which he lived, and one in which he had the support of
most Nevadans. It is not true that Bill Harrah was responsible
for Nevada's Right to Work law, but almost. "I contributed
and spoke for it to anybody who would listen to me." It took
three statewide elections. In the end, "we won [and] I know I
was real happy with that. The Right to Work is an American
fundamental."

If he had banished the union, Bill Harrah was shrewd
enough—as was Henry Ford in the establishment of his so-
called "sociology" department to check on the mood of his
employees—to grant concessions. He would be paternalistic in

the best sense of the word. In that way, the anti-unionists among his employees could point to working conditions among the best in the industry as reason not to push for organization. "There are companies that deserve unionization because they treat their employees terribly. If everyone had treated their employees as they would like to be treated themselves over the years, there'd be no unions. So many companies have asked for it [unionization] and they deserve it.

". . . We haven't asked for it and we don't deserve it." Unlike the Ford sociology department, which was too often preoccupied with trying to redress the grievances of workers who were genuinely oppressed and eventually itself turned into an oppressive agency, Harrah's preemptive measures were clear-eyed and effective.

"One way of avoiding unionization is . . . to have a board of review, which we do, so a person can't be discharged politically. They have to be proven [to be] at fault.

"The other thing is wages and benefits."

After Harrah's death, after the acquisition of his company by Holiday Inns, the anti-union policy remained. A new Harrah employee sees a slide show emphasizing courtesy, and then another describing the organization. Half of the second show is devoted to a strong anti-union message. The voice-over oozes concern for the individual and assures every new employee of fair treatment to go along with lavish wages and perquisites. It is far too heavy-handed a sell. In fact, the wages are good ($36 per shift for a starting "21" dealer, plus an equal share of the tips or "tokes" taken in by the whole department during that shift; the tokes can exceed the wage). Benefits are as good or better than those in any other service business and there are such extras as a biannual on-the-house opening of the Tahoe and Reno showrooms to employees and guests. Drink tokens are issued with paychecks, but this is more a come-on than a benefit. All casinos know employees are players. They only have to give them an excuse to return the paychecks over the tables, and free drinks are as seductive to dealers as to bus customers.

During the writing of this book, one Reno hotel/casino's dealers voted to join a Maritime Union local. The shock waves still wash over the city. Doom is predicted, old-timers rock and spit and shake their heads. From time to time, Las Vegas is virtually shut down by strikes. There is also the taint of union corruption in the city. Every time the *Reno Evening Gazette* or its morning sister, the *Nevada State Journal*, report a Las Vegas strike, the wailing can be heard echoing from the neighboring Sierra.

Anti-unionists may be right about the dangers of allowing outsiders to negotiate over control of casino inventory. It is certain to be proven one way or the other. It is not likely, though, that any showdown will come in Reno until the later years of this decade.

Reno may thus be a union-organizer's equivalent of the Alamo. If so, Bill Harrah played Sam Houston.

8

Deep Waters
Lake Tahoe, 1955–1963, Reno

"It was on a blustery morning in January, 1955, that William F. Harrah made the decision that was to transform him, in a few months, from a middling-successful casino operator in Reno, Nevada, into the biggest gambler in the world, the Napoleon of Chance." There's a two-column head shot that accompanies the 1965 *Saturday Evening Post* piece, showing the Napoleon of Chance looking straight ahead (and doing a wonderful imitation of either the president of the world bank or a soap opera doctor reporting inoperable dandruff to the relatives), his chin cupped in his hand, his stare chilly enough to frost the lens on the camera.

"He was out at Lake Tahoe that morning, 50 miles from Reno, looking for a piece of property on which he could build a museum . . . Lake Tahoe is large and deep and beautiful and mountain-girt. It is pronounced 'tah-hoe' and is said, on little evidence, to be an Indian word meaning big water or big whiskey or damn-all-white-men or (according to Mark Twain) grasshopper soup . . .

"More important for Bill Harrah's purposes, a state boundary bisects it, and an interstate highway runs along its south shore."

All three sets of Harrah executive eyes had long since noticed the Lake. John Harrah had wondered what on earth peo-

ple saw in the place, cherubic Bob Ring had stopped on his
way from Venice to Reno at Tahoe, giving it only a passing
nod, Harrah himself had driven through—but his glance returned again and again and only his.

"Bill Harrah is not at first sight the type you would expect
to be high priest [of a gambling establishment]. He looks more
like a deacon—tall and thin, gray hair, a narrow face, horn-
rimmed glasses, a thin smile, a keen look, a quiet voice . . .
There are people in Reno who will tell you that they have
never seen Bill Harrah crack a smile, and there are some who
will tell you they have never heard him utter a word. He does
not drink, he does not smoke. As a matter of fact, he seldom
gambles."

Ah, the changes sobriety wrought. Since Harrah dried out in
1952, he had substituted work for alcohol. A somber-sided
man, he dressed like a mannequin belonging to a tailor catering to railroad lawyers and expensive morticians. He had decided that since he was shy when sober, and he was bound to
be sober from now on, he would capitalize on the shyness by
wrapping aloofness around him and suggesting it was deliber-
ate.

He was on the way toward yanking not only his own life but
the business persona of his company onto a successful path.
Until the Antabus and the Cure, his success was the fruit of
good instincts. Now it would become the consequence of planning, thoroughness, foresight, and this new relentless drive to
work—combined with that remarkable intuition. Nor did he
wait very long to get up to speed.

"I'd gone to the Lake for years and admired it up there. I
liked the south end, but I thought, 'Too bad I wasn't here before,' because everything was taken." Then one Sunday in December of 1954, Harrah persuaded his friend Virgil Smith to
go driving south on the Carson highway to look at property.
Virgil, who remembers Harrah's preoccupation with South Virginia—way out—as the direction in which the city was going
to grow, thinks there was a third member of the party that
Sunday, Ben Edwards, a real estate man. As they stopped to
look at this place and that lot, Smith thinks he recalls Edwards
mentioning something about George's Gateway Club at the

Lake being for sale for $500,000. It's Smith's memory that nothing would do but for all three of them to go charging over Mount Rose, around the north end of the Lake, and over to the club.

That is not exactly how Harrah remembered it. He had begun to sponsor the Reno Tour of the Horseless Carriage Club "and we'd go a different place every year." Since Harrah planned the route, the Tour found itself headed toward the 6,200-foot elevation of the Lake; a trial for the unprepared, a triumph for Bill Harrah. "Usually, I went [to the Lake] in September because in July and August I was very busy [in Reno]. So I never went to the Lake in the summertime.

"One year [as] part of the Tour we went to the South Shore, and we went there in July. I remember walking in the Gateway Club at the time, and it was really a crummy place, just terrible. Still, the business was unbelievable! Just the crap tables were two deep. The '21' games and the slot machines, well, it was busy, busy, busy. We had a very nice place and George's was a crummy place and he was doin' two or three times the business we were."

These crowds, frantic to throw money at Lake Tahoe gamblers, had not gone unnoticed by the wheel and table men in Reno. Unfortunately Tahoe, however alluring in the summer, was not that far from the famous winter picnic site of the Donner party. Tahoe's season was June to September. After Labor Day, said conventional wisdom, it was a three-dog town, buried beneath the snow; a fit place only for arctic explorers and madmen. The single convention Bill Harrah observed when it came to wisdom was an invariable consultation with himself. He ached to go to Lake Tahoe, but: "It's too late. Everything's taken and everybody's doin' good; nobody's gonna want to sell. So I didn't even think of approaching anybody." At which moment came the casual mention by Ben Edwards of the offering of George's Gateway.

Harrah's version of his move to the Lake has him visiting the banker who had staked him to his bond in the Russian battle during the bingo wars, Eddie Questa of First National. "I came to Eddie and asked him, 'Which way is the town gonna grow—east, west, or south?'" Questa promised to think about it, "And then he said, 'By the way, did you know George's Gateway Club is for sale?'

"I was amazed . . . and then I asked him for a name of a good realtor. He said the best one he knew of [was] Ben Edwards." Harrah took himself straightaway to Edwards and, in a typically oblique opening, told him he was interested in buying one hundred acres for a museum on South Virginia. "And *he's* the one that said, 'By the way, did you know that George's Gateway Club is for sale for $500,000?' "

It was not, then, a state secret. Anybody in Reno—the Harolds Club Smiths for example—would have had the same information. But Tahoe was simply out of the question. Nobody in Reno cared. Nobody but Bill Harrah.

"And I said, 'Boy, if that's true, you got a deal!' " The deal was for a twenty-three-year lease on a truly ramshackle building —literally a quonset hut—on the lake side of the highway, across from the present Harrah's hotel and casino, next to a club belonging to Harvey Gross. "So we went to work on it, and this Ben was a super guy at puttin' deals together 'cause there were all sorts of subleases to be signed and there were three or four partners, and there was a restaurant there that had three or four partners in it, and just on and on.

"Ben just worked twenty-four hours a day, put the whole deal together in five days. And we had the place. That was in January of '55. We opened around the twentieth of June that year."

An uncharacteristic case of modesty seems to have struck Harrah when he told that story. Virgil Smith is very clear that he reminded Harrah that as part of the acquisition, he should gather up surrounding space for a parking lot. What good was a club at the Lake if people couldn't drive right to the door? Trouble was, George's Gateway was next to a trailer park. "So Bill went up," Virgil said after Harrah's death, "and it was about the only negotiation I think he ever did absolutely by himself, and he went down the road to a much fancier trailer place and he asked them how many spaces they had to lease. When they told him, he said he'd take 'em all.

"Then he went back to the people who owned the trailer

court [next to George's] and he started dealin' with them. But it got to the point where they said, 'What do we do with the people we have here with long leases?'

"Of course, Bill already had the answer to that one. He just said to move them down to the other park—which was nicer, so they were delighted. And that was the end of that problem. He got the property, and he blacktopped it and he had his places to park."

There were other things to do. Harrah had not changed his mind that the Gateway "was a terrible run-down place—just awful" and if it were going to have Harrah's name on it, it had to have the Harrah touch put to it as well. "We couldn't afford to tear it down. But we covered it so you couldn't tell it was a quonset hut. We put a false front on it. Inside we cleaned it up, really made it nice. We cleaned up the restaurant and put in some of our typical Reno slot machines," making the odds as liberal as Reno's, a departure since the gamblers at the Lake had to set theirs to make enough money during the season to last all winter.

"Then the place at the Lake was an instant success—one of the few we've had where we didn't have to really push hard to make it go. It was just needed up there. It was full from the day it opened."

Yes and no. That is to say it was a success, but it wasn't exactly instant and it didn't quite come so naturally. Harrah had understood something about Tahoe none of his competitors could see: There could be a solution to the short season problem if imagination and energy would provide it, and he had full supplies of both on hand. Customers would not drive up in the winter? Very well, he would bring them up; and he would use buses.

The genesis of the bus program is shrouded in the mists of too many memories. Everyone agrees it was Harrah's idea and his alone. Everyone concedes it turned Lake Tahoe into a year-round resort. Everyone believes it revolutionized the gambling business. Trouble comes when memories are stretched to recall how it was put into motion.

Harrah dismissed the whole thing airily. "When Labor Day

came [business] really fell off so that's when we started running buses—Greyhound buses and refunding part of their ticket—which worked out very successfully."

Bob Ring is even less helpful: "Our first promotion at Lake Tahoe was Greyhound Bus."

Mark Curtis, now Harrah's vice-president for advertising and public relations, thinks the idea was turned over to the new San Francisco ad agency, which then shaped it into its assembly line form.

Maurice Sheppard, then Harrah's office manager, recalls someone got in touch with a Reno man who specialized in transportation to negotiate details with Greyhound.

Harper's magazine saw it more dramatically: "Harrah has quietly become America's biggest professional gambler—and one of the West's powerful men—by doing what nobody ever did before," it said in 1962. "He has garnered various findings of sociology and psychology and has used them to transform Harrah's Club of Reno and Lake Tahoe into an ever-growing supermarket of gambling for masses of middle-class and lower-class Americans. As part of his study, he paid some $16,000 to the tax-free Stanford Research Institute . . . for a special report on some of his own prospective customers. And as one result of what SRI's study showed, he is smoothly operating a vast interstate bus network which unloads passengers day by day into his gambling resort almost hourly."

There's no question but that by 1962, Harrah was using consultants like Kleenex. There's even less question about his going to SRI, not once but several times. It seems unlikely, though, that he commissioned a study between the time Ben Edwards or Eddie Questa told him George's Gateway was for sale in December and its opening in June.

It was instinct. It was unerring. And to Harrah, at least, it was simple. As Ring would say, "We made arrangements with the Greyhound Bus to haul people from the Bay Area—San Francisco and Sacramento, originally [eventually from thirty-one cities] and we'd give 'em a free bus trip. Whatever the fare was at that time, and people would pay it, and then we would refund it to them, and then we'd also give them a complimentary dinner and a split of champagne.

"People thought we were nuts doin' it and we weren't so sure we weren't nuts, I guess, but it's a long winter."

None of this is to say Harrah didn't commission a bus study *after* he saw the program's success in an effort to make it even more profitable. "In a Stanford Research Institute study made for Harrah in 1957 and entitled 'An Investigation of Factors Influencing Bus Scheduling,'" said *Harper's*, "Dr. Bertrand Klass and Dr. Harry V. Kincaid described the people who used the buses as 'elderly, in a low occupational status, unmarried, a renter rather than a home owner, and without a car.'

"Harrah set his sights on this segment, and ordered an all-out campaign to proselytize it. He spent about $450,000 in one year on newspaper and radio advertising in San Francisco, Sacramento, Stockton and twenty-eight other cities, offering round trips to lovely Lake Tahoe in chartered Greyhound buses . . .

"The advertisements never mentioned gambling. They did not need to. Once a traveler was gathered into the fold with cash in hand, human nature could be trusted to do what came naturally.

"All this seemed inordinate trouble and expense just to bring scrub women and pensioners to slot machines. But the yield was satisfying. Beginning with three buses which cost him $40,000 a month—more than he would need to charter a transatlantic liner—Harrah was soon scheduling as many as twenty buses a day from Oakland alone. Snowstorms seldom stopped them; his private fleet of plows kept the road open. One Washington's Birthday, during the worst blizzard of the winter, fifty-nine buses unloaded their cargo into Harrah's salons . . ."

Some points need to be made here. The audience described by SRI is typical of what we would now call the "transit dependent," poor and car-less. The elderly and the disadvantaged. The moralists had been arguing for a century in Nevada that gambling was nothing more than a regressive tax, that is to say it penalized those who could afford it least. Now they were saying Harrah was going beyond Nevada's boundaries to tax the California poor.

Point two: If Sammy Davis, Jr., would later say that the bus program enfranchised the blacks in gambling, it only did so in-advertently, carrying Bob Ring along kicking and screaming: "First of all, we got some seedy-lookin' people . . . Some of them, all they'd want to do is just get up and get a free ride up the Lake and back, and have a dinner and a split of cham-pagne." There is absolutely no question that he is using "seedy-lookin'" as a code phrase for "black." Said Harper's: "In bus stations of cities and villages throughout Northern California, Harrah set up booths like Travelers Aid posts, manned with bright young students from college campuses whose work was to tell people about the life up yonder at Tahoe, and also to dissuade certain types from making the journey. Orientals were welcome—they are neat, meek gamblers—but not Negroes . . ."

These days the buses clog I-80 from San Francisco and Sacra-mento/Stockton to Tahoe and Reno. The New Jersey Turn-pike from Manhattan to Atlantic City has turned into a sea of buses. Ma and Pa Kettle come to New Jersey from Portland, Maine, by bus, their brothers and sisters go by bus from Portland, Oregon, to Reno, Nevada. The gambling business may be a bigger supporter of mass transit—on balance—than the Department of Transportation. For those who decry gam-bling as a social evil the bus phenomenon, which brought American blue collars to a whole new playground in numbers that stagger even financial analysts, is a wicked instrument fraying the social fabric of the nation.

For casino owners, and as this is written they include some of America's largest corporations, the bus program is an assem-bly line moving pieces into position for the manufacture of profits.

Hard-line environmentalists insist another legacy of Harrah's epiphany is the degradation of Lake Tahoe. Once a pristine al-pine pond, it now threatens to become a carny swirl of sleaze and dirt. This view ignores two things: California's own contri-bution to the threat to Tahoe, by far greater than Nevada's (much less the gambling industry's), and gaming's efforts to protect what is, after all, a business attraction. It would be wrongheaded to suggest Harrah was cavalier about the status of the Lake. While he was free to admit the busloads of peo-ple coming in encouraged building a tract of shabby motels on the California side of the state line, he did what he could to preserve Tahoe. Harrah was active in the formation of the Lake Tahoe Area Council, which was the avowed—if not spectacularly successful—guardian of the Lake. And he opened his showroom at the old Gateway to its meetings. "We believe[d] in orderly development," he said. "We sure [didn't] believe in a hundred million condominiums around the Lake [nor] the hodgepodge development at state line. [That's] blamed on the casinos. All those little motels that have popped up. [If] anything's ugly at Tahoe it's in California and it's their own darn fault.

"We've been criticized on buses. [Their occupants] are older people . . . they're enjoyin' themselves. I can't see it hurts a thing."

Except maybe John Harrah's pride. When he heard that Bill had bought George's Gateway, he wrote his son a letter: "He didn't write me much 'cause we saw each other quite a bit. So when he wrote, it was usually fatherly advice.

" 'Dear Bill, I think you made a big mistake in going to the Lake 'cause you had a lot of problems in Reno and you finally got 'em straightened out. And you got everything paid for down there. You got some money. You're independent for life if you want to be.' " Then Harrah paraphrased. His father told him "No, that wasn't good enough, you had to go up in the back woods. I don't think he said, 'You're a damn fool,' but it was a real strong letter."

The first year Harrah's new place at the Lake made $1 million and change. He got a copy of the statement for the Lake, had a copy of his father's letter made, and sent them both to John without comment.

II

Success at the Lake came only because Harrah had gotten his Reno house in order. In accomplishing that, he made use of an uncommon instrument, Maurice Sheppard, surely the most diffident gambler in the universe. Sheppard then and Sheppard now would be appalled to be thought of as a gambler. He was a numbers man who had led a Dickensian childhood. Brought up in straitened circumstances by a divorced mother, Sheppard almost does not remember a time it wasn't necessary for him to work. Before the divorce, the family traipsed around the country with a father who worked for Woolworth's. After it, Edna Sheppard and her son stopped off in Louisiana before settling in Reno, where she became the administratrix of an eighteen-bed hospital in which she lived with young Maurice, "next to the surgery."

When Sheppard was in the ninth grade at McKinley Park school, he was chosen as one of two Nevada representatives to go to Washington to meet with President Herbert Hoover. There was an almost classic problem. He couldn't afford to leave work and he couldn't afford to buy the clothes he would need to appear at the White House. There is a photo of the children, posing with the President at that meeting, and sure enough there is Maurice Sheppard, down near the front because he was a small boy and could not have been seen in a back row. He, almost alone among the eighty or so youngsters, is wearing not a jacket but a sweater; it was all the Sheppard family could scrape the money together to buy.

He graduated from Reno high school at sixteen with no hope of going to college. For a year he worked at the Washoe Market, "hauling hundred-pound sacks of sugar, $5.38, out to people's cars." After twelve months of it, he allowed himself to be persuaded by friends to give the University of Nevada a try. He could study during the day, take an afternoon break for work, go back to class, return to work, and study again at night; just as he had done in high school. When Sheppard tells it today, there is a weariness in his voice, not hard to understand, particularly since he wanted with all his heart to be a forest ranger. But UNR offered no course in forestry. Instead, he majored in botany and took a minor in economics.

College could not have been too much of a disappointment to Maurice Sheppard despite the University's failure to teach him to speak to squirrels and treat elm blight. He was a good student, he made lifelong friends, he became president of his fraternity, and he spent his summers working at the Lake for Crescent Creamery, for which he became sales manager not long after his graduation.

Unfortunately, early success coincided with the threat of the Second World War. Sheppard and his immediate circle of friends were prescient. There were four of them and all four tried for commissions in the Marine Corps two years before Pearl Harbor. Three made it, Sheppard did not; bad eyes. So he took himself to San Diego and became an inspector on Consolidated .Vultee's B-24 bomber line. It was not the quality of contribution his friends were making, but it was something. The job was a sure deferment—essential war work—but when December 7 came, Sheppard quit and went back to Reno, waiting and wanting to be drafted. The Army sent him to Wake Forest finance school, "Why, I simply can't imagine."

Sheppard was discharged in 1946, having learned finance the Army way, married a WAC finance expert named Audrey, and landing in Reno almost at the very moment Harrah was about to open the Virginia Street casino.

"Do it right, do it the way it should be done," Bill Harrah said later about the unspoken motto of his company. When Maurice Sheppard went to work as a bookkeeper at Harrah's, the gambling may have been done right, the customer service may have been done right, the design of the casino may have been done right, but the system for running the place was being done as haphazardly as a Liberian lifeboat drill.

Contemporary magazine accounts attribute extraordinary skillful management techniques to Harrah's. None of the techniques was in place when Sheppard arrived. "In the land of honky-tonk, elderly John Harrah operates a dignified gambling house on strictly business principles . . . [Harrah's] differs from honky-tonk competitors in their conservatism, and in their stern adherence to sound basic business practice." Not only was the *Saturday Evening Post* wrong about who owned and ran Harrah's, it was also wrong about the business of the business.

Sheppard had been advised to keep his head down and his mouth shut when he went to work upstairs in the Virginia Street club, in a space—irony of ironies—the bartender's union used to occupy. He would come in at 7 A.M. to be the cashier, switch to the daily routine of doing the books, go downstairs when the graveyard shift got off to balance the safe (those days, Harrah's paid at the end of each shift), go back upstairs and complete his reports. It was more busy than trying work.

Between trips up and down the stairs, Sheppard (he was universally known as Shep, "Maurice" didn't fit the frontier wheel man image) was developing something that would come to be known as the Daily Report. It listed department grosses, interest accrued daily, and pretax operating profit. It revealed immediately whether or not the company was within budget. It compared costs year to date to the same period of the year previous. "We could count the games. I could guess what the bar was doing because cost of sales was 35 percent. The figure we didn't have was the slot machines.

"So I took the payout figure and worked it backward. A kind of primitive thing," Maurice Sheppard calls it today. A later Harrah president, Lloyd Dyer, disagreed. "[It's] unheard of in any business that you get a daily P/L [profit and loss statement]. You usually get one fifteen days after the end of the month, or every three months."

The Daily Report did, in time, turn into an immensely sophisticated tool; enough so that the *Wall Street Journal* would remark on it in a major piece done on Bill Harrah in the last year of his life. Even in 1946, though, Harrah thought it was a wonderful device. In months and years to come he would encourage Shep to work out supplemental reports on each slot machine, and then each table.

If a good deal of Shep's time was spent trying to make order where there had been scattered sheets of paper, he also had to deal with an increasingly profligate Bill Harrah.

During the drinking days, it was Sheppard's job to get Scotch from suppliers, no easy thing to do at a time after World War Two during which the whisky was as hard to get as a new Ford. To buy one case of Cutty Sark, Shep had to agree to take ten cases of wine, and those were days when Americans scorned wine. But he never bought on the black market, and somehow he was able to get rid of the wine.

On the very same Sunday that Virgil Smith says Bill Harrah made up his mind to buy George's Gateway, Shep was called to the office by Harrah. Harrah had just nicked the bankroll for $250,000 to pay for Parker Lyon's Pony Express Museum.

Now he wanted $500,000 for George's Gateway. "The museum had taken every goddamn dime we had," which Harrah almost certainly had been told but chose to forget that Sunday. Said Harrah, asking for cash projections, "Can we afford to buy [the club] at Lake Tahoe?" Shep's answer was probably equivocal. It would be some time and he would shed considerable blood before he realized that you didn't equivocate with Bill Harrah. "I would have said 'no' but the next thing I knew we bought the place. When I saw it in January—it was cold as hell up there—it was just a quonset hut. I couldn't believe it. That kind of money for that kind of place? God!"

It was not Sheppard's job to question major decisions, and it's a good thing for Harrah's that he didn't take a stand on the $500,000. In later years, he would become comptroller and then president of the company. His contributions would be major. Had Shep turned stubborn that Sunday in 1954, Harrah would have reacted as he always did when challenged on matters of significance; he would have dipped his pen into his autocracy well and signed a death warrant.

Besides, it was a lesson for Sheppard in the worth of the Harrah Vision. It was another lesson as well in the hopelessness of trying to stem expenditure requests when they carried the boss's signature. Shep watched as Harrah bought antique car after antique car. "There were times when we were pinched pretty bad. I may have objected, but so what? Sometimes I felt I had to fight him for the good of the company. But he was sly about things. He would slip checks by me or past me."

Sheppard handled payables in time-honored fashion. On the first of each month he would make out all the checks. "We'd send 80 percent of the checks I'd drawn but the remaining 20 percent would represent 80 percent of the money we owed." There wasn't a housewife in Reno who wouldn't have recognized the ploy.

About this time, Harrah contributed his own innovation. It was a kind of in-the-trenches financial control to supplement the Daily Report, and it was called the Eye in the Sky. There was a crawl space beneath the upstairs office. Harrah had one-way glass installed so he could observe the activity in the ca-

sino. It is the first recorded instance of casino surveillance—
industrial spying. The security department would become enormous, its techniques demonic. Surveillance would come to be
as accepted a casino device as bells and lights on slot machines
—another Harrah brainstorm. Even the civil libertarians would
finally accept the need. Harrah saw it first; what's more, he did
something about it.

As we've discovered, Harrah saw the need for legislative control as well, and pushed for it. Now, with a club in Reno and a
club at the Lake, he was becoming increasingly nervous about
the impotence of the Tax Commission in keeping Nevada
gambling clean. He had good reason.

The state had been wracked by scandal. A coonskin-capped
Senator from Tennessee had seen in those scandals an opportunity to get his name before a television-bemused public. In
1951, Estes Kefauver's Special Committee to Investigate Organized Crime in Interstate Commerce tied notorious gangster
Bugsy Siegel to eastern mob leaders, including Joe Adonis,
Meyer Lansky, Lucky Luciano, and Frank Costello. Worse
still, the Committee report identified the lieutenant governor
of the state as having an interest in two clubs. As if that
weren't enough, it put forth proof that a member of the Tax
Commission itself, William J. Moore, was part owner of the
Last Frontier casino in Las Vegas.

Bad stuff. But in the same year the Special Committee delivered its report, a Las Vegas gambler named Benny Binion, who
was under indictment in Texas on an alleged numbers game
scheme of enormous proportions, had an attempt made on his
life. This on top of an attempt on Lincoln Fitzgerald (the very
same Fitzgerald who had run the back room game in Toledo
that had so surprised Mayme Kandis Lucille) who took a shot-
gun blast in his stomach in Reno.

There was much political maneuvering, many horrified cries
(some of which came from the Las Vegas *Sun* in a series of
1954 exposés), some abortive attempts at reform clearly tainted
by the selfish interests of part of the gambling business, and—
finally—action.

First, the legislature created an agency called the Gaming
Control Board to serve as the investigative arm of the Tax

Commission. When that didn't work, it passed legislation authorizing a Gambling Commission and put the Gaming Control Board under its wing. That is the structure that has survived. By and large it is a good one. The Gaming Control Board is tough and independent. Its recommendations on licensing are almost always accepted by the Commission. Politics rarely interfere.

If all this sounds as though the new controls came about with only a little argle-bargle, it is a misimpression. There were legislative wars fought over the measures; there was division within the industry. Throughout it all, Bill Harrah stood on the side of tight and tighter controls. He was by now terrified of federal intervention; Estes Kefauver had exacerbated his fears. He was also committed to the idea that a gambling state should control its own house. To that end, he put all his weight behind the 1955 measure to create a Gaming Control Board and the 1959 successor establishing a Gambling Commission.

During the very era that General Motors' Engine Charlie Wilson was whinnying about what was good for GM was good for the nation, Harrah was telling his people in Carson City "Whatever is good for the state is good for Harrah's."

It wasn't Engine Charlie who made the statesmanlike call on that one.

9

Maxwells and Smarts

Reno, 1948–1972
Rochester, Minnesota

A great deal more than brass and sheet metal came into Bill Harrah's life when he bought the Maxwell from Johnny Vogel's mother. A passport to a new world, in the form of an application for membership in the Horseless Carriage Club, was hidden in the papers for the car. Not for long. Harrah unearthed it, joined the club, and discovered an old world waiting.

"They had a magazine and there were other collectors—oh! That was wonderful." There was a tour from Los Angeles to San Diego coming up, Harrah sent in his application, "showed up with the Maxwell and didn't know anybody. It was almost like the first day of school; I was kinda scared." With reason. Car clubs are elitist societies; exclusionary by definition, filled with purists and snobs.

Into this rarefied atmosphere chugged a Nevada gambler with his bogus car. What did Harrah know? All his life he had lusted after sensuous machinery. He had discovered the Maxwell and done to it what he had done to everything else he bought—improved its performance. With Jimmy Gullihur as his mechanic, "I hopped up the Maxwell as I hopped up about every car I owned." It was the equivalent of redefining the shape of a Rodin, sharpening the images of a Picasso, putting touch-up paint on a champlevé enamel; it was heresy.

"We [had] made a terrible mistake. An antique car should be restored authentically. A 1911 Maxwell should be restored as a 1911 Maxwell. [Gullihur and Harrah had made his car look like a 1907, and entered it as such in the tour.] But I was all on my own and I didn't recognize that at the time." So Harrah did the equivalent of showing up at Madison Square Garden for the Westminster Kennel Club show with a part Dalmatian, part Chihuahua.

Nor was that the end of it. He botched the driving. By the time he had the controls sorted, he had fallen far behind the rest of the tour. "The lunch stop was in Long Beach, and I got there just as they were all leaving." Salvation came at the second stop at Oceanside in the form of Bud Catlett, a policeman from Sacramento. "I'll never forget. He came up to me and he was so polite. 'Mr. Harrah, I'm Bud Catlett, how do you do?' And he looked at the Maxwell and instead of sayin', 'This is wrong, the radiator's wrong, the upholstery's wrong, the fender's wrong,' and not even talkin' about the hop-up part, he said, 'Gee that's a nice car.'"

Harrah could have encountered a thousand people who would have gone out of their way to humiliate him. Instead he found perhaps the one man who encouraged his interest. Admirers of the Harrah's Automobile Collection owe much to Bud Catlett's decency, restraint, and diplomacy that 1947 day at Oceanside.

Right then and there Catlett undertook the education of Bill Harrah, suggesting in the kindest way that a 1907 radiator was not in fashion for a 1911 car and telling him, "I *think* the early ones had semi-elliptic springs and yours has full elliptic." The result was to convince Harrah of two things: his was *not* a 1907 Maxwell and that Bud Catlett was a man to be brought within the Harrah embrace. "When I got home and I really researched the car, I found he was absolutely right and I was as wrong as could be.

"We became real close friends. [Catlett] and his wife would come [to Reno] and we'd go visit them. We'd go on trips together, we just became *very* close friends.

"Here he was a policeman in Sacramento and I was a casino operator in Reno; you just couldn't imagine two people [with] less in common." On the surface, perhaps, but both Catlett and Harrah shared a pursuit of perfection and a love of cars. The consequence was that Catlett became Harrah's automotive guru. He would go to work as a car buyer for Harrah when he retired from the police force.

Together they visited many of the western regional groups of the Horseless Carriage Club. Given Harrah's character, it is not surprising to find him dissatisfied with the way his new car associates were doing things and bound and determined to effect change.

"We had a president in the national Horseless Carriage Club that'd been in there for nine years or somethin'. He had a board of directors.

"Unfortunately [for him] he got *me* on the board and I discovered what was goin' on. He had some figureheads on the board and a lot of 'em weren't even car people . . ." That last is Harrah's most damning indictment. For the rest of his life, he would divide the world into two categories of people: car and non-car. The car people ("car guys") he would and could talk to almost as though he were a normal, relaxed, gregarious man. The rest were pariahs—unless they worked at Harrah's, in which case they got temporary citizen status in Bill Harrah's world.

By Harrah's lights, the Horseless Carriage Club was a mess. So he wrote letters to all the members and campaigned actively against the incumbent president—an extremely powerful, wealthy car man in Southern California who would later become embroiled in a struggle to see who would control road racing in the Los Angeles area. Harrah's profession did not help him in the campaign. "Some places where [the president] was very popular we'd go in and we'd be insulted—almost run out of the place because I was in the gambling business [and] they'd use that.

"We kept at it and [when] they had the election, we beat

him hands down. We just put in all our people and turned the club around.

"Since then it's been good."

Three years later, A. J. Liebling came out from *The New Yorker* to take a look at Nevada gambling and ended up talking about Bill Harrah and the Horseless Carriage Club.

"While I was in Reno, young Bill Harrah . . . acted as host, to a degree, to an organization known as the Horseless Carriage Club of Northern California. The members of this confraternity own automobiles built before 1915 and take them on road runs that restore to automobiling the aleatory charm it once had.

"Horseless Carriage Clubs have been established in many parts of the country, and their activities have increased the resale value of early cars until they cost, in some instances, more than new ones. The Horseless Carriage women build up wardrobes of the period to go along on the runs. This keeps them happy and at the same time makes it clear—to me, at least—that women's fashions were more becoming from 1900 to 1915 than they have been since . . .

"When the Horseless Carriage Club visited Reno, the Harrah equipage led the parade through the streets and the visitors were entertained with free drinks (but no free chips) at Harrah's before a dinner and dance at the old Hotel Golden. Next morning, there was a tremendous Nevada breakfast—liquor ad lib and large steaks surmounted by pairs of eggs . . . and the Honorable Tank Smith, the mayor of Reno . . . made a speech praising the vision and civic enterprise that, he said, had always distinguished the Harrahs."

The New Yorker's Footloose Correspondent had looked into a part of Bill Harrah's life that would become increasingly important. During his later years, Harrah traveled to Australia, Japan, Germany, England, and South Africa so that he could participate in old car tours. It was his joy; it was his métier and his milieu; it was *almost* as important to him as the hotels and casinos bearing his name.

The car fever had always been there. It simply lay inchoate until Harrah set eyes on Johnny Vogel's Maxwell. From that moment on there was no stopping him.

"You have two cars. Then four cars. All I can tell you [is] the cars came real fast. I was makin' money, so I could afford to buy a car here and there.

"I bought a Duesenberg, I bought this and that.

"I lived on South Virginia then and I remember I had a backyard [with] at one time eight or ten cars out there. [That] worried me and I had to move them.

"So I started renting vacant buildings around. And pretty soon there were twenty and then fifty. Eventually you take a look, and, well, what are you gonna do with one hundred cars?"

It wouldn't be long before he came up with an answer for *that* one.

II

It was, in fact, a car problem that brought young Bill Harrah to an appreciation of the worth of outside expertise; a first confrontation with a consultant, if that's how to classify a flamboyant Hollywood lawyer. Bill had so exasperated the juvenile authorities in and around Venice with his driving that they finally arrested him for having a faulty muffler and instead of sending him—once again—to juvenile hall, they scheduled an appearance before a Los Angeles municipal judge. John Harrah took alarm and called his friend Jerry Geisler, the best-known "bomber" of his age. The case was laughed out of court, but Harrah never forgot that when a problem appeared the solution was to be found in the best help money could buy.

It was a lesson reinforced by the architect who did the little bar in Southern California and the bar in the Virginia Street Club.

Two years after Harrah bought George's Gateway, he commissioned Stanford Research to study his audience, as we've seen. A year after that, he seems to have helped support an out-of-state visitor survey conducted by the Nevada Department of Highways and the University of Nevada College of Business Administration. At any rate, a copy of the work appears in the collection of consultant reports commissioned by

Harrah's. If it was not paid for—at least in part—by the club
or by Harrah personally, it is the only study in Harrah's files
that was not. One sentence in that 1958 study leaps out of the
page: "Presentation of statistical data was planned to provide
highway builders with information of a nature that could be
adapted for use in present and in long-range building programs . . ."

This was a critical matter to Harrah for the state and federal
governments were planning a route for the present I-80, the
highway that ties San Francisco to the George Washington
Bridge across the belly of America and on the way crests the
Donner Summit and slices past Reno. Would the path favor
the downtown area? Or would the recommended route take
perfectly good gamblers out of Harrah's reach?

Harrah being Harrah, he attacked on all fronts. He pressured
Nevada's representative Walter Baring and he buttressed his
arguments with studies from Economics Research Associates in
Los Angeles.

"Our position right from the start was we wanted the free-
way and we wanted it as close as feasible to downtown Reno.
Walter Baring—I think somebody paid him. It got to be a political football." However, the results were satisfactory. "I'm
happy where it is. It could've gone a lot of places, but I sure
didn't want it ten miles north or ten miles south. So I think
it's fine where it is." Now, though, Harrah had consultant
fever.

"We grew just as businesses that start with six employees
and get to thousands.

"But on the management end, we still tried to operate the
old way and we knew we were spinnin' our wheels." It could
very well have been Maurice Sheppard's Daily Report that trig-
gered the notion of rationalizing management; at any rate it
was becoming clear that *something* had to be done if Harrah's
were to be run in Harrah style. There was a problem with
that—Harrah didn't know how to do it. So he did what was
coming to be instinctive: "I think I read about the George
May Company in *Time*. They were called 'business engineers.'

"So we got in touch with them. They came in and they really turned us around. I mean—we were doin' so many things just like a bunch of little kids. It's just what evolved, just hit-and-miss.

"Our chain of command and our management chart—we were just terrible."

Whether it was the George May Company or another business consultant is unclear, but Harrah also discovered early on that he needed to deal with his experts as he did with his suppliers; keep a sharp eye on them and a sharper pencil at hand. In one of his few moments of displayed anger, Harrah described a consultant lesson he would never forget: "They were excellent except this was a real gyppo outfit in that they wouldn't get out; that was their policy.

"They'd come in and they'd say, 'Well, this survey's gonna take maybe six or eight weeks.' And it was so much a week—it was expensive—like $1,000 or $500 or maybe more. But then their six weeks went by and nothin' happened. [They'd say,] 'Oh, now we're into this. Gee, we gotta study this on the food department,' or the so-and-so department.

"And so bein' polite, and it's new—okay, fine.

"So I think they went along at least twenty weeks. There were plenty of things to find, no question about that. But they'd still be here if we hadn't kicked 'em out.

"Finally, I went, 'Goddammit! Get out of here, you guys! Give me a bill and get out!'

"They did us a lot of good, but they left a bad taste." The bad taste lasted for several years until Harrah's unceasing search for perfection struck again. "Then I read another article [about] some very good [consultants]. McKinsey in New York [was one]. I tried to get them. They were kinda snooty then [but] we've used them several times since."

Indeed he did. In the McKinsey file—that tiny part of it the company will allow outsiders to see—are studies on a considerable range of subjects: "Capital Investment Project Options," "Strategic Issue Analysis," "Implications of Alternative Retirement-oriented Programs," "Marketing Organization Proposal," "Planning/Operations Analysis," and "Harrah's Automobile Collection Relocation" are only a few examples.

Certainly by the time of the bus study, Harrah's was committed to the idea of bringing in consultants on most major decisions. It is Maurice Sheppard's view that these consultants served a dual purpose. The substance of their reports was important, of course. But they were also there to make recommendations reinforcing decisions that Bill Harrah had already made. In many cases this entailed acting as Cassandra, for surely if there was one part of his job that Harrah hated, it was being the bearer of bad tidings.

"We must have had four or five or six or eight [consultants]. We've learned [that] every two, three, four years [they] should come in and take a look.

"They're super, and that's why we are as efficient as we are. We get credit for being very efficient and our accounting system and all that, which, of course, is our doing. But the incentive came from these concerns, these business specialists."

At least one of these experts was hired to do something more than provide a new table of organization. By 1972, Harrah's had long since discovered the uses of private aircraft not only for the boss's convenience, but to bring in high rollers. The company had owned a Queen Air, replaced it with a King Air and then a Jet Commander. Now the jet was beginning to feel cramped. Bigger and better ones were coming on the market and (in the words of one senior Harrah executive), "It wasn't so much that they were newer, they were *faster*." If there was one thing Bill Harrah could not abide, it was going slower than he had to, even two miles an hour slower.

Ostensibly to devise a rational plan to update the corporate airplane but in fact to support Harrah's own insistence on owning and flying in the fastest private jet in the world, the company commissioned Marlett and Associates to do "The Economics of Upgrading Harrah's Jet Airplane."

Surprise. The study recommended a Lockheed Dash 8 Jet-Star and a Grumman Gulfstream II. While the report is fascinating in its exhaustive detail of who used the jet and when and how (leading user of the Jet Commander had been the Entertainment Department, 105.6 hours in a six-month period from April to September 1971 compared to Harrah's own 56.4 hours, but Harrah's average round-trip length was much longer than anyone else's; the anatomy of junketeering and the bringing in of qualified players is exposed to daylight in the report as well), the *real* facts of consequence appear in two tables toward the end of the report. The Dash 8's maximum speed was 570; the G2's, 590 mph. Marlett recommended the JetStar; Harrah bought the Gulfstream.

Thus consultants could serve a variety of purposes, including rationalizing Harrah's need to scream through the sky like a comet. But they also brought problems, and they brought them not only to Harrah's but to themselves.

Eric Duckstad remembers Bill Harrah and Maurice Sheppard coming down to Menlo Park, California, to talk to Stanford Research when he was a junior employee of the place. He recalls that the question involved the annoying debate over locating the Coliseum. Harrah wanted data to support his view; SRI was only too happy to give them to him. Except. Except at the time, SRI was not the independent think tank it is now. It was a part of Stanford University and Stanford University was in the middle of a fund drive. Somehow the word got out that SRI, a mere department of Stanford, was working for a— gasp!—gambler. Duckstad, now a parchment-colored, shy man who puts a visitor to mind of a carved wooden figure from some primitive culture, sits smiling in his office in what has come to be called the Strategic Environment Group of SRI, remembering what happened when the news hit. The howls, the protests, the hurling of principles could have been heard in Japan.

"He [Stanford's president] said he was sorry, but the alumni wouldn't stand for it. That was the end of that."

When *Harper's* did its piece on Harrah's in 1962, it noticed the same problem. "An employee of a motivation-research company once said, jokingly, that his firm would not draw the line at working for a house of prostitution. Outsiders have no way of knowing whether the Stanford Research Institute would go along with this view of its job, because it refuses to reveal who its clients are.

"The work for Harrah [the bus study] was 'cleared through SRI's top levels of management' according to SRI executives. However, an assistant to Dr. J. E. Wallace Sterling, president of Stanford University and chairman of the board of directors of SRI, wrote . . . 'This Board did not consider the project undertaken for Harrah's Club . . . SRI is engaged in doing contracted research for hundreds of organizations at any given time with an annual volume of $25 million in contracts. The research undertaken for Harrah's, I have learned, consisted of a simple data-gathering project in 1957 concerning . . . free bus service . . .'

"SRI hedged when asked whether they were still willing to gather data for Harrah." SRI may have hedged when it talked to *Harper's*. It was pretty clear about how it felt when Bill Harrah and Maurice Sheppard came around.

Harrah's enchantment with consultants never stopped. In 1972 a discovered aneurysm required him to undergo a heart operation at the Mayo Clinic. There is good reason to believe the Mayo surgeons told him then that another operation would be necessary, probably in five or six years, and that chances for success would not be good.

No sooner did Harrah return to Reno than he ordered what used to be called an efficiency expert to tell him how he could better use his time. At the end of a week following Harrah around and recording everything he did, the man told him he was sorry, he could offer Harrah no efficiencies he was not already practicing.

A second operation did indeed follow the first, and it came six years later. Harrah did not survive it. He spent the intervening years wisely and well; certainly reassured by the report of his personal time consultant that he was not squandering the years he had left.

10

Brother, Will
You Buy My Act?

Reno—Lake Tahoe—
Las Vegas, 1941–1978

Flash and glitter, boobs and bums; to the outside world they
are as much trademarks of Reno and Las Vegas as slot machines. In fact, big name entertainment came to the casino industry late and by way of a cow county hotelier named Newton Crumley, Jr.

Elko, Nevada, is as western as a worn Stetson. It's a four-
hour drive due east from Reno, which is highly satisfactory to
citizens of both communities. Flush toilets arrived in Elko
about the same time Omaha got some, but no one would con-
fuse the town with Louis XIV's Paris.

Newton Crumley's father had bought the Commercial Hotel
in Elko. About the time Harrah arrived in Reno, Crumley, Sr.,
began implementing plans to enlarge the hotel and put his son
at the helm. There was a large public room on the first floor
called the Commercial Lounge, and Newton, Jr., decided to
make it clear he was the boss by booking a "female dancer"
into the place. It was unheard of—at least in the memories of
Nevadans not old enough to have caroused in the dance halls
of Virginia City during Comstock Days—and it packed the
place.

An ebullient Crumley promptly booked Ted Lewis into his hotel. Lewis was a showman/big band leader of enormous stature in the entertainment industry; what on earth did Crumley think he was doing? Nevada's Bicentennial Book picks up the story:

"When this startling announcement hit the local papers it shocked the residents of Elko and Elko County . . . It was the general feeling that the brash young man would send the Commercial Hotel into bankruptcy.

"To say that Lewis brought down the house is almost understating. Although unverified by the management, it was rumored Lewis and the band spent more at the tables than the $12,000 tab—so much more, in fact, Lewis came back for a repeat at little or no expense to the Commercial.

"In any event 'young Newt' was joyful over his gamble and in ensuing months he booked [among others] Paul Whiteman, Jimmy Dorsey, Sophie Tucker, the Ritz Brothers, Chico Marx, Phil Harris, and Lawrence Welk . . ."

For once, someone had beaten Harrah to the innovation. Which is not to say that he wasn't casting an eye on the entertainment arena himself; at the very least he was something more than just aware of it. When Harrah opened the Blackout Bar in the back of Murray Jacob's clothing store and next to the Reno Club (during the time its Japanese proprietors were keeping their heads very much down), he brought in a pianist he had used in Venice, by name Jack McCarg, but known to everyone as Jackson. "He was very good. And there wasn't much entertainment in Reno at that time."

Virgil Smith would have quarreled with that. He remembers that Joe Zemansky of the Fortune Club had been using Liberace and the Will Masten Trio. He *also* remembers Bill Harrah being horrified at the salaries Zemansky was paying his entertainers—as much as $275 a week. "Bill would say, 'You're just throwin' your money down the sewer,'" a significant failure of farsightedness for the man who could see into the next century, and a nice irony considering Harrah's would be competing with hotel/casinos that were willing to write stratospheric checks not thirty years later. "But that's one of the reasons I think Bill Harrah was the most flexible man I ever knew," said Smith later. "He felt so strongly against them at the time and he changed from a guy who didn't believe in entertainment to becoming the biggest purchaser maybe in the country."

When Harrah opened the Virginia Street Club in 1946, he said, "We put a little stage bar in the corner there and it went quite well . . . The space we had was pretty classy and Wayne Newton worked [there]." That last one is a little odd, perhaps the consequence of failing memory of an aging man whose life had been filled with momentous events. Later he would say, "We had entertainment at the Lake which we didn't have in Reno." Considering the Lake didn't open until 1955, either Harrah was confused or his opinion of Wayne Newton (born in 1942!) was very low.

Sammy Davis, Jr., who was one third of the Will Masten Trio with his father and his uncle, is not much help. He remembers playing Reno before he ever worked Harrah's. He was at the Riverside during the Mert Wertheimer years—which would be the '50s—and he worked for Charlie Mapes at the Mapes Hotel. But he does not mention the Fortune Club or Joe Zemansky or the $275 a week.

In any case, it is clear that entertainment came to Harrah's when Harrah's went to the Lake. It came—in some measure—at the old Gateway. It came with a vengeance when Harrah moved across the street to go medium time—an entertaining story in itself.

The Stateline Country Club sat across from the Gateway. "It had more land than we had. At least from the outside [the building] looked pretty good." Besides the land, the Stateline Country Club had something irresistibly alluring to Bill Harrah: dreadful management. It was owned by the Sahati brothers, Eddie and Nick, and they were a pair to draw to. Eddie had once taken Harrah's for $40,000 during a hot streak in Reno. He damaged a few other clubs as well, running his winnings to a reported $100,000 before politely losing it all back.

Harrah described Sahati's brother, Nick, delicately. "[Nick] Sahati was the orneryest man I ever met in my life; an absolutely rude, crude, push, shove, spit, yell, scream—you name it—just absolutely no manners, morals, or anything, just an awful guy."

When Harrah discovered the Sahatis owned the property and had leased it to "some operators from the Bay Area [San Francisco] who weren't very good," he began to froth at the mouth. He turned killer when he found out that the lessees had an option to buy. The Stateline was two clubs over from its namesake; actually straddling the line was Bud Beecher's Nevada Club, and in between there was a little nook called the Main Entrance.

Harrah saw the campaign he was about to launch to buy the Stateline Country Club as missionary work. "The Stateline was a terrible place. And it changed hands all the time. It was just dirty." Bud Beecher, who ran the Nevada Club in July and August only, was "an honest guy." Not so the owner of the Main Entrance, which was "real crooked." Convinced then that he was about to bring purity of mind and spirit to even more Lake Tahoe gambling, Harrah set out to rid the Stateline Country Club and the Main Entrance of their evil reputations by buying them both. "They were bad for the area."

The Bay Area operators showed Harrah their lease, in which he discovered the option, a Golden Retriever having a glazed duck passed under its nose. "So we bought it. And, of course, Nick fought in all directions." To no avail. Harrah had taken over the balance of the lease, two years, and began to fix up the place. In the meantime, he was courting Bud Beecher. "Beecher, you think, is gonna be there forever 'cause they're makin' a lot of money, they're wealthy and all." Gambler's luck came to Bill Harrah on that one. "Bud, the son, was real sick . . . his father really ran it [the Nevada Club] and then, as old people do, he just came apart all of a sudden.

"So Bud called me up and he and I made the deal in two minutes. I said, 'What do you want?' And he said, 'I want two million dollars,' and just zing, zing, zing we got the place."

There was a little more trouble with the Main Entrance. It belonged to a Basque brickmason. "He was a real quiet guy and kinda bashful. He was a brickmason and he did wonderful work. We had him do—but how many chimneys can you

build?" As it turned out, it wasn't Harrah's deviousness that
brought the two together, it was the brickmason's. Apart from
his mortar money, the Basque was evidently picking up the
odd dollar as a tort-feasor. What's more, he had a specialty. He
had the uncanny good luck always to find a piece of glass in
whatever blue plate special he ordered in a restaurant. He had
the further good luck always to find himself crunching it in his
mouth. Harrah is kind. "He had a phobia that he would come
in the restaurant, and he would get a piece of glass; he'd bring
it in his pocket. And somehow, he had it worked out real good.
'Oh!' (he always ate at the lunch counter), and he'd pull the
glass from his mouth and his mouth's cut.

"So the first time we settled for $800 or somethin' and the
second time my guy said, 'Well, gee, he's just a phony. He's
done it across the street, he's done it in Carson City, he's done
it all over.'

"And I said, 'No, no, no. Pay 'im!'

"And he said, 'Whad'ya payin' him for?'

"I said, 'Never mind! Pay 'im!' "

In the meantime negotiations were going on in the most
civilized fashion imaginable. "My friend Bill," the brickmason
would say to Harrah, "some of your people think [I'm] phony.
That's not true." Eventually Harrah paid sufficient tribute and
the Basque agreed to sell. "He was a good guy otherwise," Harrah would say. "He was a good citizen. He didn't get drunk,
and when he did a job for you he did it."

That was about it for George's Gateway. Harrah worked
both sides of the street for a while, calling the old Gateway the
Lake Club, but it was only kept open during the summer and
eventually sold to Harvey Gross for $5,250,000 in cash.

"Then we built the South Shore Room, which opened in
December of '59. We did have our big room and we concentrated on our stars." Once again, Harrah is glossing over a few
problems he had on the way. Harvey Gross's five million came
somewhat later than was convenient, and before it arrived
there was a substantial money crunch.

The *Saturday Evening Post* was admiring if merciless on the
subject: "Soon [George's Gateway] was bursting at the seams
and had to be enlarged. It was still too small. Turning people

away was unthinkable, so Harrah, for $3 million this time, acquired two small clubs across the highway. They weren't big enough either, and he drew up plans for merging them and adding to them to form the world's biggest single structure devoted to gambling [this was 1959, remember, and the piece was written only six years later].

"It would have a theatre-restaurant, known as the South Shore Room, bigger than any then known (850 seats) with Vegas-type stars performing every night of the year.

"The late Eddie Questa [whom we last saw going surety for Harrah during the Russian battle of the bingo wars, who had been killed in the crash of a private plane whose other passenger—also killed—was Newton Crumley, Jr.] had bankrolled many gamblers in his day. He tried to dissuade Harrah from the project, but an hour's conversation converted him and he pledged his bank's credit to the maximum. When construction delays and mounting costs pushed the price up—Harrah was spending half a million a month, and nothing coming in—Questa went outside the bank to get more."

The South Shore Room opened to a disaster. At least so it seemed in the short run. The Winter Olympics had come to town. This did not exactly surprise Harrah—his public relations man, Mark Curtis, had touted the worth of the coincidence for almost a year. In fact, Curtis had been flying travel writers and sports writers and entertainment writers to the yet unfinished South Shore Room for months. He had gone further.

"We took them all on a tour of the Olympic Village. We did a preview film on the Olympics, which we syndicated. We had all our employees write in for season tickets and by the luck of the draw we got about two hundred of them.

"For the eleven days of the Olympics we put those tickets in the hands of two hundred key people a day.

"We rented a house in [Squaw] Valley just a hundred yards from the entrance gate. We did everything imaginable to tie in with the Olympics because we figured it was a really made-in-heaven opportunity to capitalize on [our new place] as well as to show everybody where Tahoe was—Reno for that matter."

There was just one problem with all this. After a day

watching mini and giant slaloms, hockey and biathlon, speed skaters in aerodynamic second skins, nobody had the energy to wander to the other side of the Lake to the new South Shore Room. Business *looked* good because the house was papered. But revenue there was not.

Still, the media blitz did everything Curtis had hoped. It put Harrah's at the Lake on the map. And when the Olympics went away, the players began to arrive.

"Bill Harrah never lost heart," said the *Saturday Evening Post*, "and by April everyone was coming to agree that Harrah was right after all. From that day to this the flow has been golden."

That it has. It has also been black, which was even more astonishing considering the times and considering Harrah's prejudice. Holmes Hendricksen, these days the Entertainment Commodore for Harrah's, was working at the Lake fresh out of school. "I remember when Louis Armstrong worked here [Harrah's Lake Tahoe] he could not [walk around] in the casino." Despite discouragement by the scrubbed children working Harrah's bus embarkation points in Northern California, blacks were beginning to make the trip to the Lake in increasing numbers. It was a shocker to most other operators in the state that Harrah would not only eventually allow blacks to wander freely in the casino but was actually paying to get them there. Very likely it was a cold business decision, but the letting down of the color barrier could also have come because of Harrah's increasing friendship with Sammy Davis, Jr. Davis does not think that Harrah was a bigot in the sense we use the word now: "He was opinionated and he bought his ticket and he picked his seat. I think that was part of the old school.

"But to his credit, he changed this whole goddamn Lake. To his credit he changed Reno. You go into [casinos in Reno and Tahoe] now and you see black pit bosses, you see black dealers." A remarkable achievement to attribute to Harrah from a man who had seen a lily white Reno and Tahoe and who should know.

At the time, though, Harrah was certainly more concerned with seeing to the success of his new club at the Lake than he was for taking credit for a great social change. He was trying to twist and turn entertainment to fit the Harrah mold and he was having trouble finding the man to get it done. "We felt an entertainment director had to be an ex-show business personality, which wasn't true." It would take him eleven years to find just the right man. When he did, it turned out to be a kid who went to work in the cashier's cage at the old Gateway in '57, Holmes Hendricksen.

Hendricksen—who hates his first name enough to welcome being called "Homer" instead—is a Tim Conway replica in an extra large with the demeanor of a hanging judge on vacation. He grew up near Twin Falls, Idaho (during the same era as a soon-to-be Twin Falls High enchantress named Verna Harrison, who would become the last Mrs. Bill Harrah), was a frustrated jock at the University of Utah, and allowed himself to be persuaded by a fraternity brother to spend a summer working for Harrah's at the Lake. The summer would turn into a lifetime. He was variously bus boy, cashier, assistant credit manager, credit manager, and "a kind of relief shift manager. During several years, I had every job in the place," including, by 1967, general manager of Harrah's Tahoe.

Hendricksen, whose brother Lowell would join him at Harrah's and become vice-president in charge of the Collection, was like a pig in the sunshine as general manager. Harrah was known as a marvelous delegator (which carried with it the benefit of being able to put enormous responsibility on others). One of the results of the Harrah policy of giving to others what he didn't want to be bothered with himself was autonomy for middle- and high-level managers. Of all such jobs, the one carrying the most freedom was that of GM at the Lake, more so than GM in Reno only because the Lake is a long climb from town.

"In 1971 they said my new job was vice-president of entertainment," says a moderately expansive Hendricksen today. "I didn't like it all." How could he not? All those glamorous people, all that attention, all that *importance*. For openers, he didn't know anything at all about entertainment. Then, "I knew how difficult it was going to be to deal with people in the entertainment business." What's more, the new job required a move to Reno, and Hendricksen, who had been living at the Lake for fifteen years and loved it, wanted no part of the Big City. Hendricksen also considered being anointed ambassador to Oz a slap in the face. "We had just gotten approval to build our hotel. We had worked awful hard to stay competitive with the Sahara and Harvey's [Gross had built his hotel, the very one in which an enormous bomb would explode —on national television—in 1980] up there without a hotel, which is pretty difficult particularly if the customer is a high roller.

"Finally we were going to get a hotel and I really thought I deserved to be up there. I thought, at the time, [I was getting] a demotion."

Hendricksen is not giving himself credit when he says he didn't know anything about entertainment when he was elevated. The general managers of both Reno and Tahoe sat on the entertainment committee at Harrah's and each had an absolute veto over who was going to play his club. The veto and the committee were all part of the New Harrah's, the systematized Harrah's. In his vice-presidency, Hendricksen would carry the systems to a point of exquisite refinement, so today when Harrah's buys an act, it is confident the performer will adhere to Harrah's standards—which are still rigid—and he will pack the room.

II

As confident as homework will permit, at any rate. If there is a department within Harrah's today that can be looked on as bearing the full Bill Harrah imprint, it is entertainment. It had better be. Entertainment became a Harrah specialty. From scoffer he became a fan. In his treatment of personalities, he displayed an increasingly lighthearted, relaxed side of the Harrah character.

"[The] important thing is to hire stars that bring in the customers and to keep [those] stars happy so they come back," said Harrah. Hendricksen hires using the miracle of homework and a buying budget of $19 million a year. He brings them back by treating each star as though he were the reincarnation of Bill Harrah himself.

When Hendricksen's department (Holmes plus a vice-president of entertainment under whom is an entertainment manager at each club, a cabaret manager in each club, the full complement of back lot professionals *plus* an "executive assistant" who coordinates a surprisingly large staff of domestics to wait hand and foot on the heavies) scouts an act, they embark on their own endless sequence of one-night stands.

It all starts with the Harrah criteria. Number one: Will the act do business for the club and will it draw the kind of customer the company wants wandering, bankroll in hand, from table to table in the casino? Two: Will Harrah's standards be met? Is the material suitable? "Does the act do—have—a particular situation that we can't control or isn't acceptable?" By that Hendricksen no longer means "Does the act bare its nipples or use horrifying language?" which is what it used to mean during the banker's suit days. That changed one day in 1972 when Bill Harrah himself asked—in an entertainment committee meeting—how come his club never had any topless revues. The wave of shock was so palpable they almost had to call the paramedics to revive Harrah's senior management. Nowadays, the standards are much relaxed except in one area, promptness. If there's trouble with an act's meeting its schedule it might as well look to the Iowa State Fair; it will never play Harrah's.

Then there's money. A $19 million budget sounds comfortable. How much can a guy in a clown suit or wearing twelve sets of bracelets cost? A lot. There are hotel/casinos paying $400,000 a week in Las Vegas. That is substantially beyond Harrah's willingness to go. Hendricksen makes it all sound very real when he says, "The list of big names who will work a nightclub and whom we can afford is [very] small. You end up with about twenty names.

"Now, when you consider availability, the list of twenty becomes three. So many of our bookings are determined by what's available, not by what we want. Not our first choice or our second choice or our third choice."

But even if it's a fifth choice, Harrah's has its scouting reports since Hendricksen and his vice-presidential deputy have been out to look. Not once but many times. "We have a policy that we don't buy an act unless we see it work in a situation as similar to our setup as possible. That's the rule. Period. No exceptions." It is a rule straight from the Book of Harrah. Sometimes they see the act work five times, sometimes more.

The act is booked; another comic, another guitar plucker. Once they're in, you sit back and watch the "golden flow of money," no?

Absolutely not. "Bill's philosophy was very simple. These people are stars and they should be treated like stars." Star sniffing? Only if you forget the second part of the Harrah entertainment mandate: "to keep [those] stars happy so they come back."

Hendricksen, who took his mandates from the sole proprietor, would have us all believe Harrah's doesn't do anything out of the ordinary for its performers. Judge for yourself.

First off, it is the only hotel/casino that routinely sends its company airplane to pick up (and return) its headliners. But that is and was the *second* step in the Harrah Coddle. First, the entertainment department has done a little more research. Harrah always insisted that, if the star were playing Harrah's for the first time, Hendricksen's people "make an effort to find out what they like and don't like." This is a throwaway line, since "what they like and don't like" becomes more important to Harrah's when the stars arrive than to the stars; at least that's the way it seems.

There is domestic attention. Each headliner has his choice of staying in a "star" suite or in one of two houses Harrah's maintains for their comfort. The star suites are not available to hotel customers—period. Not at any price. Which is not to say that the hotels couldn't charge a decent dollar by moonlighting the occasional overnight to a Genentec Insider. The suite at Tahoe is no larger than any decent $3 million duplex on Fifth Avenue, nor more lavish. Its living room/library/bar is at the end of a corridor sealed off from the elevators by an ornate steel gate and by a security guard. Upstairs are bedrooms and a dining room occupying perhaps half the space of the downstairs, so that the living room is a two-story affair. If a star chooses to dine *en famille* in his suite, he can also indicate a choice of current movies, which are shown on a screen that descends silently from the ceiling. The view all around is of the Lake, and short of the scene outside the window of a space laboratory, there is none more spectacular.

"Mrs. [Adeline] Murphy, the executive assistant, knows every one of these stars. She has been with us for years. She knows what they like. If one likes a particular kind of cheese to snack on and he walks in the door, this cheese is waiting for him. If he drinks a certain kind of wine, that's there. If he's always fighting weight or loves fried chicken, she knows that too." Homework again, and done by the woman who had to deal with Harrah's own eccentricities for years. In addition— and once more in accordance with the Book of Harrah— Hendricksen's scouts have asked secretaries, personal managers, friends and have consulted their files. The department keeps records on habits. For example, if an entertainer sleeps until 2 P.M., the domestic staff adjusts its schedule to oblige. "We know which ones will have a house full of people. We know which ones won't have anybody around," and Adeline Murphy's shock troops are prepared in either instance.

A Harrah headliner also has a car provided, a choice of a Rolls-Royce or a Mercedes or a Jeep (it still snows a lot at Tahoe). Sometimes, as when comic/singer/race driver Dick Smothers played Harrah's, even a Ferrari—although he was politely asked to pay his own speeding tickets.

Hendricksen thinks it was pure self-indulgence, but two years before he died, Harrah had his FAA-certified aircraft/ boat and automobile fabrication department build a four-wheel-drive limousine—the only one in the world—because he would never have dreamed of having a star chauffeured in a mere sedan. Also, because it gets icy at 6,200 feet, he would not trust their safety to a standard limo, which he correctly understood to be a vehicle that tends to trip all over itself in bad weather.

Like other casinos with entertainers to please, Harrah's often sends its stars presents. Unlike other casinos, and in consequence of Bill Harrah's own huge regard for his performers, the company doesn't simply grab up a handful of star sapphires and ship them off Federal Express. "I think when we give a gift we do our homework a little better [than the competition]." Accurate only if you consider checking with: secretaries, hairdressers, friends, friends of friends and, for all anyone knows, astrologers, "doing homework a little better." And then only better if you also think it conscientious to decide on, say, fine art and further try to discover whether the piece should be of a particular period or whether it might fit in a specific room in the star's house.

"We've given pieces of western art."

"Originals?"

"We have given a Remington."

Might the department someday consider a Picasso appropriate?

"We never have but we would."

And cars. "Not as many as everybody thinks but we have given several," including Rollers, Mercedes, Jeeps, and Ferraris. (Sometimes it worked the other way round. Bill Cosby bought Harrah a Mercedes Grosser limousine for Christmas. He lured Harrah's secretary into a plot to deliver it with a card under one windshield wiper reading: "What do you give a guy who has 1,400 cars? Another car of course.")

When Harrah was alive the Entertainment Department, at his insistence, would call a performer playing the Club to ask if it would be convenient for the boss to drop by that night to catch the show. Harrah was aware everyone had off nights. He didn't want to embarrass an entertainer, nor did he want to see a show before the performer himself felt all the bugs were worked out. Another star perquisite at Harrah's, then, and it remains: consideration.

Sammy Davis, Jr., says it nicely—it's obvious he's said it many times before—"It used to be the old saying that when you leave New York, you're camping out. Any place you play when you leave Harrah's is roughing it."

III

Davis used to call Bill Harrah "Lamont Cranston—he had the power to cloud men's minds." In the early days, Davis was as impressed by Harrah's distance and the mystery about the man as he was by the way he was treated. Soon enough, the

two became unlikely friends. Davis is an enormously bright
man. Hendricksen says of Harrah: "To say that Bill was very
bright would be a misstatement; Bill was brilliant. [He] was
alert and smart enough to know that times change and things
change and that people's likes and dislikes change." That is as
good an explanation for the Davis/Harrah mutual regard as
there is. It seemed to be an appreciation of each other's understanding of the business. It was Davis' pleasure at seeing Harrah fight his own prejudice and open his hotels and clubs to
blacks. It was understanding at an emotional level, which is
one of the first sights we get of Harrah's sentimentalism. He
considered Davis "family." But here we have to be cautious.
"Nobody ever got too close to Bill because those who did got
hurt," said one of Harrah's presidents. True. The Davis/Har-
rah friendship was of a different order; the notion of "family"
which they held was clearly apart from normal context. Being
"family" was being loyal and reciprocating that loyalty, which
both of them certainly did. Being family also meant bringing
in business on one side and paying well on the other, neither
one of which was much mentioned by one to the other.
"There was a rule made by Bill that no one would ever work
here and get more money than I would get," says Davis today.
"The appendage to that statement is I never asked for a raise
at Harrah's. They just came and gave them to me. Every raise
I got, to $25,000, $30,000, $50,000 came from Bill."

Another big component of the friendship between Davis and
Harrah was their shared agony with women; still another, their
constant striving to stay current, to remain flexible in tastes.
Much of this was certainly based on the fact that they viewed
each other as equals. We do not see Harrah in any other cir-
cumstance offering warmth to anyone. "There was no ass-kiss-
ing, you know that subservient jazz just [because anyone] was
a star," says Davis. Almost in the same breath, he wants it
known he considered his treatment at Harrah's to be beyond
comparison. "Harrah's spend[s] more money in the advertising
media than anyone else for a performer." And, "If a person
was going through a phase [by which Davis meant acting
strangely or slipping *slightly* in popularity] he would hang in
with him, to protect him, to protect her." Further, there was

the extraordinary length to which Harrah had gone to give top-level professionals top-level professional support: "There isn't anything in any Broadway show that we haven't got in that showroom [the South Shore Room at the Lake]. Bill Harrah constructed a room you could house Jumbo in. You could do *My Fair Lady* [there] and he was still dealing with the individual performer where the only thing he would have needed was two curtains, a little scrim, and a bandstand."

That the friendship continued was the direct result of the change—and the extraordinary ability to change—in both men. Davis on Harrah: "He never stopped growing." Harrah on Davis was equally complimentary (although in his words he felt like a "tongue-tied oaf" around him). He admired him for his professionalism, his perseverance, and his arduous and successful attempts at self-education. Best of all, he was a "car guy."

In another sense the friendship—if not its intensity—was predictable. Hendricksen would say over and over that Harrah was a fan, that he "really, truly admired entertainers. He really did."

But not all of them. Marlene Dietrich behaved disagreeably according to Harrah's lights and he didn't forget it. "She called everybody all over the world. Her telephone bill was unbelievable. The second time [she played Harrah's] we told her that was all over. She paid no attention and still called all over the world. Our operators didn't have nerve enough, which you can't blame them, not to put a call through." The Blue Angel ended up stiffing Harrah's for $900 in phone bills.

Nor was he enchanted by Ethel Merman's standard of conduct. She had been booked into the Lake and done "terrible business, fifty people or somethin'." Harrah's minions tried to accommodate Merman and her entourage but only on the basis of lowering her fee. No dice.

"Can we cut the money down?" they proposed. Not a chance.

"Can't we call it off?" they asked. Positively not.

Harrah said the Merman-bloc position "irritated" him. It must have done more than that because he ordered the contract bought up and the show closed right then and there— "the only show we ever closed."

By and large Hendricksen was right; Harrah *was* a fan, although to Holmes's anguish he was particularly a fan of his own entertainment standards and woe be to the act that challenged them. Hendricksen had some firsthand knowledge of what happened then.

One winter, he booked the Rockettes into the Lake. Since the stage in the South Shore Room was considerably smaller than that at Radio City, Hendricksen decided he wouldn't need *all* the Rockettes, just thirty of them. His prudence was induced by a budget squeeze and so he went a step further. After consulting with the president of Harrah's, by then Maurice Sheppard, he decided he could risk putting a little faith in commercial air service. Usually the Rockettes had a couple of standbys in case of holocaust or flu; Hendricksen decided any one of several common carriers could probably move a frail dancer from Kennedy to Reno in case of emergency. He told the Rockettes management to hold three girls in New York and airmail the thirty on out.

Naturally, not one but two Rockettes came down with some dread disease on opening night. Even more naturally, Bill Harrah decided to make an unannounced visit for the first show. And even more naturally than *that*, no sooner had he sat down than he began, from right to left, to count the number of Rockettes high-stepping in the South Shore Room.

There were twenty-eight. Kennedy was snowed in, not a plane could get in, not a plane could get out—which meant Hendricksen's emergency plan was worthless.

Now if there was one excuse Bill Harrah would not tolerate, it was failure of service because of what it might cost. He had already begun to enunciate in public his credo that return on investment was an accountant's vision and had nothing to do with the hotel business. According to the index Harrah used, quality of service came first, cost came eleventh. So when Harrah summoned Holmes Hendricksen, "the finest entertainment man in the business," to solve the mystery of the two missing Rockettes, Hendricksen had absolutely nowhere to go. He stood in front of Harrah—reddening in embarrassment.

Hendricksen said Harrah wouldn't speak to him for two weeks after. When he complained to his fiancée, Christine

Hinesman, who was a flight attendant on the Harrah Gulf-stream, he didn't get much solace. "Who are the Rockettes?" she asked.

On balance, Harrah *did* like his entertainers. He was fond and admiring of Bill Cosby; he thought very highly of Lawrence Welk as a man and a performer. He was aware of Frank Sinatra's faults—among them a hot temper and the frequent moment of ill-considered judgment (of which more later)—but he thought Sinatra "a super nice fella [who wants] everything exactly so." Far from being a criticism, that was a virtue on the Harrah scale. There might have been another reason for his regard: "We pay him much less than he's offered elsewhere," Harrah would say, "and he's happy with us because we do things the way he wants them done." Holmes Hendricksen has yet another explanation for the closeness of the Harrah-Sinatra connection. "They were very much alike. Bill was a fanatic on details, Frank's the same way. Frank's a fanatic on cleanliness. Bill was the same way. Probably the two most prompt people I have ever met in my life are Bill Harrah and Frank Sinatra." Likes did not repel with Sinatra and Harrah.

Harrah was not on such secure ground with Don Rickles. "Don *is* really a likable fella when he's not on stage, although he's *on* stage all the time. But he's very funny." This last was secondhand information. Verna Harrah remembers one night in the Headliner Room at Reno when her husband watched Rickles totally perplexed, and then spent the rest of the show watching the audience react—which it did with laughter and obvious pleasure. Bill Harrah could not understand the humor. He could and did understand the appeal since he saw it for himself. It was just not his kind of stuff.

There was a problem of a different sort, Verna recalls, with Willie Nelson. First off, the show started half an hour late. Normally that would have put paid to Nelson on the spot. Two seconds early or two seconds late, Verna would say, and Bill Harrah would go nova. When the show *did* start, Holmes Hendricksen got instant elevator stomach. First off, Willie Nelson's mother leaped on stage, cracked a bottle of beer, and sat down to quench her thirst. Then the audience began to vault onto the tables for a singalong. At the show's end, Bill asked his wife what she thought and Verna replied that it was "her kind of music." At that very moment, Hendricksen came charging up filled with apologies and a promise that Willie Nelson, his mother and her empty bottle of beer would be out of sight forever before Harrah could take another breath. "But we thought he was wonderful," Harrah said. A stunned Hendricksen retreated in disorder, to book Willie Nelson again at the first opportunity.

Hendricksen thinks the great days are soon to be over. "The nightclub business is dying." Hell, he says, it's already dead everywhere but Nevada. Even Atlantic City is having dismal success with big-name entertainment. The acts are pricing themselves out of the business, having already made themselves uneconomic for the hundreds of clubs that used to dot fashionable urbs across the nation. Revues are taking the place of names. It's all a matter of money.

There will always be room for Sammy Davis, Jr., at Harrah's. But it may be in among the T and A.

IV

Frank Sinatra and Bill Harrah may have been alike in many ways. In the face of authority they were different men. After Kefauver, Washington had, as always, chased the national spotlight only now and then tagging gambling along the way.

But when Robert Kennedy became attorney general in his brother's administration, the glare was once more on Nevada. Harrah reacted typically; he was a brooding eagle with stiff lips. Sinatra's style was opposite. He attacked.

The Sinatra episode revolved around Nevada's Black Book. "Who first proposed the Black Book is unclear," says Jerome Skolnick. "In 1960, a loose-leaf binder was compiled by the Gaming Control Board with the names and pictures of eleven men the board thought to be of 'notorious or unsavory reputation.'

"The thrust of the book was simple: Nevada gambling casino operators were to keep certain underworld figures off their premises or else face revocation of their gambling license."

A thousand Black Books wouldn't have satisfied Bobby Kennedy. He was convinced that Nevada, and Las Vegas in particular, was the bank for organized crime in the United States. In consequence, he sent in wave after wave of commandos beginning with the FBI but eventually, with the cooperation of the Chief Executive, to include what seemed to be every regulatory agency in the District of Columbia except the Coast Guard.

In the meanwhile, Frank Sinatra, encapsulated for corporate purposes in a cocoon known as Park Lake Enterprises, had taken a position in the Sands Hotel in Las Vegas and a much larger one in the Cal Neva Lodge, across the Lake from Harrah at Tahoe.

There with (according to the State Gaming Control Board) or without (according to Sinatra) his knowledge, the hotel accommodated Sam Giancana, a certified member of Nevada's most exclusive club: the Black Book Society.

Ed Olsen, the Control Board's chairman, took exception. He sent a team to investigate only to have one member come back reporting that a Cal Neva executive had denied all while at the same time carefully tucking a $100 bill in the crook of the investigator's elbow. At the same time, there was evidence enough that Giancana had indeed been at the Lodge, so Olsen was prompted to begin initial steps to revoke Sinatra's license. It was the incident of the $100 bill that infuriated him, however, and he phoned Sinatra's lawyer demanding a dual explanation. The return call came from Sinatra himself, although not until Olsen made it pretty clear that no one else would be able to handle Sinatra's troubles on this one but Sinatra himself.

Olsen was an ex-Associated Press reporter. He did not record the conversation but he put two deputies on extension phones and the moment he hung up, he wrote a memorandum while the words were fresh in his memory.

OBSCENE   OBSCENE

CONFIDENTIAL   CONFIDENTIAL

said the memo on its top. (Olsen was later to muse: "It is interesting to note how only nine years ago language which today is commonplace on protest signs, in magazines, et cetera, was sealed in large envelopes and labeled 'obscene' to protect the pristine eyes of young women file clerks.") *

The memorandum was dated September 4, 1963, entitled "Memo Gaming Control Board: Re: Frank Sinatra, Sam Giancana," and its prologue reads, "The following . . . conversation[s] which occurred on August 29, 30 and 31 and September 1 and 2, 1963, are recounted here to the best of my memory and knowledge." There is an account of a snakes and ladders chase through Sinatra's recent Nevada activities with the Gaming Control people panting behind, but the moments of interest to us are those in that final phone conversation with Sinatra in which Olsen faced him with the Giancana presence at the Lodge and with the matter of the $100 bill.

". . . about 4 P.M., my telephone rang again. It was Mr. Sinatra" reads the memorandum. "To describe him as 'irritated' was a masterful understatement. He was infuriated.

"He asked why I couldn't come up to Cal Neva to see him. [To this Olsen replied as he had done before to Sinatra's accountant, that he felt it "would be inappropriate under the circumstances" and that it would "be better for such a meeting to be held in my office in the presence of others, including my secretary, who would make a record of the conversation."]

"I gave [Sinatra] the same reasons as I had given [his accountant]. To which he replied, 'You're acting like a fucking cop . . . I just want to talk to you off the record.'

"I asked him why he couldn't just as easily come to my office. He indicated he didn't wish to encounter reporters. As I started to assure him such would not be the case, he said in essence: 'Listen, Ed, I haven't had to take this kind of shit from anybody in the country and I'm not going to take it from you people.'" There followed acrimonious mutual accusations, ending with this:

" 'I'm never coming to see you again,' said Sinatra. I told him if I wanted to see him I would send a subpoena.

" 'You just try and find me,' he said. 'And if you do, you can look for a big, fat surprise . . . a big, fat, fucking surprise. You remember that. Now listen to me, Ed . . . Don't fuck with me. Don't fuck with me. Just don't fuck with me.' " Olsen, ever the understating reporter, opined, "The tone of his voice was menacing and I asked, 'Are you threatening me?'

"He replied, 'No . . . just don't fuck with me and you can tell that to your fucking board and that fucking commission, too' . . .

"I suggested it might be better for all concerned if he concentrated on his enterprises elsewhere and departed the Nevada gambling scene. He replied, 'I might just do that . . . and when I do, I'm going to tell the world what a bunch of fucking idiots run things in this state.'

"At this point he renewed his invitation to me and my friends to come up for dinner . . ."

In the event the Gaming Control Board filed a formal complaint. Its filing certainly discommoded Sinatra, but it was an unpleasant surprise to Nevada governor Grant Sawyer as well. "When I told Sawyer that I was going to file . . . for the revocation of Sinatra's license, well, the man just dropped his teeth!"

The complaint alleged Park Lake Enterprises had broken the laws and regulations covering gambling in Nevada. It detailed the times between July 17 and July 28, 1963, that Giancana "sojourned to Chalet No. 50 at Cal Neva Lodge with the knowledge and consent of the licensee, Park Lake Enterprises, its officers, directors, agents, representatives, and employees." It put forth four other counts, including one about the phone conversation, saying that "Frank Sinatra maligned and vilified the State Gaming Control Board, the Nevada Gaming Commission, and members of both said Board and Commission by the use of foul and repulsive language which was venomous in the extreme."

Sinatra was repulsed in bloody defeat from his charge on Carson City. On October 7, 1963, a spokesman issued a statement on his behalf saying he had "decided . . . that it would be in my best interest to devote most, if not all of my time to the entertainment industry . . ." and that as part of that plan "I intend[ed] to divest myself completely from any involvement with the gaming industry in Nevada . . ."

Said Olsen, "The Cal Neva was closed, of course, shortly

after the complaint was filed. It would have closed anyway because it was a seasonal operation and it was right at the end of the season. We subsequently, as I recall, reached an agreement with Mr. Sinatra, giving him sixty or ninety days to sell the stock of his Las Vegas hotel, which he did on schedule. And that closed the formal aspects of the Sinatra matter."

But not an extraordinary informal one. "There was one other significant episode in the Sinatra matter," Olsen would say. It had taken place in a motorcade for President John F. Kennedy in Las Vegas prior to the Great Memorandum Incident in conversation with Governor Grant Sawyer. "During the course of that ride, Mr. Kennedy did say to Governor Sawyer, 'Aren't you people being a little hard on Frank out here?'"

That absolutely shocked the shorts off Olsen.

"Now, that's about the highest degree of political pressure that you could ever put into the thing! Sawyer merely replied that it was out of his hands . . ."

Harrah never did make an attempt to excuse his friend. "He was dead wrong on that thing at Cal Neva. That was wrong; the rules were clearly spelled out. And there's certain kinds of people he couldn't have around, and he had 'em around. He was wrong."

It wasn't the extirpation of the evil Sinatra influence that marked a turn toward respectability for Nevada in the public eye; rather it was the appearance of a legend of a different stripe. "Late in 1966, a private train secretively brought one of America's wealthiest men to Las Vegas," wrote Skolnick. "The arrival of Howard Hughes, who was to buy within the year three of the hotels reputedly controlled by organized crime, was a watershed for Nevada." (As well, it marked the passing of a Reno watershed when Hughes bought Harolds Club.) It was also a demotion for Harrah, who, with Hughes's arrival became suddenly the *second* largest gambler in the state.

Those two great gambling sumos never really got a grip on one another. Although Harrah promised (with a characteristic dry chuckle) to "reveal everything about my clandestine relationship with Howard Hughes," his death prevented it.

We do know they stared at each other from opposite ends of

the state, at one moment with flaring nostrils and pawing the ground, at the next with bouquets in their hands, prepared to come courting.

Harrah alluded to their circling one another. He says that Hughes longtime deputy Robert Maheu called him during the time "Hughes was buyin' everything," wanting to see him. Harrah agreed to meet with Maheu in private.

"We talked, and they were interested in buying." Maheu (whom Harrah thought "a very sharp guy") asked, "Do you wanna sell?" Harrah played coy, "No, but anything's for sale.

"If you want to pay me double what it's worth, I'll consider it, but [there] are no bargains around here."

That was more or less the end of that, but for a postscript by Scherry. According to her, Harrah and Maheu played spy and counterspy with one another. Maheu liked early morning appointments, say, 2 A.M.; and Harrah would oblige, setting the meetings for his house in the Washoe Valley. There were evidently a number of these encounters, most if not all of them at some Bela Lugosi hour of the night. Certainly all of these goings-on diverted—if not infuriated—Scherry, but she took it as a mother might react to the sight of an eight-year-old son coming home from a mud lunch. "Bill never had any intentions of sellin' the place. He just liked the intrigue."

11

The Louvre–
Internal
Combustion Style

Sparks, Nevada, 1961–1978

Bill Harrah's writer friend Ken Purdy sat down one day and put a polish on the Harrah automotive philosophy: "Few material things have been as important to America as the automobile. The manufacture of the automobile was the root of our industrial growth . . . We are all tied to the automobile by history, business, by emotion. The automobile deserves to be preserved and remembered."

Fourteen *hundred* of them? By one man? To a value of almost $40 million? Bill Harrah would have been puzzled by the questions. Despite his grand statement about the role of the car in the industrial growth of the nation, all he was really doing—at least at first—was scratching an itch. "First it started out he had one car, then two, then he had a dozen, then he had fifty, then one hundred. And then the goal was five hundred.

"When we got to 500 . . . with over 4,000 [different kinds] made, there really weren't that many. So then 500 became 750.

After you got to 750, that wasn't enough either. So we go to 1,000. Then 1,100, 1,200. Then 1,500. The goal was 1,500 without a doubt."

Dandy Don Meredith is speaking. Well, not the *real* Meredith, a Dandy Don replica, Huck Finn smile and all, by the name of Clyde Wade—correct that—Emris Clyde Wade, general manager of Harrah's Automobile Collection and keeper of the flame.

The Collection's three great buildings, large enough to house a mothballed Pacific Fleet, sit like an abandoned boot camp in the midst of an industrial slum in the railroad town of Sparks, Nevada.

The physical plant is not prepossessing. Thirty years ago the place was an icehouse belonging to John Dermody, who agreed to lease it on a year-to-year basis to Harrah as storage for all those cars. Today it is three huge, ugly showrooms—still leased year-to-year—plus a fourth building (the original icehouse) housing: administrative offices, the Pony Express Museum, four rows of slots, and a long, western bar. There is a frontier sense of security about the place. It is a compound surrounded by chain-link fence. The three warehouses and the administration building form three boundaries of the Collection. On its western edge is the FAA-certified airframe shop. The HAC is flanked on its northern border by the Southern Pacific right of way. Its southern line is Glendale Boulevard, a paved path through the municipal junkyard of industrial Sparks. The landmark indicating the entrance to Harrah's monument to America is a Chinese restaurant.

Emris Clyde has been coming here from Reno, a fifteen-minute drive reminiscent of the trips from San Francisco to Brisbane or Beverly Hills to Torrance or Manhattan to Long Island City, for two decades. Emris Clyde has time in grade. He fought the grand battles of empire at his commander's side. Today he defends Festung Harrah against the assaults of the bottom-line philistines.

From the first he was a likely candidate to sit at Bill Harrah's desk at the Collection after the Patron's death. Wade has been a car guy in the broadest sense of the word since the Creation. He has been, among other things: a teenage *American*

Graffiti menace cruising main and street racing, an Otto cycle sorcerer's apprentice, a military motor pool nursemaid, a diplomate of the ad hoc College of Southern California Drag Racing, a backwoods kid who fell in love with the first Mercedes sports car he ever saw, and a good ol' boy who drives truck.

Most of this behavior was crammed into a car-dense adolescence. When Wade emerged from the Army he made his way with only a few detours to that first icehouse in Sparks. Although it was not his initial encounter with the automotive persona of William F. Harrah—Clyde had bagged groceries for Scherry and carried them out to her supercharged Cadillac, he had watched the fleet of white Chrysler 300s belonging to Harrah execs scream across the Washoe Valley—he was still not prepared for what he saw.

"I came in here [the date is December 18, 1961] and I just absolutely couldn't believe what I was looking at.

"Here's this 1910 Mercer and a '38 Rolls-Royce. There were restorations under way—I think I recall an '03 Packard in chassis form. I couldn't believe the workmanship. My God, to look at the frame was like looking at the finished product on the outside of a body. It was just gorgeous." There was a payroll of about twenty people, the cars had accumulated to almost three hundred fifty. "But the thing that really impressed me was the pink floor in the shop. It was so clean. I mean it just shined." Emris Clyde Wade, aged twenty-one, simply couldn't comprehend this was happening to him, a Nevada car kid, whose most extravagant hopes might have been—someday —to work in the service department of a dealership. Now he was an apprentice in the Hall of the Automotive Gods.

A unit mechanic, actually. Master mechanics worked on specific parts of cars: engines, chassis, transmissions. Unit mechanics "removed units, like you could pull an engine out and put another engine in." Not only that, but Wade actually got paid for doing it; his starting salary was about $125 take home a week. From the beginning, Wade was shot through with luck in his work at the Collection. He was assigned to assist George Herman, a legendary master technician who could *knit* a Franklin fender if there was no other way of fabricating one.

Wade's arrival coincided with preparations for opening the

Collection to the public. "I remember we had to go to the warehouse. This was when I first found out how many cars they owned. We went to sort motorcycle parts [with another unit mechanic]. We sorted parts for three days. Two of us. We had to inventory them and we did that for three days."

After his three-day swim through the motorcycle parts, Wade helped get the first showroom ready, painting the floor pink, then bringing car after car after car from a handful of other warehouses. For three months he did nothing but polish cars. "We'd pretty much pick our cars [to wax]. You could go over every inch of the thing. See how they were made. What was different about them." A first clue, other than his car-depraved boyhood, about what thrust Wade into Harrah's view: he was fascinated by everything he saw. There were to be a number of remarkable episodes in Wade's life, times when he showed how open he was to new experiences and new ideas, but those first months at the Collection were extraordinary. Like Harrah, Wade simply loved cars. All cars. Any cars. That is not the way of most enthusiasts. They pick an area of hyperinterest, automobiles built before 1930, perhaps, or great European racing cars of the postwar era, collect them if they can afford it, amass information in disgusting detail if they can't. To these people—and they make up the majority of the dedicated car lovers in America—nothing outside their own province is worthy of notice. They might be polite to a fire engine freak, but beneath the manners is a pool of scorn.

For Bill Harrah to have tastes catholic enough so that his collection was not constricted by such provincialism was one thing. For a kid from the Nevada outback to understand automotive eclecticism was quite another.

Wade's first big job was donkey work: a trip to Oregon on a holiday to pick up a 1908 Pierce-Arrow body and haul it back to Sparks. "I never said no [to any job]. There was never any time-and-a-half or any of that business, but I didn't care. So here I was driving a Dodge pickup in Harrah's colors, and that thing is super clean, had pipes on it, chrome wheels, whitewalls . . .

"And to be able to do this on an expense account, my God, man, are you kidding me?"

Harrah loved anything on four wheels, or two or three or six. So did Wade. Harrah demanded monklike dedication of himself and his employees. So did Wade. That was only the beginning of their shared attributes, but it was also the beginning of their mutual appreciation.

Wade's first solo assignment was the restoration of a 1930 Model A roadster pickup. "Here's your car, restore it," they said to him. "I was a little scared, but I didn't hesitate. 'Damn rights I can do it,' I said to myself," and with George Herman's help damn rights he did.

About this time, Wade began to exercise initiative. He noticed that almost everyone worked as George Herman did, by experience and through memory. It occurred to him that it would be valuable to keep records as a car was being torn down, so that if its mechanic were called to do a six-month job on another piece before getting back to the original, he would have a reference work. Harrah's had the beginnings of a good library as well as a photographic department. The connection was not hard to make, it just hadn't been thought of before. So Wade went to the librarian and to the photographer and asked if a sort of continuing record book could be kept on each restoration, complete with photographs. It was the beginning of one of the most impressive and useful tools in the restoration business: the manual for each car that today includes samples of original paint, upholstery, headliner, brightwork, and step-by-step descriptions of disassembly.

By now Emris Clyde was coming face to face, even foot to face, with Bill Harrah. In a series of encounters they would discover matched souls, although it would not seem so at first.

"If I ran out of work, I'd go to the next guy and help him out and then the next guy until I got an assignment. Well, I was standing there and I was filing something, leaning up against my bench with my legs crossed." At that very moment the man Wade described as "very distinguished [looking], not a hair out of place, never smiling, always looking like a sourpuss" strolled by. Within five minutes Wade heard about his "attitude."

But then Harrah heard about the restoration book "and he just loved it." Better still, he was taking to wandering over to

HAC at night and one evening he came across a pair of feet sticking out from under an Essex. The air above the car was blue and not with exhaust. When Wade pushed the creeper out from under the car he found himself staring at the Sourpuss, who was laughing his head off.

Another pair of incidents, another pair of rungs up the ladder for Emris Clyde. If Wade was unsure of his status at HAC, he would have been reassured if he had known why Harrah was avoiding the place in the daylight and sneaking around when everyone was gone. For months, he had strained at an inability by his Collection managers to carry out his orders. His reaction was typically Harrah; he hired a consultant to tell him what he already knew. The place needed a housecleaning.

By this time, Wade had been invited to go as pit crew on a pair of Harrah old car tours, one to Washington during which he played bearer to Harrah's White Hunter. On the second trip he arrived before the boss and had the wit to check out his room. It was a disgrace. "So here I was, a truck driver, demanding they change Mr. Harrah's room." They did, Mr. Harrah found out about it, and he was pleased with Wade's initiative.

So when the Collection senior management was purged, Clyde Wade found himself in a key position. From unit mechanic to master mechanic to assistant supervisor, he was jumped three grades to Collection technical assistant and then assistant general manager. This put him three offices down from Harrah, who went to the Collection now in the daytime (and went almost every day at that), and it made him responsible for all restorations.

That is to say, it made him responsible for seeing to it that all restorations were carried out. There was no question who chose the cars to be restored and passed on the quality of the work. That was the man three offices up from Emris Clyde.

II

The process of choosing the cars came much before the assistant general manager for technical affairs even laid eyes on them. First came the "Want List."

This was an almost after-the-fact device; the fact was the existence of three hundred fifty cars and a goal of everything Harrah could get his hands on. But within those generous guidelines there were specifics. "I'm my own decision-maker where cars are concerned," Harrah said, which would have been a little like Gordian the Goth's saying, eyes cast downward in modesty, that he more or less made up his own mind who he was going to ravage next. "I like many cars. Fortunately, I can see something good in a Duesenberg or a Star or a Chevrolet or a Stutz. That's why our Collection is so broad.

"But we also have to look at it business-wise. You know, it just can't all be fun 'cause there's so much money involved. It has to make some sense. [The Collection] has to be the most interesting in the world because of its size plus we have something for everybody."

Something for everybody meant a big want list, something to satisfy Bill Harrah meant a bigger one. There *were* some initial criteria, for instance that the Collection acquire an example of every car Bill Harrah remembered his family's owning. And one of every Ford ever made. As many Duesenbergs as possible, more models of Franklins than could be counted by an average IBM 370, and whatever collections of worth came up for sale.

The process of filling the want list was specific. "Well, first of all, we would subscribe to every major newspaper in the country," says Wade. "Texas, New York, California, Oregon, Washington; and then we would take the classified sections and give them to the guys in the tower who have a lot of time and who would go through the paper and clip the pages." By "guys in the tower," Wade meant the overseers who perch on Martello-like structures in all three buildings watching that tourist hands are as empty on leaving as they were when they arrived. "[Anyway] they would paste [the classifieds] on colored paper and give them to the car buyer, who would then compare it to the want list.

"If [an interesting car from the classifieds] wasn't on the list, maybe something that had been overlooked, [the car buyer] would mark it and send it to B.H." (Downtown and at the Lake, Harrah was always called "Mister." At the Collection, the top managers called him "B.H." It is as clear a reflection of how close everyone in Harrah's car world felt toward him as it is a clue to the chill of his casino-hotel personality.)

If a car were identified from the tower search, the HAC would call one of its scouts. Like the entertainment department, the Collection maintained a cadre of part-time lookers across the nation. "We would get a lead on something, contact them and give them the information, pay their expenses, and they would send back the report."

The next step was a patrol in force. "[Harrah] hears about a Studebaker Duplex Phaeton, which is on his want list," said *Car and Driver* in 1978. "But then he's already got a '26 Big Six [Studebaker] Sedan and it's only got 12,000 miles on it.

"He starts negotiating for the Duplex Phaeton—all the while knowing *just* what he's going to pay for it. So carefully, carefully, he probes the status of the Phaeton, quite willing to lose it . . ."

Exactly. Some of the nicest of the Collection stories come from the very point. Like the time a car buyer went out to get a Model A Ford at an agreed-upon price of $5,000. "When [he] got there the guy wanted $300 for some extra parts. Bill Harrah said to [the buyer], 'Don't you dare come home with that car.' So [the buyer] goes and says, 'I'm sorry, bud, but you just talked yourself out of a deal.' The guy wanted to give in but no way."

Harrah, no question about it, bought cars at the right price. He bought the Rockefeller and Nethercutt collections, beauties both, at rock bottom. Nonetheless, he brought a compassion to his car negotiations he left at home when it came to doing casino business. One old friend was the beneficiary of his automotive decency—Harrah went long for Austie Clark.

Henry Austin Clark, a distinguished man and a well-known collector, fell on difficult times when his family's sugar holdings in Cuba were discovered to be the wrong political flavor. "He didn't go broke but it was just a whole different life," said Harrah. "He had this style of living and he just couldn't realize that it was over.

"But when he did, then he wanted to sell some cars and one of 'em we got was the 'Around the World' Thomas Flyer." There was doubt about the car's authenticity until George

Schuster, Sr., who had driven the Thomas to its New York to Paris victory in 1908, was shown some rough chassis repairs he had made during the Siberian stretch of the race. Schuster had been flown to Nevada as Harrah's guest. When he saw indeed that it was the car in which he had driven around the world, he wept. The next time he saw Bill Harrah he gave him a present: the winner's trophy.

Not all acquisitions had happy endings. One at least was downright vicious. It all began at an auction when Harrah was high bidder on a car called a Lafayette belonging to a citizen who had divided the country in half in his own mind. The East was his, the West Harrah's. Trouble was, he had failed to tell Harrah about the treaty. So when B.H. traveled to Pennsylvania to buy the Lafayette the easterner felt his territory had been outright invaded and would not allow the auctioneer to knock it down to Harrah. "The guy comes up no sale," is the way Clyde Wade puts it. "So we go to court. We get it. Then Bill Harrah calls me in and says he wants to restore the car for [the old car meet in] Hershey, Pennsylvania, because [its previous owner] lives in Hershey and we want to rub his nose in it." They showed it at Hershey and they won. Then they showed it in a more elaborate class and they won again. And then, "We showed it as many times as we could."

It was Bill Harrah's way of saying the same thing his friend Sinatra had said to the chairman of the Nevada Gaming Control Board.

Once bought, a car had to be restored, which marked the moment the bell rang for Emris Clyde.

There were (and are) three grades of restoration at HAC. Right away, Wade had something to say about *that* since a Class One (frame up) was a one-year job. The problem—as most problems at the Collection did—came straight from the Maestro. No sooner would he acquire a car than he wanted it restored. Trouble was, there were already cars on a list he had prepared himself waiting for the very same treatment.

"When I was first promoted we would have twenty-three or twenty-six cars already under way and everybody was trying to work on all of them at the same time. There's no way in hell you can do that." So Clyde slipped over a few offices and braced B.H. "Why don't we just take five or ten cars and establish a priority line and get them out of the way?" he asked. Wade was proposing that cars almost finished be completed right away; those not quite ready be put further down on the list, basket cases left in their litters for a while.

Harrah thought it was yet another wonderful idea. Wade thought Harrah meant what he said. They had not yet gotten to know each other quite well enough.

It was this kind of problem Wade would fight the rest of Harrah's life:

"I was walkin' through one of the [restoration] shops and I saw this car. It'd been sittin' there for, oh, six or eight years." So Harrah called over his current manager.

"When the hell are we gonna get [that car] finished?" he asked.

"Well," said a put-upon manager, "when I took this job that car was third in line. You've put twenty-five cars in front of it."

The annual buying budget was about $50,000, Wade seems to remember; the restoration equivalent was more like $1.5 million, spent by and on fifty people, including five body men, one welder, fifteen mechanics, master and unit. Of course all restorations were not Class Ones. Class Two was an almost and Class Three was a cosmetic. The "almosts" were done on good cars, cars that needed only minimal work to recondition. Cosmetics were put on cars while they waited for more thorough restoration or if they were wonderful runners but aesthetic blots on Harrah's landscape.

When a car was finished, it had to by God run, and HAC had a chief test driver whose standards were high. Particularly in the case of the '29 Ford. It was a duplicate of one of the cars Harrah had owned as a high schooler in Hollywood. ("And I dolled it all up. I did a *real* good job on it and I did the work myself. I put on special wheels and overhead valves. It was about a 60 mph car and when I finished with it it'd do 80.") Not only, then, was the '29 required to meet the usual Harrah standards—as new, no excuses accepted—but *this* one had to be better.

"One car [the restoration people] could never get to go fast enough was the custom '29 Model A.

"That was one of those cars that until he gave his blessing you weren't going to get out of your hair. So I just took it on." Since Clyde Wade in his twenties was a Nevada iteration of Harrah as a young man, he instinctively performed the same magic tricks on the '29 that Harrah had.

In fact, Harrah's car had been able to make 85 mph while Wade's reincarnation of the Ford only went 82. But that was good enough, since Sparks sits almost a mile above sea level, which reduces internal combustion engine efficiency by about 12 percent.

"So [Harrah] came up to me and said, 'What did you do to make it run?' I told him we changed the carburetor jets, we went to heavier push rods, we changed valves, we changed the valve timing. . . .

"And he laughed. 'I had to do the same thing on mine.' "

Score another one for Emris Clyde.

Actually, there was a fourth classification of restoration, more properly creation: the building of a unit from the ground up, into which category the four-wheel-drive limo for the Lake fit and which also covered the parthenogenesis of a fire engine.

By this time, Harrah had spent enough time and money in Idaho that he not only had a rough-hewn lodge at the Middle Fork of the Salmon River, but was well on his way to buying the entire town of Stanley.

Stanley did not have a population density problem. It counted forty-eight residents. It had a hotel, of sorts, and a restaurant and a gas station, but it didn't have a fire engine. So Harrah set out to supply the deprived citizens of the town with a rolling squirter.

The Stanley Fire Truck file still exists but it is a baffling collection of specification hieroglyphics combined with photos combined with mysterious memoranda. The story seems to follow a typical Harrah pattern.

Without consulting anyone but himself, Harrah decided Stanley should have a fire engine and that he, Harrah, would provide it.

Available fire engines were unacceptable.

Used fire engines were legion; but was any of them good enough?

Obviously what was required here was a little homework.

"To: Clyde Wade. Re: Fire Equipment for Stanley, Idaho. I just had a long conversation with Chief Kissinger of the Truckee Meadows Fire District concerning fire units to be used at Stanley . . ." and the memorandum goes on to talk about "Army surplus two-and-a-half-ton 6 × 6s mounted with a 750-gallon tank and a two-cylinder Wisconsin pump unit."

It was only the beginning. Memoranda must have flown like geese in the fall around the Collection. One crisp rundown of costs carries Wade's penciled addendum, "Don't use Harrah's name." The inference is clear. It has nothing to do with humility on B.H.'s part; rather, with the idea that using his name would raise the price of the listed equipment.

"To: Clyde Wade. Re: Stanley Fire Truck Pricing. The best buy I have been able to find in a fire truck, with the able assistance of Chief Kissinger . . . is a 330 Golden Comet Reo 6 × 6 . . . [followed by an exhaustive description and then], the total cost will be $11,188.10."

"To: Bob Hudgens. From: Clyde Wade: How far do you want us to go? The price is good for what you're getting." On the bottom of *that* one is a note from Hudgens: "Buy it. Sell Road Grader." Sell road grader? Well, you can't buy a town and rebuild it without *some* equipment.

There are price quotes and bills of sale for add ons; there are Polaroids and color prints and three pages of specifications for the final vehicle.

Item: All piping, fitting, nipples, tees, unions, etc. shall meet or exceed United States Department of Agriculture Forest Service specifications.

Item: Workmanship—(a) The outside surface of the tank shall have a smooth tack-free finish. (b) All surfaces shall be ample (sic) coated with resin so that no glass fibers are exposed. (c) . . . There shall be no blisters, pin holes, pits, sink marks, wrinkles, exposed fibers, delaminations, moisture, foreign material, or visible cracks.

The Collection collected itself for an all-out effort on the Fire Engine, forgetting only a detail: "One item that was overlooked in the original cost . . . was the red light and siren."

Bill Harrah in his unlimited hydroplane *Tahoe Miss*. (Courtesy Harrah's)

Bill Harrah had loosened up considerably by 1973. Here he casts his mind back to the driving of a family car in Venice. Somebody *must* have sneaked this shot by the Sole Proprietor; it's impossible to imagine he saw it before it was first printed. (Courtesy Harrah's)

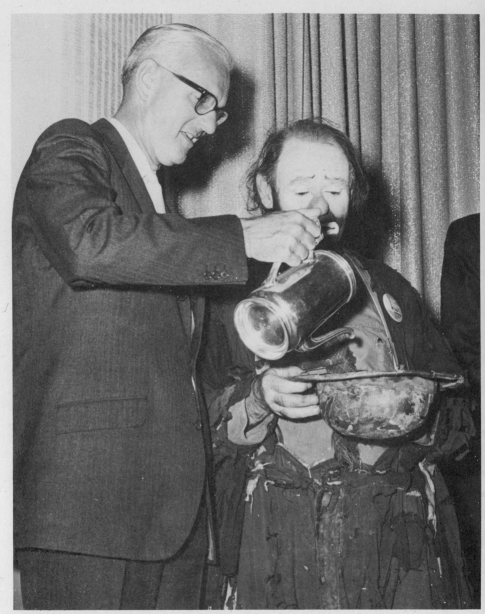

The famous clown Emmett Kelly was an annual summer attraction at Harrah's Tahoe for years. He would walk around the casino, sweeping up cigarette butts; he even went so far as to clean up the stage before the show. (Courtesy Harrah's)

Many of Harrah's entertainers shared his love for wheeled devices. Sammy Davis, Jr., donated his three-wheeled Honda custom bike to the Collection. (Courtesy Harrah's)

Bill Harrah with his first collectible: the famous counterfeit 1907 (really a 1911) Maxwell. (Courtesy Harrah's)

There are six of these behemoths in the world. Harrah's owns two of them, each worth perhaps $1 million. Notice the elegant background. (Humphrey Sutton photo)

One Lincoln is nice, two are better, fifty are better still. Another small part of the Collection. (Humphrey Sutton photo)

Cheek by jowl, a tiny portion of the Harrah's Automobile Collection. The rear car in the second row, a Delahaye with gold inside trim, was a favorite of Bobbie Gentry's. Because she drove it occasionally Harrah had his master technicians build in a roll-over bar. (Humphrey Sutton photo)

Bill Harrah, sixty-seven, in front of the Round the World Thomas Flyer. This is the for-real Harrah Smile. (Humphrey Sutton photo)

Jack Benny's first nightclub engagement was at Harrah's Tahoe in 1960 — the first full year of operation for the South Shore Room. Harrah had a Maxwell brought up from Reno for the photo; it's doubtful that Benny could drive it, although Harrah certainly could. (Courtesy Harrah's)

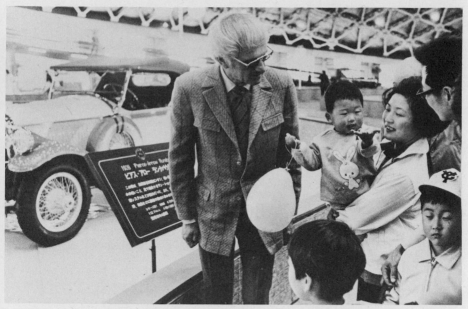

Three times, the Collection has shipped a few of its cars for display overseas, once (here, in 1971 for the World Classic Car Festival) to Japan, twice to Germany. The reception for all three visits was beyond belief; huge crowds, staggering amounts of press. (Courtesy Harrah's)

Emris Clyde Wade, general manager of Harrah's Automobile Collection and Keeper of the Flame. (Courtesy *The Seattle Times*)

With his friend Sammy Davis, Jr., Harrah pretends the replica hotel is a cake. Bill Harrah was tough enough to chew nails, but he would have had a difficult time with this much plywood. (Courtesy Harrah's)

Going public. This is the moment gambling turned from outlaw to corporate citizen. On the far left, financial wizard George Drews; two over, holding the left end of the ticker tape, Harrah's president Lloyd Dyer. Mark Curtis, Harrah's public relations specialist, in his usual gaudy dress, is at the far right. (Courtesy Harrah's)

Late in life with Verna at Villa Harrah, Lake Tahoe. Kenny Rogers on the left, Steve Martin on the right. (Courtesy Harrah's)

Frank Sinatra on the left, John Denver on the right. Sinatra and Harrah were alike in many ways: compulsively prompt, meticulous, attenders to detail. Harrah was also close to Denver, who sang at his funeral. (Courtesy Harrah's)

The Sinatra family appeared for the first and only time at Harrah's. It was billed: Sinatra, Sinatra and Sinatra, Frank, Nancy and Frank, Jr. (not shown). Nancy Sr. is next to Frank, Bill and Verna Harrah are in the center, and Nancy and her husband, Hugh Lambert, are all at the far right. (Courtesy Harrah's)

Roxana Darlene Carlson Harrah. Married October 1972, divorced November 1973. (Courtesy Harrah's)

By the time he married Bobbie Gentry, Harrah was practiced at cake cutting. He was not practiced at smiling. (Courtesy Harrah's)

Bill and Verna Harrah at home in 1977 at Rancharrah. (Courtesy Harrah's)

If Bill Harrah could, by God, have a Bugatti, so could his sons, John Adam (closest to him) and Tony Lee. (Courtesy Scherry Harrah)

John Adam Harrah.

Tony Lee Harrah.

Bill Harrah was not a believer in charity, so it's unlikely he bought the honor bestowed by the University of Nevada in 1972. Here he becomes officially a Distinguished Nevadan. (Courtesy Harrah's)

Red Skelton opened the South Shore Room and returned for its 20th Anniversary despite leaving Harrah's for another Reno hotel/casino. He was one of very few entertainers who deserted the ship. (Courtesy Harrah's)

It was ultimately finished. The truck was something over $11,000; a 1,000-gallon tank cost another $6,200 installed, the Collection spent $2977.73 on materials and $12,040.00 on labor —not so astonishing considering that the specification sheet was insistent on a Class One restoration.

How did the locals react to Harrah's generosity? Immediately upon his death some Stanleyites proposed they sell the fire engine and distribute the proceeds among the residents.

But the Great Fire Engine episode is illustrative of more than Harrah's compulsion to find and rebuild the best and the brightest. It spoke eloquently to his memorandum management style. That, in turn, said a great deal about how concerned with Collection minutiae Harrah had always been. For example, if a part was taken off one car for use to make a pattern for another, a memorandum had to be on Harrah's desk to the effect. The alternative was to have B.H. descend in silent fury having strolled through the buildings and seen a car on display with a piece absent from it. ("We have borrowed an aluminum serial number plate . . . so that Tom Maycock can copy the art work and has been sent to the sign shop.")

There were memoranda about trading parts with other collectors, about readying a '32 Ford Phaeton for Dick Smothers to drive ("Make sure the license plates ["DICKIE"] and the side curtains are installed also"), about completed restorations ("This completes the car [a 1930 Bucciali Display Chassis] which can be classified as a 'Gold Star Restoration' and also eliminated from our Scheduled Restoration List. It is very beautiful" to which B.H. added in ink, "Yes, thanks."), about cars being considered for purchase ("The 1940 Ford Lakester is in excellent condition and would make a nice addition to our race car display," but only, said Harrah at the bottom of that one, "if roll bar is removed. I think it was added later."), about a "suitable flagpole on the Main Shop building" and even catching Harrah out on rare occasions: "We have been unable to locate the toy Ferrari which was lost by your son. We have searched the new Showroom where [an employee] saw the boys playing—and, the Main Shop. We will, however, keep an eye out for it." The note initialed by Harrah is sheepish: "I found it at home and forgot to tell you."

But most of what Harrah himself memorialized had to do with the condition of the cars on display. He made lists, and next to each car on the list was a cryptic message. This is typical: "'32 Plymouth—missing car behind. '48 Playboy, wheel and tires shabby. '06 Packard—where? '33 Chrysler—Rockefeller, awful lot of copy [presumably on the identifying sign]. '06 Franklin—1976 Trek Sticker [a car Harrah had taken on a Franklin Tour which obviously did not carry the sticker that identified it as a participant]. '27 Franklin Tandem Sport—rag under, why?"

Clearly Bill Harrah was the autocrat of the Collection. That did not mean by any stretch of the imagination he was being encouraged in his hobby by the downtown managers.

"Often I was put in a position where he would request that things be done," says Clyde Wade somewhat wistfully from the big desk in Harrah's office, "and then he would get after me because it wasn't going as quickly as he thought it should have.

"He'd ask me what the problem was. I'd say I'm trying to get it done without using your name. So he says, 'Look, if it won't stand on its own merit then I want you to use my name.' I never did."

Harrah knew perfectly well he had opposition from some of his senior people. What's more, he understood their point of view. When he was asked in late life if he would give up the cars before the hotel/casinos and the suggestion was made that of course he would keep the cars, his answer was brief. "No."

"You've got to be realistic, you know. They're expensive at present. They're a drain. It would not be a pleasant decision but it'd be a real easy one."

In fact, he might have been prepared to give up the Collection, but he would certainly have kept a handful of cars. Those cars allowed him his greatest pleasure, that of traveling all over the world on Tours and Treks and Runs and Rallies.

By this time he was taking Clyde Wade everywhere. The South African experience tells us why.

Harrah had selected a 1918 dual-valve Pierce-Arrow for a transcontinental tour to end in Capetown, put the whole proj-

ect in Wade's hands, and gone off into a world of his own.
Easy for B.H., an enormous job of work for Wade. First, he
had to be sure the car was right. However good it was in
Sparks, its performance was to be judged not in Nevada but on
a continent some distance away. So Wade had to be sure the
car would be where it was needed, when it was needed. There
were only two ships scheduled to sail from the West Coast in
time to make the Tour. Wade chose the earlier one just in
case.

In the meanwhile, Emris Clyde embarked via Rio de
Janeiro, arriving in Durban to discover that the early boat had
suddenly become the later one and maybe even a latter-day
version of the *Flying Dutchman*. Nobody seemed to know
where it was, much less when it was due to arrive.

Wade, sensing the Harrah shadow descending, discovered a
small collection outside Durban, took himself thither, and
rented a '29 Packard from its proprietor.

Since the episode occurred late in Harrah's life, he had by
then divorced Scherry—married a brace of ladies we will meet
in a later chapter—and settled on Verna Rae Harrison as the
latest (and last) Mrs. William F. Harrah. Verna was his junior
by a third of a century; she was a spectacular blonde. Together
they were almost a caricature of what traffickers in gossip loved
most dearly—a clearly scandalous pair. South Africa had its
full quota of these magpies and no sooner had the Harrahs arrived in Durban when talk started.

It began with delicious speculation about the possibility that
the two were unmarried. When that arena had been circled a
few hundred times, it moved to the notion that the famous
museum owner had not then nor had he ever had any intention whatsoever of bringing over a car—much less one so spectacular as the Pierce-Arrow. Harrah remained tight-lipped
throughout, despite slander-by-slander accounts brought to him
by Wade.

When the missing ship was two days out of Capetown, word
of it arrived and Harrah dispatched Emris Clyde to get the car
off-loaded and out to him. Wade arrived at the Capetown
docks on a Saturday. He had no local influence. He knew one

thing and one thing only; if the Pierce-Arrow didn't slide itself under William Fisk Harrah before the Tour ended, Emris Clyde might have to look for work on the Dark Continent.

Somehow, some way—even during a fuel shortage—he bullied, cajoled, bribed, browbeat, and slickered the dockside lumpers into unloading the Pierce. Having done that (after an all-night drive) he managed through using the same delicate techniques to get a gas station owner to come down and open on the Sabbath. With heart and prayer in mouth Wade set out for the spa that was the Tour's penultimate stop. "They had these little huts like African-type bungalows. He was standing in front of his and here I came. Compared to the [local] restorations, [the Pierce-Arrow] was just awesome.

"So when I got there, I kicked open the [exhaust] cutout so that sucker was just roaring. I made it just as noisy as I could so the whole world would know." Nor was that the end of it.

"That evening we wanted to go up and have dinner which was in another building, maybe a hundred yards away. We had to drive, of course.

"So I fired it up. We go up there and have dinner and a couple of bottles of wine and we're feeling pretty good. He's letting his hair down a little bit and we're kidding around because we're both pretty happy.

"Then we go back out to the car after dinner and there's a big crowd of people around it. I get in and prime it and I prime it a little more and the thing just does 'Grrrrrr' and roars to life.

"He reaches over and pats me on the knee and says, 'Good show, Clyde, good show.' "

The Hershey, Pennsylvania, Lafayette deal all over again; don't get mad, get even.

Wade did not go to the Pikes Peak hillclimb where Harrah had to back his car up the hill because it got sick and wouldn't pull in first gear. But he often went on the Brighton Run, the most prestigious old car meet in the world.

For that one, Harrah always brought out the best; particularly since the rules were strict about models that qualified to run the event, which meant a wonderfully restored car would be not just a rarity but a rarity among the rare.

Nor was the thing a casual affair. Here is Harrah's 1973 schedule, by no means atypical. He was staying at the Savoy in London, from which he was picked up by limousine at 7:30 A.M. and taken to Hyde Park. He drove his 1904 Franklin to the start line, which he was required to cross by 8:55. "Participants must have completed the run no later than 1600 hours by crossing the finish line at the aquarium in Brighton," and so on and so on, including plans for a cocktail party given by the lord mayor of Brighton and another by the Veteran Car Club of Great Britain and then a banquet. It is important to understand that a 1904 Franklin would have had its problems making Brighton in the required time in 1904. Seventy years later, well, Harrah was only one of one hundred or so people who thought running the Brighton in the rain—which seemed to be the required weather condition—was car heaven.

III

If that seems odd, consider his everyday driving behavior. We have already seen him spending much of his time in juvenile court in Southern California in consequence of terrorizing whole towns with his Joie Chitwood driving style. We watch him push a little old lady through downtown Reno simply because she was driving too slowly to suit his tastes. Scherry's quick-wittedness captured our attention when she slid behind the wheel of his car, while it was careening all over Virginia Street with its ace pilot lying on his head on the pavement. *Car and Driver:* "For a Bill Harrah bodyguard, life is all diamond-encrusted frustration. First he finds out he gets a Dino [Ferrari] as his company car. Then he is told he has to keep Harrah in sight at all times, which is the same thing as being told to take a Siberian tiger for a stroll down Fifth Avenue. Because whether Bill Harrah is in the 630CSi [BMW] or the 6.9 [Mercedes], in a 308GTB [Ferrari] or his station wagon, sooner or later he's going to take it into his head he doesn't need a nursemaid.

"And there will be the bodyguard—a hunter of men, a relentless tracker—left at a stoplight or sideways in a turn or spinning harmlessly in the dust while this 66-year-old street racer, who knows more about cars than almost anyone this side of Rudolf Uhlenhaut [a famous Daimler-Benz racing engineer] and drives almost as well as another senior citizen named Fangio [Juan Manuel Fangio, considered the greatest of the postwar world driving champions], disappears into the flecked sunlight of the Sierra Nevada."

In fact, Harrah was a notorious highway carnivore all his life. He never gave up chasing hot-rodding kids on the Carson Highway; one of them remembers to this day a drive on a warm spring afternoon in his recently completed Austin-Healey. The boy had put a Chevrolet engine in the lightweight roadster which made it enormously fast. The incident took place during Nevada's highway enlightenment period when the state had no speed limit, and the Austin-Healey was lazing along at about 100 when its driver looked in his rear-view mirror to see a red dot growing bigger and bigger until he could make it out as an exotic Italian sports car called a Lamborghini.

This, clearly, was a signal to battle. The young man stretched his homemade screamer to the limit, managing to keep the Lamborghini behind him in a pair of S curves. But then the road straightened out. "Vvvvwow, Vvvvwow" is the closest he can come to imitating the speed shifts from third to fourth and fourth to fifth that Harrah made as slickly as Richard Petty. "And that Lamborghini just sailed by at maybe 125 and kept going up. It was out of sight within two miles," which is probably hyperbole but nonetheless says Harrah had his boot firmly in the firewall to the tune of maybe 175 mph.

B.H. did not usually need the likes of Lamborghinis to indulge himself in such diversions. Obviously he had them at his disposal. But with the exception of Ferrari—for which he became the west coast distributor—he did not like obvious cars. No indeed; it was Harrah's style on the highway to drive a car that looked perfectly, absolutely showroom stock.

Clyde Wade had encountered this aberration first—the Harrah highway spoor—when he saw Scherry's supercharged Cadillac, definitely *not* a factory-built car. "She told me her husband had this one built for her to take care of the smart-aleck kids . . ."

Harrah had a few cars built for himself to take care of the smart-aleck kids who, by the late '60s, were pretty much on to B.H. and his ambushes, so before they raced any silver-haired gentleman they checked to see who it was.

At various times he built: a 1962 Chevrolet Nova [the economy model] station wagon with fuel injection, a four-speed floor shifter and Borrani wire wheels ("It would do about 130–35, which is scooting pretty good"); a Plymouth Barracuda with a full-race "hemi" engine, the most powerful production motor built in America and one used almost exclusively by drag racers and the drivers on the late model stock car racing circuit. He bought two Pontiacs sometime during the late '60s, one because it had a high-powered engine in it, the other because it was small and light. And then he had his people put the powerful engine in the light car.

The most notorious of his cars was a Jeep Wagoneer with a difference. Harrah liked Jeeps but he didn't like their performance. So into the shop went the big wagon and into the big wagon went the largest engine Ferrari made and a five-speed Ferrari gearbox as well. The car was a terror, but it was a prima donna too. So Harrah tried *another* version of the same thing. The earlier car used the Ferrari nose; it was a distinctive car. For the second project, Harrah insisted that no one be able to tell the difference between his Wagoneer and anyone else's Wagoneer.

To accommodate the Ferrari motor, the engine compartment had to be stretched two inches. The Jeep's cooling system was inadequate, so the restorations shops fabricated a pair of new radiators to sit outboard and forward of the engine. The next step was a helicopter oil cooler just beneath the splash pan, and, finally, the car was instrumented as though it were the Space Shuttle.

Finally, with this car, Harrah could undertake what he felt was appropriate highway behavior. *Car and Driver* again: "If [Harrah] could love an inanimate object, he would actually love cars. Admire and respect them. And so when he gets out on the road, driving becomes very personal. Even now, going up to the Lake, for example, he will pass some driver (pretending not to be aware of what he's doing for the benefit of anybody who might be looking) just to annoy the guy.

"He needs to say he likes people, but he doesn't like *people in cars*. They're antagonists. Competitors. And in his view, people in cars feel the same way about him; at least people who are 'car guys.' Most of Bill Harrah's friends are car guys. They're friends in his office or his home, but they're the enemy on the highway . . ."

Harrah never made any excuses for the way he drove. He saw nothing wrong in his highway raids. If anybody else did, that was *his* problem.

He spent months of his life talking about the cars he owned and drove, most of the stories familiar accounts of how he bought this Chrysler or that Jaguar. You can hear the same kind of talk at the bar of any Elks Club in the country. There was this difference: When Bill Harrah talked about his latest car it was like Björn Borg telling a listener his choice in tennis racquets, Ted Turner talking about the one-design he recently acquired, E. B. White extolling a book he'd just put next to his bed.

12

Monuments and Money

Lake Tahoe—Reno, 1964–1978

All this national attention, all this star-girt foofawraw, all this churning and steaming to change an industry; yet in 1959, the Harrah Empire was about as tall as an elephant's knuckle.

Virgil Smith had a hotel in Reno (the Riverside), Harvey Gross had a hotel at the Lake (Harvey's). When Bill Harrah had guests to put up he called his competitors.

The time had come for a New World Ritz, and William Harrah was just the man to build it. First, though, he had to make plans. More accurately, *hire* someone to make plans based on Harrah-style research. "We knew we needed a hotel at Tahoe and Reno. Harvey had hotel rooms [at the Lake] and the Sahara came along. What money we had, we [had] put into shows. We had good acts and we had good food. We just didn't have the money for a hotel.

"Scherry and I had thought for years if we ever built a hotel how we'd build it. Every place we ever went, we copied every idea. We'd measure the size of rooms. We'd measure the bed. We'd measure this and that. I had a file of 'hotel ideas.'"

The jury was in on the move to the Lake; it was a stroke of genius. The jury was also in on Harrah's failure to build a facil-

ity to house his best customers—but the jury wasn't talking
about that one. After Harrah's death, his lawyer, executor, and
successor as chairman of the board, Mead Dixon, rendered
public judgment. By the time Harrah got going, he had already
gone too far. Not, Dixon hastens to say, in the notion of building hotels. Not at all. In fact, he was late in Reno. But it was
his compulsion to build in his own image in Tahoe that would
have far-reaching consequences, among them, the failure to ex-
ploit his beachhead to the fullest.

He had a point. Planning for the hotel at the Lake began
earlier than for the hotel in Reno. That could have been ex-
cused if—at the same time—Harrah's was buying land in the
gambling zone of the city. It was not. The problem was
money.

No matter what the Smith family had done to make gambling a legitimate business in their massive ad campaign for
Harolds; whatever Harrah had achieved in the rationalizing of
the industry by application of sound business practices; the
financial community, like Stanford Research Institute a couple
of years earlier, lifted its skirts and turned its head when hotel/
casinos were mentioned. Gamblers? Goodness gracious, only
the Teamsters would lend money to *them*.

There is no record of Harrah's ever knocking at the
Teamster door. No surprise, given his feelings about unions
and his horror of losing sole proprietorship in his clubs. But if
the banks wouldn't lend, and the insurance companies
wouldn't lend, where was the company to get the money to
build one hotel, let alone two?

Particularly since the plans for the hotel at the Lake were
becoming grandiose. Bob Ring talks about room mockups.
Mead Dixon says with some sadness that Harrah's insistence
on perfection was running cost projections through the tropo-
sphere. Arthur D. Little Company would put it in perspective
in a post-construction audit, condemning Harrah's for spending $115,000 per room at a time upscale hotels were assigning
costs of $40,000 and a perfectly adequate Holiday Inn room
was setting its builders back $16,000 to $20,000. ("Most company officers had copies of [the Arthur D. Little study] but
they hid them when Bill got mad at the report," said Dixon.)

Worse, Harrah had gotten into a vicious quarrel with his architect. It was so bad it went to litigation. "We got badly hurt [in court]," according to Dixon.

When the bus pulled out, it was the final straw. Lloyd Dyer (whom we're about to meet) was Maurice Sheppard's deputy for real estate and finance. It fell to him to tackle the bean-counters in the legitimate money markets, and he thought he had found the solution with the Greyhound Corporation.

"We were trying to get financing for the first Tahoe hotel and we had a package all wrapped up with Greyhound. Greyhound's president had a house at the Lake and at the time he had a board member from Daimler-Benz [manufacturers of Mercedes] staying with him. And he was going over Harrah's financial statements and assets.

"This gentleman [from Daimler-Benz] told the president of Greyhound that the best asset Harrah had was the automobile collection. We probably had 800 or 900 cars then. That is why he went with the loan. He thought this was a really sound company because we had some assets that didn't show on the books. [In fact] they did show but at book value instead of market.

"Then the president of Greyhound jumped the goddamn interest rate on the loan at the very last minute and we told him, 'To hell with it, it's just too strong.' Why he did it nobody knows. He left Greyhound after that."

That first hotel had been budgeted at $12 million. By the time Bill and Scherry Harrah were finished planning, replanning, changing, rechanging, adding, deleting, modifying, altering, and otherwise shifting the face of the map, the bill was going to come to "$24 to $28 million. We couldn't build it," says Dixon. "We had to scrap the plans and that cost $1.2 million [in fees]."

"About that time the Golden Hotel property became available," said Bill Harrah offhandedly. The Golden was directly behind the Virginia Street Club, across the longitudinal alley, facing Center Street; a mirror frontage one block to the east.

The Golden's history was filled with the same rich historical threads that Harrah seemed to pull along with him wherever he went.

Reno's siamesed newspapers, the *Nevada State Journal* and the *Reno Evening Gazette* did a thorough, handsome history in a special section about the downtown area. From it comes the story of the Golden. "A Carson City jeweler named Frank Golden envisioned the largest hotel in the state on a choice piece of property in downtown Reno. And that's exactly what he built.

"Construction began in 1906 . . . shortly after the hotel opened, Golden suddenly died. The George Wingfield family, a well-known business group, took over." (Calling the George Wingfield family a "well-known business group" is a little like saying the Rockefellers dabbled in oil. Wingfield, a veteran of the Tonopah/Goldfield strikes, virtually ran Nevada in the first half of the century. In Reno, he was partners with Bill Graham and Jim McKay. The *Gazette/Journal* is right about this at least: the Wingfield name was well known.)

The hotel went through a series of owners. With each its personality remained restrained until a California hotel man was brought in. "He began by tearing out the bar, stores, barbershop, and banquet room and replaced them with a spacious casino area. The hotel was then dubbed the 'Glittering Golden' and its image forever changed.

"The west end of the room was all bar area. And beyond that was a theater-restaurant called the Gay Nineties Room.

"The Golden then became known as the political center of Northern Nevada. Casual conversations in the old marble lobby or secret huddles in upstairs rooms decided the course of many an election.

"After the changes in the hotel's profile were completed [the California hotel man] suddenly skipped town, and it was discovered why: 325 creditors had been left unpaid with the total bill amounting to more than $100,000. [The debts were eventually paid by the Californian.]

"In 1952 [a Texan] bought the Golden . . . two years later the Tomerlin brothers, James and William, who owned a hotel in Long Beach [California], traded it for the Golden."

The Golden burned to the ground in April 1962. Well, not exactly to the ground. The steel skeleton was left; the girders were sound if scorched. The Golden's timing couldn't have been better.

Bill Harrah's refrain is familiar. "The Tomerlin boys had [the Golden] and didn't operate it too well 'cause they were good fellas but just young kids. It was a very poor operation. And then somehow they started to rebuild and ran out of money. Things just got worse and worse—I forget the touchoff—but we could acquire the property, which we did. [It] filled in beautifully with what we already had.

"Then we rebuilt the hotel. The steel had been standing for several years and had become rusty. I believe we took it down and reused some of it.

"We just about completely rebuilt to our specs, which are pretty good—not as good as Tahoe amenity-wise, but it's a good hotel."

Forgive Harrah his ugly jargon, forgive him more his boosterism, credit him with hiding disappointment. Mead Dixon: "After the first Tahoe experience we came to Reno and finished the Golden Hotel at a much more reasonable cost, $7 million perhaps. But the Reno Hotel was not what Bill Harrah wanted." Certainly building a hotel already constrained by existing property lines deprived Harrah of some latitude. That is not to say he objected to the existing property lines. On the contrary. They fell within the boundaries of the gambling zone in downtown Reno, and those boundaries were as sacred to Harrah as a cave entrance to a mother wolverine.

It all had to do with something called the Redline. The Redline was code for official recognition of a *fait accompli*: the closing off of a downtown area for gambling. Harrah and his entrepreneurial colleagues had not combined in a formal bloc. There was simply *agreement* that all proprietors of clubs in the two-block area would devote their efforts to seeing that gambling did not expand beyond it. It was no more important to them than the Ruhr was to prewar Germany; nor South Korea to Douglas MacArthur. Harrah put a nice face on their reasons. "I feel that it's something that was definitely needed and beneficial to the gaming industry, and beneficial to the state of Nevada and the city of Reno.

"You get your honky-tonkers, people come in operatin' on a shoestring and the town would be the worse for it. They wouldn't operate with the ethics of a major casino." In other words, the downtown area belonged to the gamblers who had already staked out claims there. No one else was welcome. What's more, it was important to Reno that gambling be restricted to downtown. Who could tell whether a new Bill Harrah might come to Reno and open a bingo parlor in a whole new neighborhood? Why, gambling could spread through its own momentum and be totally free of the grip the established owners had upon it.

The Redline question was nothing more or less than a game of real world monopoly—in every sense of the word. Expectably, it stirred a few spleens in Reno. Bill #1670 was before the city council, a measure to formalize the Redline. Around its passage grew a storm of debate.

Doubtless the company's spokesman was tactful in his 1962 testimony. Harrah's position was put in much blunter fashion somewhat later: "We intend to oppose in every way possible any change which will permit more small casinos in the downtown Reno area. By small casinos, we mean those with a few games, many slots, no rooms, no entertainment, and no advertising budget designed to promote new customers. We view such things as a threat to our investment; and when we see a threat to our investment, we become really serious."

A. M. Smith, a member of the mayor's Committee on Gaming Licensing, had his doubts. "It is only reasonable to question whether the original concept [of a Redline] was designed by and for the protection of small nongambler/businessmen, or whether it was done by gaming-controlled businessmen for the benefit of the gaming industry.

"Assuming [it] was in fact the gaming influence which really promoted the Redline, the only remaining question is 'Why?' . . . the answer to this must lie in the economic motives which the industry could have been desirous of promoting.

"First, and most obvious, control of entry by a few over any potential competitor is highly advantageous in any industry.

Usually this is called oligopoly and is highly frowned upon by the federal government. If this control could be exerted through the city government, the few would not only enforce their will but would be completely exonerated from having done it.

"Second, the establishment of prescribed boundaries outside of which gambling would not be allowed would permit the few to quietly purchase or otherwise take options on most of the property within the boundaries. Not only would this prohibit any potential competition from moving in, it would have the additional benefit of allowing them to charge a premium on leases made in a highly desirable downtown business section.

"Finally, if the few were able to exert this type of control through 'just and proper' city government, the ultimate of this pressure might well extend beyond the realm of the gaming industry and could influence every service industry associated with gambling."

Smith insisted that there was a gambling conspiracy he called the "Big Ten" in Reno. He claimed the Big Ten had bought out "potential troublemakers." That they had succeeded "in loading the local political organization with 'their men.'" He insisted this consortium had "acquired control of over 85 percent of the property within the Redline." He found this appalling, particularly since he saw no opposition coming from nongambling businessmen in Reno, many of whom were absolutely dependent on supplying gambling with goods and services and therefore could not afford to speak up.

In one of his complaints, Smith was justified. Harrah had gazed across Virginia Street at a structure called the Byington Building. He decided it was all well and good for gambling to exist on the *east* side of Virginia—after all, his own club was there—but the *west* side, where the Byington Building sat, was tainted. And threatening. So he and Shep trekked down to Northern California and took a lease on the building through the year 2000. A preemptive move, his colleagues would have called it. The fruits of oligopoly, A. M. Smith might have said.

In any case, Bill #1670 was placed into effect May 27, 1963, by a vote of four to three with Mayor Bud Baker casting the tie-breaker. Outside the Redline, the ordinance said, no gambling establishment smaller than a prescribed size would be permitted to open.

The Redline served Harrah well. His claim that it also served the city of Reno was not entirely self-serving. If the Redline kept fly-by-nights out of a golden rectangle, it also kept the gamblers in. That was not the case in Las Vegas, whose gambling establishment spread like leprosy, making the city all but uninhabitable by ordinary folk.

Thus, the Redline explains much of the difference between Nevada's two gambling centers. Las Vegas is a wheel, table, and convention town—and a new one at that. Reno is old-time residential, with gambling in the city core. It is a town of neighborhoods with strong cultural institutions—frontier style. The Nevada Opera Association, for example, is in Reno, not in much larger Las Vegas. The more prestigious of the University of Nevada's campuses is the one in Reno, not Las Vegas. Las Vegas lives to entertain laid-back Los Angelinos. Reno receives more formal San Franciscans as weekend guests. Las Vegas is an adult sandbox, a wonderful place to spend recess. Reno is a city, a good place to live.

Harrah's Reno hotel opened in 1969, square in the middle of the Redline zone. All the while it was under construction, its chief innkeeper was planning the hotel he really wanted to build for Tahoe.

"We had the casino [the South Shore Room at the Lake] going. We had money coming in every day. And we didn't have to open the hotel [at Tahoe] any certain date. So we could just do it at our leisure and do it the way we wanted."

The Reno hotel had been built on short-term money, and through delaying payables until "the merchants screamed." With income (the "golden flow") pouring in and a brand-new financial base, plans for the Tahoe hotel were revived in full grandeur.

Mead Dixon: "Tahoe was Bill's hotel. It represented everything he was trying to say about himself." Harrah did not want an institutional architect for Tahoe—in all likelihood he accepted the idea of an architect as he did many of his consultants; an expert to confirm his own judgment about a decision already made. The shape of what he would construct had come from his "Hotel File." The result is stunning.

Tahoe is not a hotel after the grand fashion. Instead, it is the ultimate expression of convenience-contemporary. It is to the Dorchester in London what a Cadillac is to a Rolls-Royce. The rooms (only 250 were built at first. When environmental pressures were being felt at the Lake, a second and final 250 rooms were added) are all tones and textures. "Bill Harrah was an understated, earth-tone man," said Warren Lerude, former publisher of Reno's newspapers. If the hotel at the Lake was a reflection of the whole Harrah, each room is an image of the personal Harrah, the bedtime Harrah. In addition, then, to a soothing environment (the opposite of the Las Vegas philosophy of glaring room colors to instill a sense of unease in a customer who insists on sleeping instead of going downstairs to the tables), Harrah demanded his hotel offer amenities—American style. Each room has: a stocked bar, a bedstead with so many built-in controls that it seems its occupants can sleep, read, make love, and fly a 747 all from the same place, a view that would stun Lowell Thomas, and two bathrooms, each with a television set and a telephone. It is this lavish furnishing that prompted Mead Dixon to say, "Harrah . . . misunderstood the management of . . . capital resources. For the same amount of money we could have built one thousand rooms at Lake Tahoe and have been a more successful company."

Bill Harrah not only *would* have disagreed, he did. And vehemently. "We knew what we wanted. And we got it. There was no compromise. I'm real proud of that 'cause [it] was a little difficult. We have members on the board and in our management that are Return on Investment [people].

"Harrah's can't run on ROI 'cause we'd lose all of the qualities that have made us as good as we are. Our service would go down. Our cleanliness would go down. Our everything would go down.

"One of the most difficult things is to keep up the standard. 'The hell with the ol' ROI.' I'm proud of that hotel."

That pride showed in more than fixtures. It also showed—
and would still show if Harrah were alive—in service.

II

Bill Harrah was as much concerned about the quality of
service as he was about the authenticity of Franklin restorations. By the time the two hotels were in place (Tahoe opened
in 1973) he had entrusted the maintenance of his standards to
a new president, Lloyd Dyer, who, except for his characteristic
heavy glasses and penchant for suede, could be lost in any
crowd, anytime.

Dyer had come up through the ranks, not only *like* Holmes
Hendricksen, but *with* him. Dyer was a mixture of self-
confident manager and brash overlord. He was the first—and
last—Harrah president to feel entitled to the perquisites of
command. In all likelihood, it was a symptom of his upbring-
ing.

Dyer's mother was a borderline heiress. His father spent
most of his time unemployed. After a comfortable childhood
in western New York state, and a stint in the Army as a
finance noncom, Dyer launched himself on a wildly eclectic
program of higher education. It was not meant to prepare him
for any craft in particular. In fact, it trained him superbly for a
life on the business and finance side of the hotel/casino industry.

He studied finance as an undergraduate at Brigham Young
University. He spent time in the hotel school at Denver University. He graduated from the University of Utah in banking
and finance, after which he decided he needed some legal frost-
ing. First, though, he needed the money to put himself
through law school.

Dyer did not cringe at working. He had attacked a variety of
jobs in college. When he graduated he was Fagin to a clutch
of scurrying newsies. He had been a brakeman for the Southern Pacific railroad, and he seems to have actually played with
the idea of making brakesmanship his career. Then his fraternity brother Holmes Hendricksen mentioned that not only was
there money to be made working summers at Harrah's at Lake

Tahoe, there was *lots* of money. Not so much that the pay was high, mind you, but Harrah's non-union employee family was allowed to put in the hours it chose. Hendricksen was recommending twelve-hour shifts, seven days a week. So far as Dyer could see, this was the perfect arrangement. He would put in a killer summer, amass a cache for law school, and return to Utah.

The man who quit Denver's hotel school, saying that "the only way you're going to make it in the hotel field is if your father owns the hotel; otherwise you're going to wind up being the goddamn cook," ended devoting his life and career to the hotel business.

Dyer began at Harrah's working as a cashier for eight hours a day and then moving above the cashier's office for a continued four hours of making up change bags. He was rooming with Hendricksen, but that was about to change. Dyer didn't take a day off all summer, in fact he waited until the February Tournament of Champions Golf orgy in Las Vegas to steal some time. There he met an extremely attractive, dazzlingly bright woman named Joan Louise Pearson Nicolson, who was deeply preoccupied being unhappily married.

That meeting was to turn into a long and continuing marriage, productive of good, strong issue. Also a second income.

"By the time I married Joan, I'd had about three promotions. I'm getting to really like this business and I'm also getting old. Hell, I'd started college when I was twenty-one and I'd been screwing around for ten years." There is a hint of the influence of the new Madame Dyer's growing will of chromemoly steel in that, particularly since it is followed by Dyer's proud boast that his new wife started at Harrah's as a switchboard operator and then went to payroll, where she had memorized the names and salaries of everyone she dealt with. "That's like memorizing the phone book."

Dyer underwent a graduate version of the same broad training during his first decade at Harrah's that he had given himself in college. He was a cashier and later ran a shift of cashiers. He was a scheduling supervisor. (Ever since the great snowstorm of 1946, Harrah's had kept a close eye on numbers of shift personnel. If there were too many for the day's trade, the scheduling supervisor would call his counterpart for the next shift suggesting a cutback in the oncoming force.) He was Harrah's first employee counselor. In time he switched mentors, from Hendricksen, who had been his first boss, to Maurice Sheppard, then comptroller, soon to be president. No question: Lloyd Dyer was an ambitious man ("I told Joan in 1962 that I could be the president of Harrah's if I wanted to be").

Under Sheppard's protection (the protection was mutual; later on Sheppard would say, "Lloyd was my backbone") he zoomed up the executive ladder. Shep, who was then vice-president of community affairs, brought Dyer to Reno from the Lake to handle real estate and acquisitions. It was Dyer who negotiated the Golden Hotel property deal. It was also Dyer who was the point man in leasing property for a casino in Carson City—a project Harrah's later abandoned. Not a great deal later, Dyer found himself dealing with a representative of the principality of Monaco which wanted Harrah's to run that country's gambling. The company declined.

All this was rocketing Dyer onward and upward. But everywhere he went, he kept foremost in his mind that personal success would be predicated on carrying out the Harrah standards of service excellence.

Those were specific. Harrah had studied the territory and he knew what he wanted. That began with his knowing what he *didn't* want. "Many of our customers [would go] to Vegas. And they [came] back just horrified that their reservations weren't honored. They got a terrible table. The waiter was rude. The food was lousy. The star was very, very dirty [by which he meant obscene or scatological].

"Not all places in Vegas are bad. But there's a philosophy—it's not only Vegas, it's worldwide, I guess." The world traveler considered New York attitudes "just terrible, about the worst there [are]." There was "lots of courtesy" in London but not in Paris. "So there's a national philosophy, and then a city philosophy," and then a Harrah philosophy.

Which again began with homework. "Whether it's a kitchen or an elevator or a hotel, I'm a great believer in getting the experts in. Be sure you get good ones, pay 'em what they want, and let them help you."

Then you add your own ideas, which in Bill Harrah's case were many and varied. The hoped-for result was largely achieved. "It's treating the customers as we would like to be treated. When they check you in at the hotel, the desk clerks should smile. If the customer has a reservation, the clerk should find it as fast as you can snap your fingers. The room should be available unless it's 10 A.M. and then it should be ready by one.

"If the customer wants a certain kind of suite and it was confirmed they should get it. When they get to their room it should be clean and made up and a fresh rose should be there.

"It should be quiet. The customer shouldn't be bugged. The lock should be secured on the door. The maid should be prompt. When they call room service . . ."

Room service was a Harrah challenge and a Harrah triumph. To the same measure he was annoyed at the primitive one-bathroom hotel rooms he had encountered all over the world, he was impressed with the grand style of London hotels when it came to room service. Each floor had a little butler's pantry, he would say, and you could get breakfast in five minutes. On the continent, he had seen special room service kitchens located high in the hotel, the better to serve the guest floors. He went all of them one better.

Not only did the hotel at the Lake have a special kitchen to fill room service orders, not only was any order not delivered in nineteen minutes or less required to be reported to a full management committee, Harrah had installed a special elevator to carry orders, and room service orders only. It all came down to attitudes.

"People should do their jobs. That's what they're gettin' paid for. I like a comfortable life. I don't like trouble. I like things to go smoothly. I like everybody to be happy, having a good time.

"[Even] when things are like that there's plenty of problems without makin' them. And that's when we're *trying*. If you're *not* trying, it's just—well, then it's *really* super awful."

Lloyd Dyer's job was shortly to be one in which he was responsible for delivering Harrah's comfortable life and being sure the empire's minions were *really* tryin'.

III

Perhaps because he was so concerned with his own placid existence, Dyer did an excellent job at both.

Time took a trip to Harrah's in 1977 and came away impressed. "Harrah's approach to managing the chaotic business of gambling is to leave nothing to chance . . .

"Harrah's is literally run by the book. More than fifty operations manuals, written by executives over the past quarter of a century, spell out everything from window-washing policy to the importance of maintaining a businesslike decorum. The company's pit bosses are referred to as administrators, and cocktail waitresses taking orders at the craps tables are instructed to call out, to the bartender, say, 'Two double Scotches for C' instead of shouting the word craps.

"Every effort is made to dispel the rowdy, green eyeshade image of gambling . . .

"Department heads are required to write daily reports on customer complaints and answer them by letter or telephone . . .

"The 1,600 seats in Harrah's showrooms are almost always filled every night, and top performers sell out nearly a month in advance . . . During the fiscal year that ended June 30, 1977, Harrah's hotels averaged a high 92% occupancy rate and net profit rose 25%. Unlike many casinos in Las Vegas that cater primarily to heavy-spending Eastern gamblers, Harrah's has boosted its earnings—an average of 19% a year, compounded, for more than two decades—mainly by mass-merchandising its casinos and shows.

"Last year it spent $36 million on promotion and brought in more than a quarter of a million patrons by bus, mostly from nearby California. Acknowledges President Lloyd Dyer, 'We are the Safeway of the industry.'

"The supermarket approach, though, is slowly giving way to a new opulence as Harrah's tries to upgrade the quality of its clientele. Each room at its recently expanded Tahoe hotel cost $100,000 to construct and contains two baths with telephones and miniature Sony TV sets. A similarly posh addition is planned eventually for Reno."

Very well then, we have Dyer's personality and presence, Harrah's standards and *Time*'s evaluation of how the former implemented the latter. Are we to take all these things at face value?

No question that Harrah meant everything he said about standards of service. He certainly had built the hotel for a new level of customer treatment at Tahoe. Reno was not all *that* far behind. Harrah gets full marks for ordering a push beyond the level of care in most hotels.

In Dyer, Harrah's had a president who was skilled, able, and thoroughly indoctrinated in the right way of doing things. There are differing judgments about his effectiveness. Dyer himself insists he demanded—and got—wide authority from Harrah, more than any of his predecessors except the sole proprietor himself. So if Harrah's was what it should have been in the years of the Dyer administration, he gets a great deal of the credit. Mead Dixon does not address the issue directly, only to say that the company was "stagnant" in the last years of Harrah's life. Dixon is inclined to attribute the falling momentum to Harrah's own distractions: his cars, his new wife, his compulsion to acquire what amounted to an almost separate province within the state of Idaho. There is some reason, though, to believe Harrah was dissatisfied with Dyer's stewardship. We will never know for certain.

What's left is inference and a view inside Harrah's in the final year of Dyer's presidency, for that is about what he had left in the office after Harrah's death.

The place did indeed run by the book. Dozens and dozens of them; *Time* was right. Likely, though, *Time* never saw a Harrah procedure book, nor stood in a personnel line at Harrah's bleak employment office, nor listened to the people in the trenches talk about the company on their breaks, nor watched an obnoxious customer handled as though she were a Fabergé bomb, nor troubled itself to meet the people who populate Reno's sixth city: the City of the Black-and-Whites.

Harrah's greets new employees with changing expressions. It is stern about unions. There will be no truck with them, and that point is made clear within minutes during a job interview. Harrah's is benign—paternalistic in the best sense—when its people talk about the tradition of service. The company truly believes it can indoctrinate its attitudes into its often transient hirees. Harrah's is sly. There is a salacious wink in its eye when it talks about entry level benefits. All the traditional ones are there, an interviewer will hasten to say, but in addition there are the informal attractions of becoming a part of the band of brothers and sisters who wear the mandatory black bottoms and white tops identifying casino floor employees. During their shifts it will be all business. But Reno is a players' town, the employment people make clear, and Harrah's is the best club in town in which to play. So there is emphasis on after-work pleasures, gambling and drinking. "When we talk about the job, we talk about broads and booze, we emphasize party-ing," said one interviewer.

If a new Harrah employee has difficulty reading, he's in gen-uine trouble. During the first days of his job—even if it's a me-nial one—he is shipped into a corner with a notebook outlin-ing the specifics of his work. And telling him about acceptable dress. And about his hair style. And the little, annoying things that might get him fired; for instance, putting his hands in his pockets if his job takes him into moment-to-moment contact with cash. He is expected to know his job well and quickly. That is why the procedure book was put together. It has worked at Harrah's for decades. It will work with the new em-ployee, or he will be replaced with a newer employee.

But no simple manual can prepare an innocent for the cacophony of the floor. Casinos are crowded places, there are bells and whistles going off without mercy. Sound, glare, shuffle, seethe, action, hustle; it's what a casino is all about, what makes it work. For the employee, it is exhausting and stimulating, it is never-ending, it is pushing between crowds. It is mind-numbing repetition of a single job. It is awareness at every second that the Eye in the Sky is not there to serve only the Keepers of Rectitude. It is there also to be sure black-and-whites on Harrah's payroll are not standing around doing nothing. It is surveillance also by two or three or five or eight sets of supervisors on the floor, constantly patrolling, constantly watching. It is factory work.

Nan sits in her cashier's kiosk in the old part of the Club, the Virginia Street side, watching over a parade ground of slots, standing like a gaudy troop of imperial guards, each with a dull silver-colored saber in the crook of its arm. She is in her early thirties, blonde and very attractive. She is the mother ship to the patrolling suppliers of change. She registers and approves jackpots. She stamps parking checks.

As a Harrah veteran, she sponsors new employees; not by choice, by direction. In Nan's case a sponsorship consists of a sisterly lecture in the company cafeteria about courtesy and hard work. The message could come straight from the *Reader's Digest*, except that Nan means every word she is saying. *She* believes it. Nan's effort to pass along a flame could be as superficial as a California fast-food waitress's greeting. Somehow, it is not.

If Nan is patient with a novice, she is crisp and businesslike with George. He is probably just as happy that "Gilligan's Island" is no longer shown in prime time, for George is a slimmer version of the Captain. He is in his fifties, his hair is white and caps his head in hard uncrested waves. George is a key man, the second lowest job slot in the department. Once he was a supervisor, but he didn't like the responsibility. Now he comes to work on shifts he can more or less pick because of his seniority. George is a large man but he manages to stay in constant movement with a change apron weighing thirty-two pounds around his waist. He is here, fixing a slot machine. He is there, advising and counciling an anguished woman player. George moves in and around the rows of machines with unexpected grace. He rarely smiles, not out of discontent, but because he is too concerned that something, somewhere might be wrong. That would be a personal affront. What's more, it would reflect badly on his professionalism.

David, an engineering student at the University, works day shift in slots because he needs the money. He is Taiwanese. His father brought the family over only four years ago. Their joint ambition is to own a 7-11 store. In the meanwhile, David needs to study and David needs to work. David works as though he owned the place. His speech is noodles-in-the-mouth unintelligible, but in any case he does not have time to speak; he is forever in motion. When he is not making change, or paying off a jackpot, David is shaking out ashtrays, moving glasses from the slot counter to a shelf beneath it. Perhaps this is the Taiwanese work ethic. If so, it is strangely close to Harrah's.

Harrah's cafeteria is bright, its food good grade institutional, its atmosphere cheerful; not because of the decor or the Jell-O, because the place pulses with energy. This is in considerable contrast to the solemnity of the employees' lounge, which is like a loser's locker room. The employee/players are exhausted. They read (procedure books much of the time), they watch television, they sleep. Breaks are longish (twenty minutes) but they are as badly needed as those from General Motors Assembly Division lines. There is the usual gossip about the job, centered around this or that announcement, but mainly the customers on the floor. Scorn for the uninitiated, for civilians, is as prevalent in the lounge as it might be in a similar place at Macy's. But there is a noticeable lack of malice. Humor, yes. And often at the expense of Harrah's clientele. But it is not bitter humor.

The tenor becomes more sober on the floor, particularly when there is a problem. Here is a middle-aged woman squeezed into designer jeans a size too small. Her face, elaborately painted perhaps two days before, is beginning to crack like the façade of a long-abandoned boom town saloon. She has taken more than her share of the generosity of circling cocktail waitresses. Now she is complaining about being cheated on a $7.50 jackpot. Two young men appear at her elbow, talking to her as a pair of psychiatric nurses might. They are patient and firm. She will have her problem solved. If she persists in her shrill complaining, she will be asked to leave.

It does not take long to realize that the secret to Harrah's service is insistence that the people who wear its badge give good weight. That they do is apparent. Why they do is not so discernible.

It has to do with Harrah employee morale. Harrah's people consider themselves an elite among casino folk. The very fact of working at Harrah's sets them apart. So if Harrah's employee controls are as strict as its financial ones, the employee side of productivity is this sense of being part of something special. It is almost as simple as that. The result of all of this is that Bill Harrah's standards of service are (in the largest measure expectable) met.

The proprietor of a small business dependent on casino worker's trade said it well: "They make bigger money at the MGM. But the people who work at Harrah's, they're the ones who are proud of their jobs."

IV

The tower for sybarites at the Lake, the $19 million annually for entertainment, the sudden expansion of the Collection—all of it was possible largely because Bill Harrah did the unthinkable.

He took a gambling joint public.

Recall that financing for the original hotel at Tahoe was unobtainable from conventional sources, that when the Greyhound deal fell through, Bill Harrah had to resort to rolling over high-cost six-month notes.

"Given [Harrah's] contradictory nature," said *Forbes* (in a piece entitled "The Two Faces of Bill") "people around Reno stopped trying to figure him out decades ago. But even they were startled last fall [1971] when Harrah sold 13% of his Harrah's to the public for $4 million (after taxes and expenses).

"None of it added up. Only a few years before, Harrah had walked away from Howard Hughes's offer of about $40 million *cash* for the whole pot [an offer, as we have seen, Harrah did not ever intend to accept]. And Harrah's $84 million (sales) company, though it was expanding, didn't seem to need the public's money either. So, why would Harrah trade the joys of private ownership for the rigors of public scrutiny?

"And there were plenty of private joys. Through the years,

Harrah's had taken special care of its sole stockholder. It paid him dividends (totaling nearly $2 million since 1967), bought lavish mountain retreats . . . bankrolled his costly hobby [the Collection] and even footed the bill for his costliest divorce . . .

"Why sell even a slice of such a bountiful company?"

Forbes speculated that Harrah's high living was simply piling up too many bills. It delved into the record to discover Harrah's had never borrowed more than $4.5 million in short-term money prior to 1968. But then the article went on to say Harrah's went looking for $12 million in long-term notes for its Tahoe addition. From the sale of stock to the public, Harrah got $2 million. ("I planned to put the money in a sack and walk past the bingo parlor where I started and then around my new Reno hotel, just swinging that sack. But all I did was pay my debts, buy an apartment house and some stock, and put the rest in certificates of deposit. Oh, yeah, I also invested in a gas well. And, funny thing, it hit.") The company got a like amount.

You do not build 500-room, 1000-plus-bathroom hotels for the $2 million that the company got from the sale of stock.

Forbes was right about the long-term borrowing. Harrah's was beginning even then to be able to go to the legitimate markets looking for money, although Lloyd Dyer's experiences, and Mead Dixon's as well, were more frequently discouraging than helpful.

No, it was not the direct proceeds from the public offering that changed the financial base of Harrah's. It was the perception of Harrah's in the financial community that changed. That change came because if the company was traded over the counter and then on the American and finally the New York Stock Exchanges, it must be as clean and hearty as General Foods.

It was a breakthrough of enormous proportions.

From an outlaw activity even in Nevada, gambling had been dragged by its hair to respectability. Bill Harrah had done the dragging. The SEC and the great national money exchanges had conferred the respectability. Well, at least the diploma. It had been Harrah who had qualified the business for its ascendancy into decent society.

"It was a good thing for the company because we then had methods of raising money [we] didn't have otherwise," says Lloyd Dyer. But it did not come easily.

"When we first went back to Wall Street, the first thing they [said] was, 'We've never been in your place in Las Vegas.' They'd heard of Lake Tahoe but they never heard of Reno [except] as the divorce capital of the world.

"Not only that, but those people looked at us like we had to be carrying machine guns under our coats. We were ashamed of what the industry's image was in the East. But we were goddamn proud of what we at Harrah's were. We developed a rapport with top investment bankers: the Merrill Lynchs, the Paine Webbers, the Dean Witters. We had excellent ratings from the rating companies [but] that was something we had to do ourselves.

"We proved ourselves in that financial community, which was a tough nut to crack."

But crack it Lloyd Dyer and Bill Harrah did. They were followed by a legion of gambling corporations going public. Yet it is critical to understand that was possible only because in the stiff, staid atmosphere of Wall Street, Harrah's, its reputation and its people, overcame "the industry's image in the East."

However much Bill Harrah needed the money to expand his empire, to buy cars, to lavish marquise diamonds on lovely women, he went through hell giving up part of what he had built.

"Everyone was in favor but me. [Harrah had a canny explanation for that: "The deep reason that they may or may not (have) known is that they (wanted) to own some of (the company)."]"

Scherry remembers, "He went public but it tore him apart inside. It was his club and he wanted it to stay his club. But what else could he do?"

"Apparently, the only heritage in America strong enough to challenge puritanism is capitalism," observes Jerome Skolnick. If so, overcoming the puritanism that made gambling a pariah industry by putting it firmly in the cradle of capitalism—the New York Stock Exchange—is a large piece of the Harrah legacy.

V

Pursuit of manifest destiny is dangerous work. Bodies crashed to the ground around Bill Harrah on his way to empire. One casualty was Harrah's wife; another was the president of his company.

Scherry and Bill Harrah were married for the first time August 5, 1948, five months after his divorce from Thelma. These, remember, were the drinking years, the "You come home at 3 A.M. one more time—leaving dinner to get cold on the dining room table—and you can wear it" era. The first marriage to Scherry lasted four years. They separated January 7, 1952, and were divorced in March. The former Mayme Kandis Lucille did not spare the accusations at the trial. Harrah was "possessed of a violent and ungovernable temper"; he was drinking to excess. He had struck her "with great force and violence" so that she had to call a doctor and keep a nurse in attendance. The grounds for the divorce were "extreme cruelty."

(Perhaps the years softened those memories. After Harrah's death, Scherry reassessed her 1952 injuries and decided—if indeed the injuries were real and not for the benefit of the court —that they must have come upon her in some other way. "Bill never hit me," she said.)

Scherry became Mrs. Harrah again in December 1954; this time, she lasted fifteen years. She filed for a divorce on grounds of incompatibility, and it was granted in March of 1969. The testimony of the second trial is sealed.

That second divorce was a tough one. By then Bill and Scherry Harrah had adopted two sons, John Adam and Tony Lee. Bill was an adoring father, much in the mold of his own. He loved the boys when they were babies; he got skittish about them as soon as they began to wander into the world; he was downright confused about how to behave when they were preadolescent. Adolescents he didn't understand at all.

Not that he didn't try. Every How-To book ever published about parenthood ended up in the Harrah library; more accurately, in the Harrah attic, although not until he had read most of them. But this stern, shy, Victorian man, no matter how many books he read, could simply not come to any real understanding of formative human clockwork.

He and Scherry took the boys to the Menninger Clinic for a routine check; preventive maintenance. When a psychiatrist on the Menninger staff asked Harrah to make a list of the problems his sons might have, particularly the elder, John Adam, he couldn't think of a single one. Was that looneythink or was it ignorance? Probably both. Harrah did not like to face ugliness. Listing problems his sons might have had, and might have had because of Harrah's treatment of them, would have brought him face to face with unpleasantness. This Harrah almost always refused to do, even in the security of his office. Growing children were messy, ugly, problem manufacturers. Harrah would spend some time with the boys, but he would never be completely at ease as a father.

He tried, as his own father had tried, to buy the badge of fatherhood. He had HAC build a maharaja's collection of toy cars for his sons. In Idaho, he kept a pair of snow machines for the boys. He encouraged John Adam to race, and he set up a team for him that might have brought admiration in the garage area at the Indianapolis Speedway.

That he worshiped his children there is no doubt. Still, time was the most precious resource Harrah had, and if he was generous with snowmobiles and toy cars, he was stingy with his time. The second divorce from Scherry was inevitable, but that didn't lessen the difficulty for Harrah; he was in terror of losing his sons.

Scherry's problem was different. From the beginning of the second marriage, from the moment Harrah discovered sobriety, Scherry felt the need and the wish to participate in the management of the Club. She had worked in the gambling business. She trusted her understanding of it. She knew her husband sufficiently well to be aware he would never invite her joint management. So she devised an arm's-length—a kind of absentee landlord—style of being a part of what was going on.

During her frequent trips to the Club, she would walk around the casinos making notes, talking to old friends. Unless Harrah brought up business problems at home, Scherry never discussed what she had seen or heard. But she *would* leave the same kind of cryptic notes on Bill's dresser as he might have given to Clyde Wade at the Collection. Scherry did not see this as interference. She would not even go so far as to call them suggestions. The notes were there simply to supply information. Bill could act or not act upon them, Scherry told him.

She did more. She claims to be the authoress of the carpet inspiration, urging Harrah to pave the alley between his Virginia Street and Center Street clubs with polyester instead of macadam.

She certainly helped in the planning for the Tahoe Hotel. It is clear also that she was as responsible as her husband for the cost overruns. Her understanding of the reason for postponing the first incarnation of the hotel at the Lake was that the architect had dotted the casino with pillars, which she found absurd. "Everything had to be changed."

Scherry was instrumental in Harrah's buying Parker Lyon's Pony Express Museum, whose artifacts now sit almost unnoticed at the Automobile Collection.

She certainly entered Harrah's world of antique cars with vigor. Scherry found and collected dozens of costumes for herself and for Bill to wear on tours and treks.

She expressed her early willingness to subordinate herself to Bill by designing Rancharrah (the enormous house just outside Reno) to fit its master.

Scherry kept track of Harrah's increasing wardrobe. She even had a glass case made for his ties so that they would not get dusty.

The burden of dual parenthood fell on Scherry, and she was up to the job. She was then and is now an attentive mother.

None of that mattered to Harrah by the time of the divorce; it all mattered a hell of a lot to Scherry. Given nineteen years of official marriage and two years unofficial, given that she enjoyed the rights conferred by a community property state during all the time Harrah's was growing, Scherry could have walked away from the second marriage a very rich woman indeed.

She did not. The settlement was on the order of $3 million. Almost certainly, it was Scherry's indiscreet behavior late in the marriage that deprived her of an enormous settlement. But it was not the reason for the divorce. Mead Dixon, Harrah's lawyer in the matter, said: "Bill and Scherry had different intellects, different desires and goals, different interests in life. The fundamental reason [for the divorce] was Bill Harrah's decision that he no longer wanted to be married to Scherry. He had a new challenge and a new frontier. He felt it was time to move on."

The blowup with Maurice Sheppard was somewhat more straightforward—if slightly bizarre.

Sheppard's linear approach to organizational problems had impressed Harrah mightily. From the moment he produced his daily Profit and Loss statement in 1946 when the Virginia Street club opened, Sheppard was on his way within Harrah's. He coordinated many if not most of the consultancies; he was as responsible as Harrah himself for shoving and pushing the executive structure until it could stand erect. Elevating him to the presidency was a perfectly logical move for Harrah to make.

But Maurice Sheppard was a flawed man, and flawed in a way that particularly irritated Harrah.

When distressed, Sheppard would withdraw diplomatic recognition from the world. He would wander the halls of Harrah's as though he alone inhabited them. If someone spoke to him during these times, he did not deign to acknowledge his presence.

Given that growth was slowing ("We were goin' along fine," said Harrah. "We were makin' a million a year or somethin' but we weren't really expanding any.") and Sheppard's terminal aloofness in times of stress ("[Sheppard] has a tremendous inner thing. It doesn't come out. It'll fester."), Harrah had reason to be displeased. That Sheppard took stubbornness to work with him every morning didn't help. "Shep would fight Bill on everything and I told Shep 'lose the little ones and win the big ones,'" says Lloyd Dyer now. "I said one of these days you're going to be sitting on your ass [at home] and somebody else is going to have that job of yours. [It turned out to be Dyer himself.]

"That's exactly what happened. He fought Bill, Shep being so bottom-line-oriented, and when Shep would get mad at Bill, he wouldn't go see him. If Shep had an unpleasant subject to talk to Bill about, he'd procrastinate." Only one man could duck unpleasantness at Harrah's and that was the man with his name on the building.

Reason upon reason. Then Sheppard gave Harrah all the excuse he needed.

"I pulled a Wilbur Mills," is the way Maurice Sheppard puts it today. Sheppard, Dyer, Dixon, and Art Smith from the bank dropped by to visit a prospective host for a new Harrah's hotel/casino: the state government of New South Wales, Australia. Negotiations had been going on for some time. Harrah himself was optimistic; Australians were great gamblers, what's more, they liked old cars. Matters were close to conclusion, and a large, formal banquet had been arranged to announce progress. As president of the company, Maurice Sheppard was the head of Harrah's delegation.

A few days before his departure, Sheppard had returned from a trip to Sacramento suffering chest pains. He had gone to the county hospital where emergency-room tests showed no heart trouble, but the doctors had written him a prescription for pain.

As a drinker, Sheppard was not in a class with the old Bill Harrah but he was not a teetotaler either. On the plane going over and in his hotel room, Sheppard swallowed a couple of beers and then a martini. The combination of pills and liquor was devastating. By the time Dyer knocked on Sheppard's door to say it was time to go to the banquet, Shep was a basket case. Dyer, who was not feeling well himself, put him to bed. Dixon and Smith carried on.

Dyer picks up the story: "Shep was in fair shape when he got on the airplane [home], but then he'd had a few beers and he was on these pills, which we never knew. Shep insisted on getting off the plane in Hawaii. "I said, 'You'd better get home and protect your goddamn job.' " No sooner had Dyer gotten back to the office than Harrah called him in, wanting to know what happened. "That was the closest I ever came to lying to Bill. [I told him] Shep was not feeling well." Dyer had not been particularly pleased to have contracted Australian flu at the time, now he was ecstatic about it. "I told [Harrah] I was in the hotel room for three days and I thought I had the flu, and I said I wasn't [at the banquet]." Smith had been there. Mead Dixon had been there. Dyer suggested Harrah talk to one of them.

"Mead went in to see Bill. And then he came to my office and said, 'Shep just lost his job.' "

The story has a happy ending. Dyer was able to argue, successfully, in committee, that Sheppard's contributions had been valuable and his loyalty strong, in fact that he was still a handsome asset. He was given a slot as vice-president for community affairs and put on leave of absence. "Bill was so pleased this whole thing with Shep had come to a head. He had not been happy with him for about two years."

It was probably inevitable from the beginning. Sheppard was a gentle soul. When challenged he balked instead of barking.

Dealing with Bill Harrah when he was being thorny required the canniness of a fox and the reflexes of a mongoose. Sheppard chose to curl up like an armadillo.

That tactic was reserved for the boss.

13

Sea Changes

Reno—Stanley—
Sun Valley, Idaho,
1968–1978

It is an endless refrain. Wives, enemies, old friends, executives, competitors say the same thing: the man had an amazing capacity for change.

Now, with the divorce and adoption of the boys, came the change noticed most. It was actually the third great alteration of Bill Harrah's character. There would be a fourth.

Each of these changes has fascinating coincident happenings. Each is marked by the influence of one important woman. In Harrah's ambitious period, each was accompanied by a great leap forward in his business. When he neared sixty, he began to look inward, and the changes were to his personal life.

Harrah's early years in Southern California were serene—unless he chose to roil the waters with his own great social splashes. He was a lively boy and a lively young man; a heller who lived at home while at the same time sharing an apartment with friends during his last year in high school, the better to wallow in innocent sin. He was swept into business by a confluence of currents: the onset of the Depression, an unforgiving University administration that reacted sternly to his having cheated on a chemistry examination, and the suicide of his mother.

At that point, Harrah launched himself with astonishing vigor into the gambling business, buying out his father's circle game in Venice.

Too much can be made of this first passage. In many ways it is simply the familiar emergence into the world of an energetic man.

That is not true of the second great change. His determination to try hard in his marriage to Scherry and to try even harder to make a success of his first club in Reno, required harsh self-discipline. He cured himself of alcoholism. He stopped smoking. He ended his career as a player. As a gambler he turned from minor tactician—operator of a child's game— to strategist; opening a serious casino, reaching for larger, long-term gains. He affected sobriety not only in his veins but also in his manner. During the next twenty years, he would establish his reputation for aloofness. He would take to wearing gray and brown and dark-blue suits. He combed his hair as though he were preparing for a day on the federal bench. In all of this Scherry had great influence. She sees herself exerting more effect on Harrah than was the case, but Harrah did listen to her. He did plan with her. He did weigh her judgments. She was a strong woman, and during most of the years of their marriages, she and Harrah were compatible. They were silent, together; almost without a discrete personal life—energies devoted entirely to the business. No coincidence that these were the years of great growth for Harrah's.

The third sea change came with the adoption of John Adam and Tony Lee and the subsequent divorce from Scherry.

Suddenly there was a new Bill Harrah, a man who wore casual clothes tailored in Italy and Beverly Hills, who wore his hair as though it were a nest of lace perched on his head, whose standards of taste changed not only for himself but were visible in the Club. Playing a topless revue is the case in point. Harrah became looser, freer, more tolerant. He married three times in as many years. Changing presidents of his company mirrored impatience with his conservative past.

This period of upheaval occupied about five years. In 1974

he married the former Verna Rae Harrison and entered a stage in his life in which he tried desperately to become something he had never been: a whole man. He sought love, although he never learned to give it. He turned away from the single-minded pursuit of success to enjoy what he had already gained. He fixed on the idea that the time had come to cram sixty-three years of missed pleasure into what time he had left.

It was not much and that brings up another shared characteristic in his changes. Each was attended by the loss of a life, the arrival of a new one, or a threat to his own.

Other than his regret at sending his mother to a quack (his word) to cure her alcoholism and depression, Harrah does not say much about how her suicide affected him. There must have been a great sense of loss, perhaps even the classic feeling of betrayal. Speculation about how the suicide marked his later attitudes toward women are fruitless. Harrah never talked about such things. It's easy to see Thelma Batchelor as an echo of his mother; a simple, comfortable woman who made no demands on him. Yet in his mind, at least, she betrayed him too. In their April 1948 divorce he accused her of having committed adultery with at least three men.

The second watershed is marked by Harrah's almost killing himself twice; the first time when he slammed into a bridge on his way to a whorehouse, the second when he bounced his head on the pavement of Virginia Street at 80 mph.

With the arrival of two babies, Harrah began to change again, an equally profound shift in his persona.

At almost the same time he married Verna, he discovered from his doctors at the Mayo Clinic that his life was coming to an end, and he changed a final time.

II

Fathers of infants wear fawn slacks and open shirts, jog or play tennis, and are married to young women. Grandfathers parade around in dark suits and somber expressions.

That is how Lucinda Wade—wife to Emris Clyde and Harrah's secretary—understands Bill Harrah's self-appraisal at about the time he began to show signs of spring.

She is worth listening to. Harrah was about to display a desperate contempt for most women by marrying as many as he could find pretty much without regard for who they were. ("Why he just didn't put an ad in the *Wall Street Journal* I simply don't know. He certainly would have done better," says a Harrah intimate about this marrying frenzy.) Cindy Wade offers no more direct reason than Harrah's unease as an ancient father. That was surely a big part of it. So was his general attitude toward women. He was comfortable with many women, but he had no great regard for them. Early on he accepted his father's view that a woman's place was in her husband's shadow. A woman's place was also in a showcase. Mainly, a Harrah's woman's place was anywhere Harrah went, helping to make his life easy.

That did not necessarily imply intimacy. Intimacy was certainly not the touchstone of the Bill Harrah/Cindy Wade relationship. In many ways, she was a perfect female companion for Harrah during those five years of late-life turmoil. She was —and is—very attractive, a Harrah prerequisite. She was as much of a perfectionist as he. She honed her sensitivity to his moods to an extraordinary, even uncanny degree. She knew his business but she did not intrude upon it. She was an anchor when the sea turned nasty.

She was close to Scherry and close to Verna. Like them, with the death of Harrah, her ties to empire were severed. But if Harrah had a support system in the last eight years of his life, much of it was put in place by Cindy Wade. Theirs was a familiar relationship, the business marriage.

Lloyd Dyer watched Harrah's metamorphosis after his divorce from Scherry with some bafflement. "He was a very lonesome man and I don't think he knew what he wanted, what he was after.

"He was searching for something, God knows what it was."

Cindy Wade could have told him. Harrah was exhibiting enormous curiosity about the Wades' family life. He was fascinated with their treatment of their three children. One Christmas Eve—to Cindy's astonishment—he went to church with the Wade family, and Harrah was not a churchgoing man.

The curiosity was tied specifically to Harrah's turmoil in finding himself a parent. There was also aimless curiosity. Cindy Wade was ordered to get such a bewildering variety of devices, gimcracks, books, artifacts—just plain *stuff*—that she had to hire a girl just to oversee Harrah's acquisition of junk, from Ziploc bags (he had seen them advertised on television and wanted to find out how they worked) to a Polaroid SX-70 camera. He sent his vice-president of public relations, Mark Curtis, on a hunt to find out the real story—still very much of a secret—of the fraudulent Clifford Irving biography of Howard Hughes. It was Curtis' inquiries that shook loose the fact it was a counterfeit.

But there was a deep malaise in Harrah that no numbers of plastic wonder bags or miracle cameras could allay. "Love to [Bill Harrah] was compatibility. He was not a deeply loving person; love was a word. He just didn't know how to have a personal life. When he died, he still didn't know what a loving, family relationship could be."

Cindy Wade spent Harrah's last night in his hospital room, alone with him. But that does not say she is exactly accurate in concluding Harrah never came to understand what a "loving, family relationship could be." There is much evidence to suggest he finally came as close as he could to that understanding with Verna, although it would remain true that life with young boys underfoot would always interfere with his patterned life—an interference he would forever resent.

In the meanwhile, there was the Cindy Wade period, the time in Bill Harrah's life during which he was as frantic as he had been as a teenager. It was a time, in Cindy's words, when he was "pathetically lonely."

The marriage madness that came on him reflects it.

On December 18, 1969, he married a spectacular singer named Bobbie Gentry. She was a one-shot show biz wonder, having hit like a meteor with a single called "Ode to Billy Joe," an absurd lament to a Mississippi railroad trestle. Nobody, much less Harrah, quite understood the marriage. Maurice Sheppard, Holmes Hendricksen, Lloyd Dyer, Emris Clyde Wade—Harrah himself—say the same thing: the marriage was doomed from the start. Gentry saw herself as having taken the first step to stardom. She was paid well as a Harrah's entertainer. She had absolutely no intention of retiring to Rancharrah and becoming a housewife—however rich.

For his part, Harrah simply didn't dream that Gentry would want to continue her career. Each was preoccupied with his own life. Neither would sacrifice for the other. They were divorced after four months.

In the desperation of loneliness, Harrah decided that the kind of affection he needed was easily bought. He took up with prostitutes. The meetings were cold and businesslike. He would be told that a woman awaited him in a particular room of a specific motel. Cindy Wade wonders how such a shy man could have conducted transactions of that kind. The answer is obvious. He was incapable of giving more than a night's attention, and unwilling to accept more than a night's exercise.

Five months after his divorce from Gentry, he married Mary Burger. They remained husband and wife for a little more than a year, divorcing in 1971. According to Harrah, they broke up because of their lack of common interests and friends, and that one day Mary "just took off."

There are fascinating undercurrents in this fifth marriage. Harrah's words about Mary's departure set the tone. She was an only child, a self-described "simple woman, [whose] eyes were opened" by Bill Harrah's world. There is some reason to believe she is not being entirely candid when she says that. She allegedly had a wide circle of men friends prior to the marriage. One piece of evidence implies a divorce in a county neighboring Reno on the same day as her marriage to Harrah in another nearby county. The divorce is not mentioned in the marriage certificate, in which she gives her name as "Mary Ann Burger." In fact, it is "Mary May Burger." Adeline Murphy, the Harrah housekeeper, recalls that she took some trouble to erase any traces of her presence when she left Rancharrah. She had been an employee of the Club when she met Harrah. For whatever reasons, her employment file was pulled. Harrah's will not say why, nor will the company volunteer information about her.

Finding Mary the Mystery Maiden a decade after her divorce from Harrah and three years after his death called for research of a special sort. Here is the report:

"Leonard Weissman Investigations, 2404 Wilshire Boulevard, Los Angeles, California: Pursuant to your request, this investigator attempted to locate the ex-wife of now deceased Mr. Bill Harrah. The only information [provided] was her maiden name and a telephone number: (805) 497-8460.

"Initial telephone contact [allowed] three working days to complete [the] assignment. Initial search was made in the State of California since the telephone number was in the Southern California area . . .

"Telephone records for 1973 were found with a listing of M. M. Burger, 2871 Instone Court, Westlake Village, California, showing the listed telephone number. Currently the number [is] assigned to a different party.

"The aforementioned address joined with the name was again checked throughout California and the only name similar was a Mary Michele Burger in Los Angeles. State records showed that the aforementioned person has a spouse . . . and since Burger was said to be the missing party's maiden name, this automatically eliminated the aforementioned individual.

"[Further information showed] Ms. Burger's date of birth. No other information was found. [Since] Ms. Burger's family had once lived in Colorado, this investigator began a statewide check. A computer run was made using the name of Mary M. Burger . . . and a driver's license in the name of Mary May Burger was found. Inquiry in a specific Colorado area was made and this investigator was told that Ms. Burger was known to people in the area and it was also known that she had once been married to Bill Harrah. This concludes my investigation."

Mary Burger sounds like a contented woman these days. She is glad she married Bill Harrah; her memories of him reflect credit on them both. It's just that nowadays Mary Burger would as soon no one in her small town know that once upon a time she was a fairy princess. She wants to be measured for what she is, not what she was.

Which is not to imply regret: "I had never experienced any-

thing on a grand scale before I met Bill. He taught me such
things were possible for me and that I was worthy of [them]."
She considered Harrah "a highly evolved person." He was "in
control of his world completely. He knew what he wanted and
he got what he wanted. I never received anything but respect
and devotion [from him]."

Whatever he was receiving from her, it was not enough.

A year after their divorce, almost to the day, Harrah married
Roxana Darlene Carlson.

In many ways, Roxana was typical of Harrah's women during the Interim Sisters period. She was a small-town girl (Yer-
ington, Nevada), whose alcoholic father left Roxana at home
with a bitter, angry mother. She migrated to Reno, existed on
eggnog and scrambled egg sandwiches, working first at Sears
and then at the telephone company. When she met Harrah,
she was modeling at tearoom lunches, a step up for her, since
before she had earned seven dollars every other week cleaning
her mother-in-law's house. Carlson, her recently divorced husband, seems to have been in every way an ordinary citizen,
fathering two sons, running a small business he had built, pal-
ling around with the guys, and actively ignoring his wife.

The picture is distorted. If Roxana was down home, she was
as shrewd as Scherry. Harrah had no patience with stupid
women. Through her eyes, then, comes a fair portrait of the
Harrah in transition, the mod Harrah, as he was being called
in Reno.

With Scherry, he had stood mute at the bar of the Wine
House on their first date. Roxana remembers him as "Chatty
Cathy. He told me stories about his past."

The second dinner together was at Rancharrah. The master
had just come back from heart surgery at the Mayo Clinic.
Again Harrah was all small talk and charm. What's more, he
seems to have come to a reconciliation with the ogres of his
past: "He could laugh about the stories he told. And enjoy
them. There was never any animosity about people in his
past." Roxana has a recollection of Harrah's telling her about
cards sent to him by both Bobbie Gentry and Mary Burger,
and his arranging dinner at the Club when one of them—Roxana can't recall which—came to town.

The new Bill Harrah may have changed his skin, but it was still squeaky clean. "He was immaculate. That was very important to me because my father became very dirty as he got older."

Roxana was (her own confession) a wisecracking woman, "flippant" she said, even "smart-mouthed," and Harrah liked that too.

She saw more: "He wanted my companionship. He wanted me to be with him." It was an echo of Cindy Wade's theme of Harrah's pathetic loneliness. Harrah was watching his weight, he was exercising. This was Mary Burger's legacy. She was "a health nut" (according to a Harrah executive who traveled with Harrah and Mary frequently). She had given Harrah some understanding of the workings of the cardiovascular system, and he had become a jogger, although he hated it. He had also allowed himself to drink wine, unafraid he might fall back into alcoholism. More shocking still, he asked Roxana if she wanted to try marijuana. He had, he told her, but didn't like it. Roxana declined.

Harrah still gave jewels to beautiful women. Roxana's temporary engagement ring was a baroque pearl with diamonds all around it; the real one was an enormous marquise diamond. Nor did Harrah stint on the cars. Roxana's engagement present was a Rolls-Royce. He clearly felt he had come to a point in his life during which he could cast aside any thought of fiscal prudence. When he took Roxana to New York, they went on a buying binge. "He loved to [take me] shopping. He loved sitting there. I couldn't believe that he could sit there for hours while I tried on clothes, but he could."

Finally, he had come to feel totally at home in Stanley, Idaho. A slight shudder passes through Roxana to this day when she thinks of the place. ". . . the first time we went to Stanley we went to this *cafe*. I mean, it was distasteful to me.

"He liked it. The meal, although it was home-cooked, was kind of like being in someone's home where you didn't trust them not to put their fingers in the food. But he liked it. That was his little town. Those people were really nice to him."

Some things never changed. Harrah lived and Harrah traveled on schedule. "Tomorrow we get up at 6 A.M. and this was

planned a month ahead, and mimeographed, and everybody's
got a copy and you follow it, too.

"I mean, don't we ever get to do what we want to do?

"Oh, no. Because doing what [he had planned] parted the
waters and he never had any upsets. He wanted everything the
way it was."

It couldn't work. It didn't work. Roxana was far too brittle,
Harrah too rigid still. The reason for the divorce was failure of
intimacy. The grounds were mental cruelty, Roxana was de-
fendant and counterclaimant. Harrah requested that the tran-
script be sealed.

Roxana was glad to oblige.

One final curiosity about these five years in Harrah's life. A
warm friendship arose between Harrah and the brilliant automotive writer/editor who polished and published Harrah's
judgment of the influence of the automobile in America, Ken
Purdy. They were both car collectors; the HAC still has one of
Purdy's Bugattis on display. There was more. Purdy had been
to Heidelberg, Germany, to the clinic of Dr. Joachim Stein, for
regular shots of youth serum. Not exactly serum, of course, but
one of those sets of treatments in which the Europeans seem
to specialize that involve injections of unborn wombat cells.
Harrah was enchanted. He had Cindy Wade book him into
the clinic. Purdy's insistence that the treatments made him a
new man kept Harrah's spirits up in Germany. Then Purdy
committed suicide. It was no way to reinforce his claim of
being a new man. Harrah took one more treatment in Heidelberg and dropped the whole thing.

By then, he had met Verna Rae, and he was about to embark on this last and most rewarding metamorphosis.

III

Verna was young, she was beautiful, and she came from
Idaho; all three important to Harrah. In common with his
other wives, her background was humble. In contradistinction
to her immediate predecessors, she was a stayer.

Nobody expected it when they married in 1974, but Verna
Harrah would domesticate the Sole Proprietor. At last he

would have a family. Finally he would feel comfortable with a woman. From skepticism at first, Harrah's high command, almost to a man, ultimately agreed that his final five years were the richest of his life. They agreed also that a good deal of credit was due Verna.

There are echoes, half-forgotten themes, shadings to her early life so reminiscent of the backgrounds of Harrah's first five wives that the conclusion is inescapable: Bill Harrah married women who offered no challenge, who were proper and subdued in their youth and continued to be, and whose childhood and early adulthood were deprived. Certainly such women were attracted to Harrah because he was rich. Perhaps that was also true of Verna; but she had a few surprises in store if Harrah had any notion that he would keep an escape route open in this marriage too. Verna turned out to be as close to a full partner in marriage as any woman could have come with Harrah, say 30–70.

She was born in the last year of the Second World War in a tiny Idaho town called Glens Ferry. Her father had been beaten as a child, her mother's family was bread-crust poor. She was a bold child. A six-year-old Verna used to hang out with railroad bums—occasionally bringing one home for a peanut butter and jelly sandwich. Every once in a while, she was taken to dine with her grandfather, a difficult and stern man. The menu was unchanging. A plate filled with hamburgers and one steak, "Because, by God, B. F. Harrison always had steak for dinner. They'd pass around the plate and I'd take the steak because I wanted it."

Her father decided about this time that his children needed a better education than Glens Ferry could offer. He tucked his family under his arm and took them off to Twin Falls. Verna was not intimidated by urban America. Indeed, she was even feistier now that her territory had expanded. "The town looked so big. What was exciting to me [about it] was that I thought it might take me two or three weeks to find my way around."

Verna Harrison's father was a railroad engineer. Her mother was working at a Singer Sewing Machine retail store. By the time she got to high school, she felt not deprived, certainly, but not quite at the level of her contemporaries. (Her mother made all her clothes. One day—struck by a compulsion to get her clothes where her friends did—she tripped down to the local department store, chose an expensive sweater and skirt, and put them on layaway at $1 a month. It never occurred to her that she wouldn't get the clothes until she paid the whole cost, about four years distant.)

In high school, she blossomed, converted to Catholicism ("I'm not sure why; I liked the ritual, the music, and I had a Catholic boy friend") and got her first and last lecture from her father about men. "I was getting ready for a date and my father was pacing outside my room. Finally he came in and put a piece of toilet paper on which he'd written '⅞ths' on my bureau.

"Seven eighths? What is that?"

"Just remember," said her father, "seven eighths of what those boys out there tell you is bullshit, just bullshit."

Verna Harrison would remember the piece of toilet paper twice in particular during the next decade. For the moment, she was off to Seattle University, a Jesuit school where the on-duty intensity of the faculty so contrasted with its off-duty indifference that she gradually lost her faith.

She also lost her health.

During her sophomore year she went to a party at what sounds like a Charles Addams house. It was as crowded as the Forty-second Street subway station at getaway time. She went out for some air and somehow pitched through a railing, landing flat on her back about ten feet down. From that moment, her life was pure misery. Perhaps some parts jarred loose, perhaps the fall gave her an excuse to choose illness as her style of guerrilla warfare. In that decision, she got a lot of help from her kidneys. She was in and out of the hospital. Between sojourns she lay in bed in her dormitory shivering and sweating so profusely her friends would change her bedclothes four and five times a night.

Verna was not only in physical anguish, her conscience was chewing at her too. Her mother had given her money for school insurance. She had spent it on a bikini. Now the bills were mounting and she had to tell her parents they had no coverage. They were amazingly understanding.

After two years of school, Verna had had enough. She spent a miserable summer and took herself to San Jose, California, in the fall to go to work. "I had always thought of myself having a dramatic life, perhaps I would become a spy," she said of her junior high school fantasies. In fact, she became a secretary, living in a California cardboard apartment, still sick, now profoundly depressed at what had become of her. "Disillusion had set in."

Her disaster period began with the fall from the house in Seattle. It was just getting started. She moved to Salt Lake City, met, married, became pregnant by, and divorced Burl Frank—almost as quickly as that. "I think what I wanted was not to be married but to be pregnant." (Strangely, it was a good instinct. The son born of that marriage, Richard Frank, would be her delight during years of agony, her strength after Harrah's death, and is her greatest pride today.)

Pregnant, in despair, lonely, Verna went back to Twin Falls where her mother allowed her to cry for three days and then shipped her out to look for work. Her father would not speak to her. Had not, in fact, for some time. Verna had profoundly disappointed her father when she left college. He had had no education (although *his* father was a lawyer), his other two children wanted no part of college, he had spent hours in political dialectic with the young Verna. Now his expectations were dust. Worse, his daughter had obviously come to a dead end.

Until somebody said Harrah's was hiring in Twin Falls. Verna went down to apply and was welcomed warmly. By this time, she had turned from scrawny chicken to a woman of striking good looks. She was not a conventional beauty, but she was a beauty. The Twin Falls Harrah's interviewer wanted her on the spot as a cocktail waitress. This was some distance from being a spy, it was better than secretarial work in San Jose, Salt Lake, and Twin Falls, but it seemed degrading. Was there something else? Certainly.

With exactly $100 in her pocketbook, she headed south. Harrah's in Reno had never heard of her, "some kind of mixup," besides which there simply wasn't "something else" available.

Verna worked cocktails in Reno, hating every second of it.

She did not like to wait on people; she did not like to be put out like a veal chop in a butcher's display case.

Then there was the problem of baby Richard. She had found a sitter and then found the sitter was a child beater. She cast around desperately for a home, some stability, some bulwark for her and her boy. His name turned out to be Ken Crobarger. He was a bartender at Harrah's. Their marriage lasted three years. Clearly, though, she was in crisis and she knew it.

Bill Harrah's good marriages were to women with a little steel in them. First Scherry, soon to be Verna. It was at this moment in her life that Verna showed her mettle. She was working cocktails at Harrah's on the midnight to eight in the morning shift. She enrolled in real estate school. The bulwark she had married wanted no part of Richard, so his care was entirely her responsibility. She was sleeping an hour a night, if that.

The real estate business in Reno had been a closed corporation, guaranteed to remain that way through use of an age-old device: the Impossible Examination. Verna Harrison Frank Crobarger saw her name second on a list of successful candidates after an examination in which one half of one percent of the examinees passed.

In no time, she was one of the best residential salespersons in town. That was 1973. Verna was twenty-nine years old, and one day a friend asked her to come along and meet Bill Harrah. For Harrah, who had no idea of what was in store for him, it was simply another courtship that ended in yet another marriage. Verna had different ideas.

Early in her marriage to Harrah, Verna learned about his new casualness and at the same time made her presence known to him and to the people who surrounded him, by this time skeptical of new wives. Three moments in the early years of the marriage opened a window.

Harrah had an appointment in Sacramento, a three-hour drive down the hill from Reno by limousine. Arrival time coincided with the lunch hour and Harrah asked his new wife if she was hungry. "Yes," she said and he instructed the chauffeur to go to the usual place. A flabbergasted Verna Harrah watched as the limo slid silently into a slot at McDonald's, as the chauffeur brought back a pair of quarter pounders w/cheese, opened the door, placed a napkin and the hamburgers on the regal laps, and withdrew.

During the day, she was left alone at Rancharrah. Enforced idleness bothered her, but the attitude of the household staff was even more upsetting. At one moment, when she was bathing, a maid knocked on the bathroom door and said, "You'll have to get out now, it's time for me to clean." It took a few months, but Verna finally got through to Harrah. This was now her house as well as his. Never mind that previous female tenants had bent to the strong will of the housekeeper. Verna had a mind of her own. Harrah sent the staff packing and Verna hired her own crew.

One evening she was in the living room totally engrossed in a book when she noticed Harrah standing over her. "When I'm around, you're not to read," he said. She looked up, stared at him for a moment, and then put herself in a totally different class from the Marys, Roxanas, and Bobbies: "This is not the eighteenth century, Bill," she said. "I'll read when I choose." The old Harrah would have stormed out. The new one smiled and said, "Oh," and the subject was never brought up again.

Verna was a good traveler and went with Harrah on his increasingly frequent trips. It was this very issue on which Scherry had chosen to take a stand; the 1968 itinerary had been so full, Scherry said, she finally had to call a halt. That was her understanding of the reason for the final split. But much of this was new to Verna and enjoyable, for Harrah was traipsing around in the same down-at-the-heels style he had begun to affect some years before. Full and complete schedule a month in advance, fly to Sun Valley or Stuttgart in the Gulfstream with the maître d'hôtel from the Lake to cook the meals aboard, limousines waiting at the destination, eight-star hotels wherever they went. "We lived Bill's life 100 percent. It happened I loved Bill's life."

She particularly loved Idaho. From the moment Harrah had gone to Stanley for his first alleged cure, he had adopted Idaho as a second home state. Even before he built the hotel at the Lake, he had acquired the Middle Fork Lodge on the Salmon River. Now, with Verna's encouragement, he was spending more and more time and more and more money in Stanley—and in Sun Valley—and in Ketchum.

With Verna at his side, Harrah went on a spending spree in Stanley and in Ketchum. Stanley became a Harrah enclave. He would buy most businesses of consequence in the town and enlarge his own house.

Harrah and Verna bought a staggeringly beautiful house in Sun Valley, built by and for the developer of the resort.

In Ketchum, the town Hemingway loved, the Harrahs acquired a travel agency, a department store, and a Volkswagen/Porsche-Audi agency. (Harrah was indulging himself in retail automobile sales in Reno too. He owned dealerships for virtually all the imported makes available, including Ferrari, Mercedes-Benz, and Rolls-Royce. He also owned the Jeep point in town.)

Mostly, though, Harrah and Verna were in Idaho to relax and to enjoy each other. This was the fourth Harrah, a contented man, still haunted by time demons, still rigid in many ways, but for the first time tender.

"We would have our best times when we were alone together. We would perhaps drink too much and get silly, we would laugh and giggle.

"Bill almost never *did* drink too much, but sometimes we would decide, 'What the hell, why don't we have a couple of brandies and make love.'"

Harrah was enormously affectionate toward Verna and it showed. "I think a lot of people tried to make Bill out as kinky. I certainly saw no signs of that. He was very old-fashioned with me, very interested in being warm and good."

Sometimes, the crazy things took Verna and Bill Harrah to Tucson, a place they liked because they were away from everybody they knew. There, both would crash off their diets and eat at Mexican restaurants every night, keeping up strength to spend the next day as they had the one before: "seeing two or three or four movies."

Harrah had also learned something about kindly humor. He had always kept his considerable wit in the dehumidifier; his humor had a dry edge. Not with Verna. When she began to speak to him about her belief in reincarnation, he gently replied, "If we all go on to a life after death, it's going to be real crowded, isn't it?"

What's more, Harrah had even come to the point that he was willing to confront prejudice. It may have stared him down but he confronted it: "Bill was from another age. He desperately wanted to be young and be a new thinker. It was difficult for him.

"Bill was still transitional. He was prejudiced but didn't want to be. He desperately wanted to be [in favor of] women's [rights]. But he couldn't be and he wasn't."

Idaho was also for the boys. Verna wanted Bill to adopt Richard Frank. He surely treated Richard as his own. With John Adam and Tony Lee, Harrah had actually gone on an overnight backpacking expedition, sleeping in a tent in a downpour, and somehow managing not only to keep up with people half a century younger, but once in a while to get ahead of them.

Harrah waffled on the adoption. His excuse was that he would be doing his own sons some injustice; but mostly if he gave Richard his name, he would have an obligation to Mary's daughter and Roxana's two sons to do likewise.

There is one sad note in Harrah's wonderful new life and likely he didn't even know about it. Cindy Wade found herself not only replaced as the woman in Harrah's life but forced to be a buffer between Verna and Scherry, whose animosity was fueled by Bill's attention to Verna's son. No getting around it; the role of intermediary embittered Cindy Wade. At the same time, there's no getting around Harrah's regard for her even after Verna filled his horizon. In a codicil to his will, signed a week before his death, he appointed Clyde and Cindy Wade guardians of the persons of Tony Lee and John Adam.

After his death, Harrah's intimates realized he had been aware every day for six years that his time was limited. He never said a word to anyone, including Verna, and to her only at the last moment. But he was helping himself by the fistful to everything that gave him pleasure during the years of his final marriage.

Of all those things, by far the most rewarding was his wife.

IV

Bill Harrah wouldn't have dreamed of going anywhere but Rochester, Minnesota, for his checkups. After all, wasn't the name of the best medical consultant in the world Mayo Clinic?

In 1972, a few weeks before he invited Roxana Carlson over to Rancharrah for dinner, he had surgery at the Mayo. We do not know and we will not know for certain what Dr. Ralph Smith told Harrah about his condition after the operation. We know the surgery was to correct an aneurysm in the aorta, that great channel from the heart so critical to the passage of blood to the body that it is spoken about to laymen as "the trunk of the tree." We know that a section of the aorta was replaced with synthetic material. From all Harrah did, and all Harrah said, the best guess is that when the surgeons went in in 1972, they saw further aneurysms. These were not so advanced that surgery was immediately required, but it was clear it soon would be. Two further conclusions push themselves forward: first, Harrah was told the surgery must surely come in four or five or six years; second, that the chances for its success would not be good.

The reaction to his first heart operation can only be explained in that context. And then we have Harrah's own words to Verna on the night before his final operations. He told her his last five years—the span of their marriage—had been the happiest of his life. It was a desperate hour for Verna Harrah. She had been puzzled by her husband's moment of pause just as he was to leave Rancharrah to go to the Mayo. Harrah had picked up his poodle, Pierre, and walked a distance onto the lawn. He had stopped there and, with sadness in his eyes, had turned a half circle, looking at the nearby Sierra as though to fix their outlines in his memory. Now, on this night, his words echoing in her mind, she remembered that scene and it struck real terror through her.

After calling Cindy Wade in Reno and asking her to come
to the Mayo immediately, Verna left to go back to her hotel.

Harrah's operation was scheduled for the following morning
at eleven. Another aneurysm had been discovered in the aortic
arch, in a place adjoining the section that had earlier been replaced. With Harrah prepped and ready, his doctor came in to
tell him that there would be a delay. An operation scheduled
earlier was taking longer than planned. Evil augury; it took
four hours longer than expected. Finally, around 4 P.M., Harrah
was wheeled into the operating room. His surgery took almost
five hours.

Again there is no firsthand information. What seems to have
happened is that Harrah's aortic arch was so deteriorated that
the Mayo surgeons simply could not secure the newly repaired
section to the previously implanted synthetic material. The
aorta's integrity had been irretrievably breached. The delta
could no longer contain its vital flow. All through the night,
Harrah was given blood in enormous quantities to no avail. At
nine the following morning, the doctors decided to go in again.
The initial operation had failed to accomplish what everyone
had hoped. Certainly Harrah, who knew the odds, might have
expected failure. Had he been aware of it, he would have understood that a second operation within twelve hours signaled
disaster.

Semiconscious after this second surgery, Harrah made two
final gestures, two statements about himself, two summaries of
who he was and how he had lived.

He was plugged into a bewildering tangle of life-support systems. His kidneys were failing for lack of blood. He was in ex-
tremis. And yet he was able to point to the area of his intes-
tines when he felt the need to move his bowels, for even in the
last hours of his life, Bill Harrah was a fastidious man.

Then, with his wife, Cindy Wade, Mead Dixon, and his personal assistant Bob Hudgens hovering over him, he suddenly
moved his arms in the manner of a swimmer doing the breast
stroke, fingers splayed, signaling for room around his bed.
William Fisk Harrah had stood alone all his life. Now, he was
saying in the only way left to him, he would die alone.

It rained all night. Verna was given a sedative and sent to

sleep in a motel across the street. Cindy Wade sat in a chair in
Harrah's room, keeping the death watch. She must have fallen
asleep, she says, because suddenly she heard voices and it was
morning. Harrah was unconscious. His vital signs had deteriorated all night, he was dying. At noon, his wife agreed to have
the life-support systems disconnected. By three, Bill Harrah,
age sixty-six, was dead.

The date was June 30, 1978. It was the last day of his company's fiscal year. The $500,000 insurance paid to the Club was
sufficient to bring the annual profit and loss statement from
stasis during the previous year into the black.

That night in Reno, the Sahara hotel opened with a planned
gala, already under way when news of Harrah's death came to
town. The grief was universal. The Sahara's opening was
squashed beneath it. Harrah would have been delighted that in
death he had not only helped his own company at a critical
moment but also subverted an important event for a competitor. The irony of his moment of death was reflected in idly
chosen words of a surviving executive a few years later: "Hell,
he didn't just feel rivalry, he wanted to *bury* his competitors."

v

Reaction to Harrah's death in Reno was extraordinary. Employees cried openly on the floor of his casinos; not just his
people, others. They wept at the Sahara opening, too. How did
it come to be that such an aloof man—a recluse in fact—could
be so mourned?

That outpouring of grief was not for the man but for what
the loss of the man represented. Harrah's friend and public
relations vice-president, Mark Curtis, had been accused of en-
larging Harrah's public presence beyond his achievements. It is
a calumny upon them both. "My message was and always had
been that Harrah's represented integrity, first-class treatment,
and absolute honesty." After Harrah's death, Curtis was grimly
insistent: "The man was not from Chicago or Detroit, he had
no tarnished image. He was from the West. Neither Harrah
nor his people had been born into gaming. They all grew up
with him. They all learned the business together, and because

they didn't come to it with preconceived ideas, they shared his first-class approach to everything.

"And then there's his Collection. A great symbol that really spoke in highest terms about this business.

"There are very few things gambling has brought to Nevada that can be called aesthetic contributions. [Harrah's] company with its high standards and his Collection represented that kind of contribution.

"Here was a so-called gambler who gave something back."

Harrah left an enormous fortune, half in a marital trust to Verna, half to John Adam and Tony Lee in trust. The inventory of his personal possessions is revealing, filled with contradictions. His houses in Sun Valley and Reno were chockablock with Lalique and Spode. From a description of its furniture and decorations, his house in Stanley could have been owned by a roughhewn rancher.

Harrah's estate was curious. He owed $13 million to a bank in Reno. He had no savings. He had a checking account with something over $80,000 in it. His personal life insurance was in the amount of $10,000. He owned a bewildering number of umbrella companies sheltering his properties in Idaho and Nevada. He left an enormous apartment complex in Florida. His holdings in Harrah's came to almost six million shares. Estate taxes were calculated at something over $35 million, but he left nothing with which to pay them. Mead Dixon, Harrah's executor, would spend a year negotiating with Holiday Inns on behalf of the heirs. On the last day of February 1980, Harrah's became a subsidiary of Holiday, its shares valued at $35.50 for purposes of the merger.

The huge estate is an American mark of success; we measure a man by his final accounting. Harrah wouldn't have given a damn. In his last years, he told Verna and he told Mead Dixon he was perfectly sanguine about his company's being sold. He was even content to have the Collection dispersed. "He told me that he was not opposed to selling the company and the cars," said Verna three years later. "I just couldn't believe it.

"I said, 'Bill, why don't you put in your will that the company *can't* sell the cars?'

" 'I'd never do that,' he answered. 'That's my thing, not theirs. They should be able to do whatever they want.' "

Verna was incredulous. "You'd sell those cars?"

"Yeah, but I'd probably start all over."

Emris Clyde Wade sensed it at Harrah's funeral. "I lost a friend. I also lost a lot of hope."

It was a small funeral considering the stature of the man. A partner in Dixon's firm delivered the eulogy. John Denver sang and played his guitar. The mourners and the city were still in shock.

Harrah's death coincided with an industry passage. Individual entrepreneurs were disappearing, the enormous MGM Grand had just opened in Reno, the megaglomerates had taken over gambling.

As a reflection of what Harrah had done, that was the real tribute.

Bibliography

Great long lists of books, said Fletcher Pratt, belong in libraries. But it would be ungrateful not to give credit where due. Herewith the principal printed sources for this book.

Elliott, Russell R. *History of Nevada*. Lincoln, Nebraska: University of Nebraska Press, 1973.

Harrah, William F. "My Recollections of the Hotel-Casino Industry, and as an Auto Collecting Enthusiast," Oral History, University of Nevada, Reno, 1980.

Laxalt, Robert. *Nevada*. New York: Coward, McCann & Geoghegan, 1971.

Lewis, Oscar. *Sagebrush Casinos: The Story of Legal Gambling in Nevada*. Garden City, New York: Doubleday & Company, Inc., 1953.

Lillard, Richard G. *Desert Challenge: An Interpretation of Nevada*. New York: Alfred A. Knopf, 1942.

Nevada Official Bicentennial Book. Stanley W. Paher, ed. Las Vegas: Nevada Publications, 1976.

Sanders, Barbara. "A History of Advertising and Promotion in the Reno Gaming Industry." University of Nevada, Reno, Journalism Master's Thesis, 1973.

Sawyer, Raymond I. *Reno, Where the Gamblers Go!* Reno: Sawston Publishing Company, 1976.

Skolnick, Jerome H. *House of Cards: The Legalization and Control of Casino Gambling*. Boston: Little, Brown & Company, 1978.

Turner, Wallace. *Gamblers' Money: The New Force in American Life*. Boston: Houghton Mifflin Company, 1965.

Index

45